50 YEARS
LOVE
AFFAIR

A Rangers fan's story

Bob MacCallum

50 YEAR LOVE AFFAIR

A Rangers fan's story

DEDICATION

For my wife, Jessica, my family and all my friends (you know who
you are) who have touched my life in so many ways.

First published in Great Britain in 2011 by Derby Books Publishing Company Limited, 3 The Parker Centre, Derby,
DE21 4SZ.

A catalogue record for this book is available from the British Library.

ISBN 978-1-85983-855-6
Printed and bound by Melita Press, Malta

CONTENTS

INTRODUCTION

I should warn readers that this book is a very subjective one. It is my account of the last 50 years I have spent going to Rangers matches. Of course, I was a fan of the club before that when I was deemed too young to go to the games at Ibrox. I didn't choose to be a Rangers fan; Rangers chose me. I was born into a family of Rangers supporters – in Govan, a few hundred yards away from Ibrox Stadium. How could I have become a fan of any other club?

Since I retired from teaching, I have had four books about Rangers published, and I honestly didn't think that I would write another one. Then, at the end of 2009, two things happened. Firstly one of my friends started sending me parts of an autobiography he was writing. This made me think about my own life now that I was nearing the ripe old age of 59. Secondly, Rangers' much-publicised financial problems came to the forefront of the news again, with some speculating that the club might have to go into administration, or even worse. It occurred to me that, by the end of 2010, I would have been going to 'Gers games for 50 years. Imagining a worse-case scenario of Rangers being no more, I realised just what this famous institution had meant to me for over half a century. That's when I decided to record my Rangers experiences. That's why this book is so subjective – it is how I felt at various times over the club's past 50 years.

I have thus written a book that combines what has happened to Rangers over the past 50 years with what has happened to me personally. I hope you forgive this indulgence. As we all know, human memory is fallible. Since my heart bypass operation, my once-brilliant memory doesn't have the accuracy that it perhaps used to. If I describe something in the following pages that you remember differently, forgive me. I am not trying to mislead deliberately. Where possible, I have tried to check facts and dates from my plethora of excellent Rangers books written by various 'Gers fans and others. Also, if your opinion of players and/or matches differs from mine, then that's the beauty of football. Friends used to joke with me that I always seemed to remember events in my personal life by connecting them with what was happening to Rangers at the time. *Mea culpa!* Perhaps this book is the ultimate example of what they meant.

If this book helps the reader to remember times past and enjoy all over again the great achievements of Rangers over the past 50 years, then I will be happy. I consider myself very lucky to have been chosen, by fate, to have become a Rangers fan. Supporting the world's most successful club has meant that the good times have far outweighed the bad. I'm sure that you will agree and hope that this book will provoke your own memories, if you, like me, are a Rangers fan who has always loved this remarkable club.

December 2010

ACKNOWLEDGEMENTS

Thanks to my son-in-law, Robert McKee, and his brother, Tam, for supplying some of the photographs and my son, Stewart who supplied others.

CHAPTER ONE

STARTING AT THE TOP

Like all good stories, I should start at the beginning. I was born on 13 December 1950 in Govan, Glasgow. in our home, the third-floor flat of a slum tenement in Burndyke Street at the junction of Govan Road. When my wee brother, Ian, was born three years later, he had the luxury of coming into this world in a hospital in the East End of Glasgow. When we grew up I took delight in reminding him that, unlike me, he wasn't actually born in Govan and thus was not a true Govanite! The name on Ian's birth certificate was actually John, and that was the name he was christened with, but nobody *ever* called him John. Don't ask me how he came to be Ian (apart from on official documents). As long as I can remember he was just Ian, my lovely wee brother.

Our flat was what was known in Glasgow as 'a room and kitchen'. It consisted of a living room and a bedroom but, due to dampness, the bedroom was only used as storage and my parents, my brother and I all slept in the living room. My brother and I slept in a 'cabinet bed', which was a piece of furniture with doors that opened to allow a fold-down bed to be brought out. My parents slept in a recessed bed behind it. We shared a communal toilet with the other two families who lived on the top-floor landing. When we wanted a bath we had to visit our gran's, a five-minute walk away.

Our tenement was in the street adjacent to Copland Road and a few hundred yards away from Ibrox Stadium. On match days, the roars of the crowd could be heard even above the noise of the traffic. We lived on the south bank of the River Clyde, a street-width across from the world-famous shipyards and Prince's Dock.

Harland and Wolf was the nearest shipyard to us but along the road were Fairfields and Stephens where my dad worked as a crane-driver and my uncle was a joiner. Apparently, in the 1950s, the shipyards on the Clyde built around 30 per cent of the world's ships. These yards were places where Rangers drew a great deal of its support from.

Sir Alex Ferguson was born in a tenement a couple of hundred yards from mine but nine years earlier. The chances are that we might have passed each other in the street. Once he left school, he became an apprentice toolmaker in one of the shipyards until his footballing ability saw him leave the yards behind for a better and more illustrious future. My parents and education would ensure that I would also have a better future, though far from illustrious.

Although we lived only about 400 yards from Ibrox, my gran's much more modern and salubrious tenement was even nearer. She was just over 100 yards away – about the distance of a Peter McCloy kick-out. Her scheme (the Scots term for 'estate') was known locally as 'The Wine Alley'. In those days it wasn't the use of drugs that was a major problem in Scottish society but booze. That is still the case. Despite its forbidding name, I used to play at my gran's place more often than at my own as my best pals lived there and never once can I remember feeling frightened or under threat. At that time, if gang members were on the prowl, they were looking for their opposite number, not innocents like me.

Because my gran lived so near Ibrox Stadium, the streets around her tenement were filled every match day with the cars of the fans. I discovered in my early childhood that there was money to be made in those vehicles. As fans arrived and parked in the streets, I watched the older kids approach the drivers and ask, 'Mister, can I watch your car?' I was amazed because invariably the driver would dig into his pocket and place a couple of coins in the outstretched palm of a dirty-kneed urchin. More amazingly, the now-paid child wouldn't actually 'watch' the aforesaid car but would move on to the next customer. When the streets could take no more cars and the match had started, the car-watchers didn't hang around. I found this very strange.

Instead, we all went to the back courts of the tenements to play football amid the roars from the simultaneous game at Ibrox. These back courts were huge spaces enclosed by the rear of the tenements on four streets that formed a rectangle. There was no grass, of course. That would have been a luxury. The ground was simply dirt, rubble and rubbish and, apart from metal poles that held up clothes lines, there were only the concrete 'middens' (dustbin enclosures) and old brick air-raid shelters from World War Two that hadn't been demolished but whose entrances had merely been bricked up. All of these structures were great for kids like us to climb and sit on, sometimes even watching the football games being played below us by the older kids. Some of the air-raid shelters' entrances had been breached through time, but it was a brave child who ventured into the dark dampness of these places, with their stale and nauseous smells of who-knew-what left by previous visitors. I always got no further than a few steps inside the entrance before the stench and fear of the unknown drove me out.

Five minutes from the end of the big game at Ibrox, the 'car-watchers' would leave our game and position themselves in the street where they had supposedly been watching the fans' cars. At least they made the effort to maintain the pretence! The returning fans gave them a look acknowledging the unspoken understanding that had passed between them, but few ever gave them any more money. The first time I ever tried to 'watch' a car I failed miserably. I used the password, 'Mister, can I watch your car?' but the man with the Rangers scarf just ignored me and walked away. Obviously I didn't exude just the right hint of menace.

A friend advised me to call drivers 'Big man' rather than 'Mister' in an effort to ingratiate myself. I couldn't do it though, especially as most of the fans weren't big, even from my child's perspective. Another friend showed me the type of face to put on when I was asking the driver. I could pick from poor and pathetic to wild and menacing. I elected to go with my 'normal' facial expression. Eventually it worked, and I can still remember how proud I felt when a driver gave me two pennies for my trouble. On a good day this could mount up to a sum that would be enough to buy some decent sweets. In those days you could buy a penny whopper, a dark-brown, slim bar of fudge-like matter, and a packet of Smiths Crisps, the only brand available at that time. They only had one 'flavour' – plain. Each packet contained a little blue bag of salt so that you could add as much, or as little, as you desired. The 'ready-salted' brand was a futuristic concept. I can also remember the emergence of a new brand of chocolate to rival the number-one selling bar, that was Cadbury's. It was called Galaxy – but it never did overtake the most popular brand. No matter how much I earned though, it never came anywhere near the sum of money I saw other kids pocketing. Those penny whoppers were about all my 'fees' could get me.

Much of the time when I asked fans if I could watch their car, they would palm me off with, 'I'll see you when I get back.' They seldom did. I remember once I was standing listening to an older boy offering to watch a fan's car, which had a big Alsatian in the back seat and the window open a tiny fraction. The driver pointed at the dog and said, 'See that big dug? Ah don't need you to watch my car.' The boy replied, 'Aye, but can it put oot fires?' With that, money changed hands. Nowadays, the ancient ritual of car-watching still takes place at Ibrox, but the kids seem to get pound coins thrust into their hands. I'm lucky enough to park in a street near the stadium where the kids are too lazy or 'minted' to need to watch cars.

When we weren't watching cars, we were playing games. Apart from playing football in the back courts, we played a number of other sports. Considering we were in deprived Govan, some of these might be surprising. In the summer, thanks to the televised ritual that was Wimbledon, we fished out our old tennis rackets and tried to play a version of the game. We would stretch a few lengths of string between two clothes poles, as the 'net'. Then we would scrape our shoes in the dirt and dust to create the lines of the 'court'. It was taken very seriously, and line-calls caused as many arguments as any decision in our football matches. John McEnroe could have learned something from us! Perhaps even more surprisingly, another game we played was cricket. We had a 'toy' cricket bat and used a tennis ball rather than a real cricket ball. The wicket was painted on to a wall and at the other end some crude 'stumps' were banged into the earth. We didn't need a wicketkeeper at one end, which was just as well because we were always short of numbers, and it was really hard work chasing a well-hit ball to the far end of the backcourt. I think we hit more windows playing cricket than we ever did playing football. When that happened, it was a case of run for our lives, wait a while and then, if deemed safe, resume our game.

Less contentious games were such ones as hide-and-seek and kick-the-can, which was an advanced version of the former. As I discovered, this could be more dangerous than football. The boy who had to find the others gradually accumulated his friends in a group where the 'base' or 'den' was. An empty can was placed there, and if one of those hiding could get to it and kick it, the others were free to run and hide all over again. It was an incident during one of those games that caused my only trip to Accident and Emergency in the local Southern General Hospital was I was a child. I was captured and standing in the den when one of my mates ran in and kicked the can, which still had the jagged edge of the lid attached. Tin openers were crude affairs in those days. Unfortunately the can took a couple of bounces and then, as if it had a mind of its own, it jumped up and cannoned off my bare calf. How the blood poured out! I distinctly remember that sick, cold-sweat feeling as I looked at the blood oozing out. I was taken straight to my gran's house where my mum was. Once it had been cleaned, she thought the wound looked deep enough to necessitate a visit to the hospital, a 10-minute walk away. It was the first time I'd ever been inside one. Thankfully, the cut wasn't wide enough to need stitches so it was merely cleaned up and bandaged, and I was given an anti-tetanus injection. I still have that scar.

I don't remember ever getting injured while playing football apart from the odd bruise. Playing football was what we kids did most of the time. It was best in the summer, though, when we would take the trouble to walk to Bellahouston Park. To play here, on grass, was almost considered a luxury. We could go into sliding tackles and throw ourselves about if in goal and know that there was no danger (apart from dog poo), unlike in the backcourts, which were full of debris and items such as nails, broken glass, crumbled bricks – and dog poo. Always when we played football we chose to be certain teams and pretended to be actual players. Usually one of the guys would even do a 'commentary' on the game as it proceeded. I don't know where they found the breath! If we wanted an exotic match, we would opt for the two best sides on the Continent at that time. One side might be Real Madrid while the other became Benfica. The guys would then pick the players they would be. For instance, I might be Ghento and Puskas of Real or Eusébio of Benfica.

Normally, though, the team that got first pick would be Rangers. That's when we had the chance to become Jim Baxter, Alex Scott or Jimmy Miller. The attacking players in blue were the most popular choices, as you'd expect, although when it was your turn to be put in goal you were always delighted to be diving about like George Niven or Billy Ritchie. Until I was 10 years old, being Rangers in the backcourts and seeing highlights of matches on television was the nearest I came to the 'Gers. The *Scotsport* highlights came to be called 'Arthur's Mad Movies' in honour of the commentator, Arthur Montford, and the crude, badly edited, black-and-white film showing 10 minutes of a game. It wasn't a rare occurrence for goals to have been missed by the sole camera used at the match.

The BBC's coverage in *Sportsreel* and then *Sportscene* was no better. In fact, when Celtic beat 'Gers in the 1957 League Cup Final (I'm too young, thankfully, to have experienced it first hand) by 7–1, a record defeat in an Old Firm match, the BBC was unable to show the second half because a lens cover had been left on at the half-time interval and the cameraman had forgotten to take it off as the second half started, thus missing five of Celtic's goals! Celtic fans saw a BBC conspiracy in this, thinking they were deliberately avoiding the showing of 'Gers' humiliation, but it was simply the primitive nature of broadcasting at that time. When I compare the coverage then, with hardly any live matches allowed, to the wall-to-wall live showings of games nowadays, with multiple cameras and replays, it's as if we're living on a different planet.

In terms of organised football, I was too young to play for my primary school, Copland Road, but I was a first pick for my Cub Scouts' side. I was a striker although in those days they were called centre-forwards. I was one of the quickest in the team and so my speciality was running onto a through pass to score. My favourite move was to draw the 'keeper off his line and then take the ball round him before tapping it into the empty goal – just like Rangers striker Ralph Brand. I can still remember what a great feeling that gave me. The one disappointing aspect of our Cub team was the football strip. Most of us would have loved the blue of Rangers but our shirt consisted of four quadrants, two yellow and two blue, diagonally opposite each other. Playing on a proper pitch with goals (but no nets) helped us imagine that we were the famous Rangers players of the day, but I still hadn't seen my heroes in the flesh yet.

All my friends were Rangers fans and we talked about them all the time, although none of us had actually ever been inside Ibrox Stadium. The adult members of my extended family were 'Gers fans, but none of them went to every game, not even every home match, so that was another reason why I hadn't made it inside Ibrox until that point, despite constantly nagging my dad to take me. Then came the great day. I can pinpoint the exact date as it was a birthday treat for me, having just become 10 years old four days earlier. As part of my birthday surprises, my parents had bought me a Rangers scarf. I still have the same type even now, known as a 'bar scarf'. It was a woollen one with the traditional design of blue with red and white bands spaced across it horizontally. In the 50 years since I got that first scarf I've had various types with different designs and materials, but that kind has always been my favourite. That scarf would be the only indication that I was going to a 'Gers match. In those days there was no such thing as a replica top. The men went to matches wearing heavy coats in the winter, with a 'bunnet' (a flat cap) and their 'Gers scarf, and that was it.

I was so proud of that scarf. It made me feel almost like an adult, like a proper Rangers fan. I even wore it around the house occasionally as I anticipated going to my first 'Gers game. That game took place on 17 December 1960. Rangers' opponents were St Mirren, from the neighbouring wee town of Paisley, and we cuffed them 5–1. As it turned out, I was very lucky because I started going to see Rangers when the greatest team in its history was almost fully developed. Nothing like starting at the top! The season prior to this had been something of a failure in Rangers' terms as the club had 'only' won the Scottish Cup, beating Kilmarnock 2–0. They had been knocked out by Eintracht Frankfurt in the semi-final of the European Cup (with the Final played at Hampden against the fabulous Real Madrid) and had finished a mere third in the League Championship, which was won by Hearts (the last time the Jambos managed to win the title). However, by the time I was looking forward to my first match at Ibrox, Rangers had already won the League Cup in October (again beating Kilmarnock by 2–0). They would go on to win the League title again and would make it to the Final of the inaugural European Cup-Winners' Cup. Near the start of this season 'Gers even managed to beat Celtic 5–1 at Parkhead – Rangers' biggest win there for 70 years.

The one blip in that great season came in the Scottish Cup in March, when a brilliant Motherwell side, led by the pre-Liverpool Ian St John, knocked 'Gers out in a replayed game at Ibrox. I missed that game because I was taking part in a school choir competition in the suburb of Pollok, three miles away from Ibrox. Little did I realise that soon I would be living near that area and going to a Pollok primary school. I remember being totally shocked as we were all returning home and being told that Well had beaten the mighty Rangers at home by 5–2. I'm not sure what upset me most – the shock of going out of the Cup or the margin of the defeat. Maybe it was just as well that I missed that particular game. I might not have seen much of it anyway because the crowd turned out to be the biggest at Ibrox in years with a whopping 90,000 fans turning up. In those days the 'normal' maximum crowd was about 80,000. Very few matches needed a ticket for entry.

It didn't lessen the pain of defeat to read next day that 'Gers' beloved centre-forward, Jimmy Millar, had missed the game due to injury and, even worse, our best player and my hero, the magical Jim Baxter, had also missed the game. Why had he suffered an enforced absence? In those days, young men had to complete their National Service. Footballers were not exempt. So, Jim Baxter missed that vital game because the Army refused to release him. It wouldn't be the last time either. At the end of the following season Slim Jim would miss out on Rangers' groundbreaking tour of the Soviet Union thanks to the British Army needing him elsewhere – and not even in battle.

How lucky was I that I began going to Rangers' games almost halfway through the great season of 1960–61? I have read and heard accounts of various guys' first experience of going to a football match and they all seem to be very detailed and vivid. However, my memories are very sketchy.

I remember walking from my home with my dad the few hundred yards up Copland Road to the stadium. I'd walked that road thousands of times before, but this time there was a funny feeling going on in my stomach stemming from the fact that the destination was Rangers' ground. There must have been thousands of 'Gers fans strolling up Copland Road, as they'd done countless times before and, with my new Rangers scarf on, I already felt like one of them. There definitely was a kind of hubbub, but I don't remember hearing any Rangers songs coming from small groups approaching the stadium that I would hear in later years. I do remember feeling that we weren't walking fast enough, so eager was I to get to the stadium.

Then we had arrived. We went to the turnstiles nearest Copland Road, which were in Cairnlea Drive. I don't remember having to queue. My dad stood behind me and then lifted me over the turnstile before paying at the gate. Lifting boys over to gain entry was common practice in those days, and already there were quite a few youngsters outside the ground asking adults, 'Can you give me a lift, Mister?' This was only possible because 90 per cent of the stadium was terracing and standing-only, so fans entering without paying were not causing any inconvenience to others – just losing the club revenue! Asking for a 'lift over' in the coming year or so was something I was never good at (just like my 'car-watching'), but I did succeed a couple of times. In we went, and I can remember the metallic clicking sounds of all the turnstiles as fans paid their way in.

Once through the turnstile I looked ahead, and there before me reared the back of the huge 'Rangers' End' – the Copland Road terracing. There was quite a space to traverse between the turnstiles and the foot of the enormous staircase. We stopped near the stairs and that gave me the chance to look up at the impressive sight before me, seemingly stretching up into the sky. Of course, I had seen the back of this terracing many times previously from the street, and naturally it had looked big, but looking up at it from the foot of the staircase made it seem like Everest. We started climbing the stairs, and what would later become a chore was like an exciting journey, heading to the top of the staircase for my first sight of the inside of Ibrox. Little did I realise that just over 10 years later this stairway would become infamous as 'Stairway 13', the site of the second Ibrox Disaster, where 66 Rangers fans would die in the worst accident in British football history to that date.

I think in those pre-Disaster days the stairway was composed of earth/cinder steps with wooden edges. It was divided into two broad sections by a wooden barrier with a fence and a hedge running down the entire length of the staircase.

Less than a year after my first visit, an accident on this same staircase caused the death of two Rangers fans. Apparently, supporters stumbled on leaving an Old Firm game, and a crush developed, which shattered the central barrier and made the fencing at the side of the stairs give way. This probably saved lives as fans were able to escape from the stairway onto the grass embankment at the side of the stairs. This tragedy caused the club to 'refine' that exit by dividing the staircase into seven narrower lanes by using steel tubing barriers, and the fencing at the edges of the staircase was replaced by much stouter, stronger material, which, ironically, did not cave in at the time of the later Ibrox Disaster and probably contributed to the injuries and deaths of some fans as there was no escape from that stairway at its sides. By then the stairway, like the rest of the stadium, had been concreted.

Looking up, Stairway 13 appeared massive and I could barely envisage what it must be like when thousands of fans were pouring down it at the end of a game. Up we climbed, and it seemed to go on forever. Finally, we reached the summit and there I saw the vast stadium spread before me. Even to an adult, Ibrox must have looked massive, but through the eyes of a 10-year-old it seemed almost unbelievable. I stood at the top of the terracing and just stared before my dad guided me towards where we were going to stand. We walked around the passageway at the rear until we were practically behind the goal at the Copland Road end. Then we walked down an aisle, past about three or four rows of crush barriers, before moving inside to the terracing. We had arrived quite early so the stadium was gradually filling up, but not all the crush barriers had been taken yet. Eventually the ground would only be half-full for a humdrum match against St Mirren, and I've since discovered that the attendance that day was 'only' 35,000. Most of the early spectators were leaning on the steel, tubular crush barriers (designed by the great football stadium engineer, Archibald Leitch) that divided up the huge bank of terracing that was composed of earth-and-cinder stepping identical to that of the staircases that allowed entry to the fans.

My first thought was how was I going to be able to see over the heads of the adults? My dad lifted me up and sat me on top of the crush barrier while holding both arms around me. Thinking back now, that must have been a most uncomfortable way for him to watch a match, but there was no other solution. I do remember that, despite him holding me, I gripped on to that barrier for dear life throughout the game. There was no waving of the arms when Rangers scored — and they would have to score five times in that game! That would be the last time for quite a while that I would watch a game from such a high vantage point on the terracing. After that, my dad would take me right down to the front of the terracing and lift me up on to the white wall surrounding the track around the pitch while he stood behind the nearest crush barrier from the front. The wall was about 4ft high on the terracing side and a bit shorter on the track side. It was where the youngest boys sat to get an uninterrupted view of a game. The only trouble was that, due to safety rules, you weren't allowed to sit with your legs over the wall on the track side. This was because the ball might hit you, resulting in a broken leg, perhaps. We all had to sit on this wall in a 'side-saddle' position, craning our neck to watch the action. It was not a comfortable experience, so maybe it's just as well we were watching a brilliant team winning most of the time.

Ironically, in view of this 'safety' measure, Ibrox, at that time and for years to come, allowed those little invalid cars to park against this perimeter wall, and the disabled fans watched the game through their plastic windscreens. Three sides of Ibrox accommodated these appropriately coloured light-blue, three-wheeler cars. I think even I had a better view of a game than they did. Can you imagine the Gauleiters of Health and Safety allowing this nowadays?

I remember almost nothing about the match itself except that Rangers gave me great pleasure by winning easily, scoring five goals from Millar (2), Brand and Wilson as well as an own-goal. I have since researched that match and discovered that this was the side that played: Niven; Shearer, Caldow; Davis, Paterson, Baxter; Scott, McMillan, Millar, Brand and Wilson. Apart from 'keeper Niven making way at the start and end of that season for Billy Ritchie, that was basically the 'Gers side for every game, aside from the very occasional injury. At last, I was able to see my heroes in the flesh: Jim Baxter, Jimmy Millar, Ralph Brand and Davie Wilson. What a brilliant attacking side to begin my 'Gers-watching life with! Over the next couple of years Greig, McKinnon and Henderson would join and form, in my opinion, the greatest Rangers team ever.

I don't recall much else about the game, but I remember asking my dad at half-time what the men were doing with the letters and numbers at the back of the terracing behind each goal. In those days there was a huge metal frame with letters A – I or maybe J. This was the method used to indicate to the crowd what the half-time scores were at the other matches. For example, the scoreboard man would slip in the numbers alongside the letter A to show that the present score at that game was 1–0. The only problem for the fans was that you had to have bought a match programme to know which teams were represented by those letters. If, on that day, you knew that Aberdeen was playing at home then you could make an educated guess that the first score on the board would be theirs. However, it would all just be surmising – unless you, or a fan near you, had a programme.

I also remember something that was to become a staple part of games at Ibrox. All around the back of the terracing and even walking through the fans, if it wasn't too crowded, you had the guys selling crisps, Lees' macaroon bars or Wrigley's spearmint chewing gum. All these goodies were contained in big cardboard boxes that the vendors had to lug around while alerting fans to their presence with the loudest voices you have ever heard. If you wanted a drink, it was Bovril or nothing at one of the primitive kiosks at the bottom of the staircases. The drink was so weak you had to wonder just how much Bovril was put into the Styrofoam cup before the hot water was added. Nowadays, you can buy Bovril, tea, coffee and soup at the ultra-modern kiosks below the stands, which also sell such delicacies as 'Blue Nose Burgers' and 'Championees Hot Dogs'.

Also at the foot of the huge staircases were the very basic toilets that were merely drains surrounded by brick walls with no roof on them. These were places I made a point of avoiding, even when I became an adult. During the game, few fans would bother to leave their place on the terracing to visit these toilets and would simply urinate into one of their now-empty beer cans (if you were lucky) or just do it onto the ground in front of them. I would be splashed many times by such activity! The feeling of a warm liquid running down your trouser leg is not a memory most people will be likely to forget or miss.

Another memory was of the sheer volume of noise created by the 35,000 Rangers fans and how exciting they seemed to find the match. In a lull in action I took the opportunity to have a good look around from my vantage point and take in as much as I could, not knowing when I might be back. The feature of the stadium that fascinated me most was the press box, perched on top of the roof of the Main Stand. This was part of the Archibald Leitch design for the stand that had been built in 1928, and it was unusual because it had a castellated roof, making it appear like a tiny castle above the drama unfolding beneath it. If the hacks couldn't get their facts right and describe a match properly from that viewing point then they really must have been useless. Having said that, compared to the current hacks, these guys wrote like Hemingway.

When the final whistle blew, my dad told me to stay where I was. A few adults did the same as us, but the majority of the fans swept towards the top of the terracing before heading for those massive staircases that would take them to the street exits. After about five minutes, holding my dad's hand, we walked to the staircase. Even then there were still thousands of fans pouring down the steps. For a brief moment I got the chance to have a good look at the tide of humanity rippling down those stairs before I, too, had to descend. We kept to the very edge of the stairway, and I couldn't see anything then, apart from all those adults surrounding me, but I trusted my dad to get me to the bottom safely. In years to come, I'd realise just how dangerous the leaving of a stadium could be if you tried to leave right at the final whistle. Hanging around on the terracing for five minutes or so before attempting an exit was easily the most sensible action to take and one that I did for years. The alternative was to exit a couple of minutes before the final whistle. The fans who do this nowadays don't do it for safety reasons but are known by their fellow fans as 'The Subway Loyal' because they leave early in order to get into the queue for the subway at Copland Road.

We walked back down Copland Road towards home and, once nearly there, my dad took me into the local 'chippie' where I was bought a bag of chips and a bottle of Vimto, my favourite soft drink, which even eclipsed the magic of Irn Bru. It was the perfect end to the perfect afternoon. If only the next 50 years of watching Rangers could have been so simple and idyllic!

That was my first game at Ibrox, but it wasn't the beginning of attending every home match. My father didn't attend every home game. I had to wait until he was going before I could accompany him because I was deemed too young to go without an adult. I probably went to another three or four matches that season. However, a bonus, now that I was 10, was that I was allowed to go with my pals to the reserve games at Ibrox. Only the Main Stand and the 'wee enclosure' were opened for such games, so we paid into the boys' gate at the enclosure because it was cheapest. Normally we went right down to the front and stood at the retaining wall. The strange thing about this wall was that although it was three or four feet high on the side we stood on, it was only about a foot high on the track side. When we were bored we could lean over and draw with our fingers on the cinder track. Also, it was great that sometimes we could get right beside the tunnel and be so close to the players as they emerged from it. It was fantastic if a star player, recovering after injury, was appearing in the reserves until deemed fit enough for first-team duty.

The thing I remember most about going to these reserve matches was spotting some young player who would become a future star in the first team. One such youngster was Willie Henderson who joined the club at the age of 15 in January 1961. The wee winger was absolutely brilliant and so exciting to watch as he sped past defenders or turned them inside out with his dribbling skills. We couldn't understand why he wasn't in the first team already – until we remembered that Rangers already had a Scottish international winger, Alex Scott, playing there. It wasn't long though before 'Wee Willie' was challenging (and eventually defeating) Scott for his position on the right wing. Going to these reserve games was great as we got quite close to the players, something that wasn't possible from behind the goals in first-team matches.

It was also at one of these reserve matches, watching from the wee enclosure, that I made my only appearance at the 'medical room'. I had taken my brother, Ian, to the game, and at one point he went to the toilet. Next thing I know there was an announcement over the tannoy system telling me to go to the St Andrew's Ambulance Room. When I arrived there was Ian with a paramedic treating his leg. Apparently, while coming back to where I was, Ian slipped and banged his leg off the concrete of the stairs, cutting it. It wasn't serious, but once he had been patched up I took him home. I wasn't looking forward to explaining how he had managed to hurt himself at a reserve game.

That first season I remember that my biggest disappointment was not being allowed to go with my dad to the Old Firm game on 2 January, which 'Gers won 2–1. How I would have loved to have been part of that 79,000 crowd, but my mother wouldn't let me go. She was of the opinion that Rangers versus Celtic games were not a suitable environment for a youngster due to the ever-present possibility of crowd trouble breaking out. I must have been so naive in those days as I couldn't understand why this match should be any more likely to produce problems than any other game. All I knew was that this was the biggest game of the season, and to beat Celtic was the greatest thing that any 'Gers team could do.

My education on this front was completed just over a year later. It happened when Celtic was playing at Ibrox – but not against Rangers. It was a Scottish Cup semi-final at the end of March, and Celtic's opponents were St Mirren, with Ibrox the chosen neutral venue. Rangers would beat Motherwell in the other semi at Hampden, and all my pals and I expected it to be an Old Firm Final. It would have been the first since the legendary Final of 1928 when Rangers had broken their Scottish Cup 'hoodoo' by beating Celtic 4–0, a Davie Meiklejohn penalty starting the rout. It was with great anticipation that my pals and I expected the inevitable Final against Celtic. That day should have taught us never to rely on the expected when it comes to football.

I was back on car-watching duty in my gran's street, but this time the cars were those of Celtic fans. Once the Celtic match had started we all played football in the street, making use of the parked cars by hiding behind them with the ball so that we couldn't be tackled by opponents and then dashing out between them to score. Wouldn't football be more fun if obstacles were allowed on the pitch nowadays? It wasn't as dangerous as it perhaps sounds because those parked cars would have been the only ones in the street – hardly any residents owned a car then – and there was no through-traffic. Strangely, some of the Celtic fans started to appear much earlier than usual and get into their cars. The first ones were asked the traditional question, 'What was the score, Mister?' to be given the gruff reply, '3–1'. Our initial reaction was one of puzzlement as to why these Celtic fans were looking so down in the mouth, and then one of them revealed that it was 3–1 to St Mirren!

We discovered later why they had appeared early at their cars after seeing the highlights of the match on *Scotsport* that night. St Mirren had amazingly gone in 3–0 up at half-time in front of a 65,000 crowd. Then, in the second half, a Celtic 'goal' had been disallowed for offside, causing fighting to start among the Celtic fans at the Copland Road terracing. In those days, when fighting began, a huge 'hole' would develop in the terracing as innocent fans would try to escape from the fists, sometimes knives and flying bottles. This time these fans jumped over the boundary wall onto the track and then onto the actual pitch. Meanwhile the police made the opposite journey to get in among the trouble-makers and make some arrests. Then, as if to copy the scenes at the other end, the fans in the Broomloan terracing invaded the pitch, cavorting around without a care in the world, even asking players for their autographs.

The referee took the players off the field, having seemingly abandoned the match. The mounted police appeared, to 'usher' the fans off the park and back into the terracing. Once order had been restored it was obvious from the big gaps in the crowd that many Celtic fans had taken the opportunity to leave as there was no way there would be a comeback. Many had thought also that the game was over. One of the later theories written in newspapers was that the Celtic fans had invaded the park in an effort to get the game abandoned. If so, they were to be sorely disappointed because, after about 16 minutes, the referee brought the players back out and the game was resumed. Celtic even scored a consolation goal but got knocked out the Cup that day.

This defeat was a shock, not only to those Celtic fans who attended but to me and my pals as we had been looking forward to a Rangers versus Celtic Final. One of the older and tougher boys watching the cars in the street seemed particularly distraught. I couldn't see the problem. Until then I had never figured out why Celtic was the team Rangers fans most liked to beat. It had always puzzled me because Celtic had never been a really good side since I had become aware of football and certainly had never challenged the supremacy of Rangers. That had come from clubs like Hearts, Kilmarnock and Dundee. A match against Celtic, in my eyes, had never been one that pitted the two best teams in the League against each other. When asked why he was so upset, this boy said something like, 'I was just looking forward to tanking the Fenians!' This was the first time I'd ever heard this word used, so I asked him what he meant. 'They're Catholics and they hate us. That's why it's so good to beat them!' Now I understood the reason why there was this intense rivalry that might cause trouble.

It didn't make any difference to me. I went to a non-denominational primary school and couldn't have told you if I even knew who was a Catholic in my neighbourhood or my gran's street. As far as I knew, all my Rangers-supporting pals were Protestants, but it was never something that I asked about even if they didn't go to the same school as me. The local Catholic primary was called St Xavier's, and sometimes I would walk past it on my way to my gran's house. Occasionally I would see kids playing around outside who hadn't gone home from school yet and they didn't look any different from the pals I had at my own school. They were dressed just as poorly as we were and lived in the same slums in Govan. I certainly don't remember any fights ever occurring between Catholic and Protestant schoolkids based on sectarianism. Probably, in those days, it was the sectarian issue that kept working-class Protestants and Catholics apart, allowing the Tories to gain a majority of Parliamentary seats and rule Glasgow Corporation, as it was known then. At least, I now understood why beating Celtic was so crucial and would give such pleasure to thousands of fans.

I didn't get to see many games, but I followed the team through the television highlights, as few games were broadcast live then. Rangers won the League title, finishing the season with a brilliant 7–3 win at Ibrox over Ayr United. That was a game I definitely remember. However, the most exciting aspect of that season was 'Gers' tremendous progress to the Final of the inaugural European Cup-Winners' Cup.

The road to the Final started in September when Hungarian cracks Ferencváros came to Ibrox to be dispatched 4–2. In the return leg, in Budapest, 'Gers lost 2–1 but went into the quarter-final to face the Germans with the longest name in European competition at the time, Borussia Mönchengladbach. This time the first leg was away. Even then, German sides were considered formidable opponents, so it was a wonderful result to beat them 3–0 on their own patch. Even better was to come in the return at Ibrox in November. What had been a drizzle all day turned into torrential rain by the kick-off. Maybe that was why the crowd was only just over 38,000. The Germans were also drowned by Rangers, who thrashed them 8–0. 'Gers had been 5–0 up at half-time. When was the last time any British side beat a German team 11–0 over two legs? It has never happened since. Rangers played a clever, close-passing game on a dreadful surface and demolished the visitors. Ian McMillan's immaculate play even outshone that of Jim Baxter, although 'Slim Jim' did score two of the goals. In the first leg, the Germans had been particularly rough and brutal, but this time, as if to acknowledge their inferiority, they took their beating like gentlemen. With 25 minutes still left in the match Rangers were 8–0 up and, rather than increase their margin of victory, contented themselves with toying with their opponents. At the end of the game, the 'Gers fans were singing in the rain, 'Bring on Real Madrid!' Pity the maestros were in a different tournament!

Rangers had made it to the semi-final of the new tournament. Their reward? They were to face the English Cup holders, Wolverhampton Wanderers. This tie was to become the original 'Battle of Britain' as it was the first competitive meeting between a Scottish and English side in European football. Thankfully Rangers made it to the Final, but over the course of the next 50 years few Scottish teams would overcome English opposition in any of the European tournaments. The first leg was at Ibrox and 'Gers won 2–0 thanks to goals from Scott and Brand in either half. This was a great result considering Rangers had been hit by injuries. The side that had played for most of the season went into this game minus attacking favourites McMillan and Millar. In their stead appeared 19-year-old Bobby Hume, who went on to become a nonentity, and centre-half Doug Baillie, who went on to become a not-so-good football writer for *The Sunday Post*. 'Gers' 'iron man' Harold Davis lived up to his nickname. He pulled a muscle early on, went off, had his leg strapped up and then came back and played on the right wing. In those days, before the use of substitutes, this was usually what happened to a 'passenger' in a side. Except Davis wasn't the type to become a 'passenger'. He took part in attacking moves and tackled, even saving a goal. In adversity, Rangers pulled off a great victory and boosted the country's morale – isn't that always the case in any victory against the English?

In the return match, neither Millar not Henderson had recovered from injury but McMillan had. He played well, but for most of the first half it was Rangers having to do most of the defending with, 'keeper Billy Ritchie making one magnificent save. Typically, the away side scored just on half-time, when Alex Scott shot low into the net. Now 'Gers were three up on aggregate. Wolves equalised 25 minutes from time, but everyone knew it was a case of too little, too late. Thousands of 'Gers fans who had made the trip down to England celebrated like a conquering army. As usual, this victory was made even sweeter by the fact that the English football writers had written Rangers off even before the first leg.

Rangers had made it to the Final of the inaugural European Cup-Winners' Cup to play against Fiorentina. Unlike the premier competition, this Final was to be played over two legs, home and away. Unfortunately Rangers were up against an Italian side who were masters of two-legged ties. Even more unfortunate was the fact that the first leg was at Ibrox.

On 17 May, Rangers became the first British team to play in the Final of a European competition. Despite the fact that there was great prestige to be had in winning this new tournament, Rangers' preparations were hindered slightly by the fact that six of their players had flown home from Czechoslovakia only two days previously, having had to play for Scotland in a World Cup qualifying match. The ref for that game was Herr Steiner, and he had sent off Pat Crerand of Scotland. Ironically, he would be the ref for the game at Ibrox against the Italians, and he would do 'Gers no favours in that game either.

Until that Wednesday evening, this was one of the few games that had been broadcast live on Scottish television. I remember being in my gran's house watching the game on her television. I also remember walking home at the end of the match and joining the thousands of Rangers fans from the 80,000 crowd walking down Broomloan Road, most in a grim mood. Fiorentina had won 2–0, having scored early on and then again in the 90th minute. In between, the visitors had tried the patience of the 'Gers players and the crowd with their cynical fouling, time-wasting, protesting and general moaning at the ref. The worst example of this came in the 17th minute when Rangers, already a goal down, were awarded a penalty. The ref was immediately surrounded by angry, gesticulating Italians, who made Roy Keane seem positively meek. Even Fiorentina's assistant trainer, Chiapella, ran on to the pitch to accost the ref. The furious Rangers fans were in an uproar. Eventually order was restored and Eric Caldow prepared to take the penalty. Italian 'keeper Albertosi was on his line, jumping around and waving his arms. He had already shown a rather eccentric nature in the way he bounced the ball while preparing to kick it out. Remember, this was in the days when the 'keeper was supposed to stand still. Even worse, as Caldow ran forward to kick the ball, so did Albertosi. By the time the ball was kicked, the 'keeper was practically on his six yard line! Caldow cracked the ball past the post and, despite the laws of the game having been broken, the ref did not order a retake. He probably didn't want to go through all that Italian hassle again.

The last-minute second goal at the end of 90 minutes of Italian skulduggery was just too much for the Ibrox crowd when the final whistle went, especially when the Fiorentina players, seemingly oblivious to the mood of the booing crowd, took a bow in the centre circle. Bottles were thrown and some of the crowd in the Broomloan Road terracing managed to haul down the Italian flag that had been fluttering from the end gable of the north enclosure. It was promptly set on fire, despite the attention of the Glasgow police, who had tried to intervene.

Most fans suspected that Rangers, with a below-par performance, had lost their chance to win this new European trophy. And so it turned out when the Italians won 2–1 in Florence. It was a disappointing end to a great adventure. At least we kids gained something – another couple of exotic names to pretend to be when we played football in the streets. You wouldn't believe the number of us who suddenly wanted to become Albertosi and bounce the ball the way he had in those 'Gers games!

That was the end of my first season going to Rangers games. It was the start of a 50-year love affair. As I've said before, I was lucky to begin my support of Rangers at that time. Over the next three seasons, Rangers would win the League twice and be runners-up in the other season; they would win the treble in 1964, for the third time in the club's history; they would earn the League Cup in two of those three seasons and complete three consecutive Scottish Cup Final victories – a very rare occurrence. So rare that Celtic has never managed to do it, 'Gers have only done it three times – the last time in 1964 – and, apart from Queen's Park and Vale of Leven in the early days of the Scottish Cup, only Ferguson's Aberdeen side of the 80s has managed the feat.

At the end of that season, at the start of summer, we moved to a new house, a council flat on the south-west boundary of the city, five minutes' walk away from the small town of Barrhead, where future Rangers' manager Alex McLeish came from. Instead of walking a few minutes up the road to Ibrox, I now had to make a half-hour bus journey on the No. 49 to Govan from our scheme, the insalubrious-sounding South Nitshill. My mother had always dreamed of having a house with her own 'front and back door', but this flat was the best she ever achieved. We lived in a newish tenement at No. 53 Whitacres Road, on the first floor. Our flat had two bedrooms, a bathroom and even a veranda – luxury! From the tiny veranda, if you looked across diagonally, a couple of hundred yards away were fields with real-live cows strolling around. I was 10 years old but I had never seen a cow before – unless you count a couple of girls in my primary school class. The tenement had two storeys. Below us were the Hamiltons. Molly Hamilton had two daughters, Jean, who was older than me, and Sandra, who was the same age as my wee brother Ian. He promptly fancied Sandra and they became great pals. Also on the ground floor were Mr and Mrs McGeeney, an old Irish couple. Mick McGeeney was like Victor McLaglen who always played the big Irish sergeant in John Wayne cavalry films. Opposite us were the Brattons, who had a son and two daughters, all younger than us. I seem to remember an old spinster lived in the flat above us and a widower opposite her flat, but I can't remember their names. All in all, it was a nice 'close' with decent, friendly neighbours who got on well. I remember that first summer Jean Hamilton constantly played her favourite record Cliff Richard's *Bachelor Boy*, on her Dansette record player. It came wafting out of her open window to where we played football. Who would have thought that almost 50 years later he'd be Sir Cliff, would have had hit records in every decade since and would still be a bachelor boy?

The things I missed most about my old place in Govan – apart from its proximity to Ibrox – were our trips in summer across the river. I remember how on lovely summer evenings my father would take my brother and me on the Govan ferry across to the north bank of the Clyde in a 'voyage' that probably took three or four minutes. The boat was pretty small and probably only carried about 20 people – not that 20 people ever used it when we were on. We called it the 'Govan ferry', but actually that one was a few hundred yards along the Govan Road from us. Strictly speaking, the ferry we used was the Finnieston ferry, and its dock was just across the road from our tenement. Even in those days large stretches of the river bank were derelict and the old dry docks on the Finnieston side of the river were crumbling, weed-infested, overgrown areas. My brother and I just loved running around the place, jumping over big capstans, climbing up and down rusty ladders that took you to the bottom of a dry dock. Talk about simple pleasures. Until then I had lived my entire life beside the River Clyde and its famous shipbuilding yards. Now I was exiled to the housing scheme on the edge of the countryside.

Apart from the fresher 'country' air, the biggest plus about living in South Nitshill was that there was a huge back green. This was where we all played football and we could make sliding tackles or dive around in goal without fear of being hurt. In years to come, when my cousin, Robert Middleton, stayed overnight at ours, he would be the goalkeeper and I would practise my shooting against him while he dived around in his all-black 'keeper's outfit with a white number one specially sewn onto the back by my mum. I remember that, even when it had got dark, we would play on by the glow of our 'floodlights' – the lights we switched on in the bedrooms of our flat that overlooked the back green. 'Middy' was fearless and, like all 'keepers, threw himself around as if his life depended upon it. He was probably a better 'keeper even then than Le Guen's favourite, Lionel Letizi.

The other bonus was going into primary six at a new school, Leithland Road Primary, near where that choir contest had been the evening Rangers had been knocked out the Cup by Motherwell. My previous primary, Copland Road, was an old Victorian building, but now I was to attend a modern school that had been built in the 50s. The only disadvantage to my new school was that, since it was about three miles away, we had to travel to it in special school buses. Ironically, months before taking our new council flat, my mum had turned one down that was a five-minute walk from this school! She had refused it because it had been on the ground floor and didn't think she'd feel safe living there, having lived on the third floor of her previous abode. It hadn't mattered that the local police station was just yards away.

The great thing about the school bus trip, especially on Mondays, was that all the boys could discuss the Rangers game that had taken place the previous Saturday (it was always a Saturday in those days) and all things Rangers for the rest of the week. I distinctly remember how excited we were on the bus that day in January 1963 when George McLean was transferred from St Mirren to Rangers for a fee of £26,500, a Scottish record. He had played against 'Gers in the previous season's Scottish Cup Final and had been one of the few successes in the Saints' side. In modern parlance, 19-year-old McLean was a cross between a midfielder and a striker. At his best, he was a Platini before anyone had ever heard of the Frenchman. At his worst, he looked as if he had two left feet. In 1967, after Rangers' disastrous 1–0 defeat in the Scottish Cup by lower division Berwick Rangers, McLean and Jim Forrest (as non-scoring strikers) were made the scapegoats and never played for the club again. None of us on that school bus could have foreseen that.

The great thing about Leithland Primary was that it had not one, but two, proper football pitches. The surface was red blaise, a coarse, grit-like surface that became muddy in winter and in summer was prone to dust-storms. But at least we had real goals. Unfortunately, at the interval and lunch-time, practically everybody played on these pitches. The bigger boys, like us, got to play from one goal to the other while the younger kids played across the width of the pitch. Meanwhile, other kids would be running around playing. Talk about chaos! We had to beat our opponents as well as dodge past all these other kids on the park. How we knew who were our teammates or opponents I have no idea. No wonder Scottish football produced so many 'tanner ba' wingers in those days.

I also made new friends at the school. One was Stewart Watson, who lived along the road from me in South Nitshill, but the others all lived near the school in Pollok. Along with Stewart and other friends, Jim Mullin and Eddie Chyc, I was one of the best footballers at the school, and in primary seven we were all in the school team, coached by Mr Alexander, the music teacher. Although I haven't met any of them for over 40 years I can still remember their names: Kenny Sinclair, Jim Stewart, the Ewart twins, Tom McHugh, Graham Fleming and Harold Unsworth – an unlikely name for a Scottish boy in Pollok. One of the nicest-looking girls in my class was called Lynn Wilson and, as I discovered nearly 40 years later, she married Jim Stewart. I discovered this fact because one of my granddaughters was taught by her at Bargarran Primary, near where I now live in Erskine. I made a point of meeting her at Sports Day one year. It really is a small world – but I wouldn't like to paint it!

The following year we all went to Crookston Castle, a secondary school that had only been open for about eight years and was now one of the first comprehensive schools in the city. There I met others from different primary schools in the catchment area. Jim Mullin was a quick centre-forward who played for us but also represented Glasgow and Scottish Schoolboys' teams. He played alongside Kenny Dalglish and Tommy Craig, among others. He was a great goal-poacher and, although on the small side, looked certain to become a star as an adult. He was a clever boy as well, but he left school at the end of the fourth year to go to London, where he signed for West Ham in 1967. This was the club that still boasted the English World Cup heroes of Bobby Moore, Geoff Hurst and Martin Peters. Jim could have signed for more successful clubs, but the glamour of West Ham and London presumably made him keen to go there. Unfortunately, after a few years, it didn't work out with him, and he didn't have a chance of getting first-team action. He came home to Glasgow and went part-time, signing for Partick Thistle. That was maybe the height of his career.

In my opinion, my friend Eddie Chyc was an even better footballer than Jim Mullin. He was barrel-chested, like a boy Dave MacKay, but he was supremely fit, had speed, determination and skill, and, like Jim Mullin, gained representative honours. He should have gone on to become the new Bobby Murdoch. He was my rival when it came to the 100 and 200-yard sprints in the school Sports Day, and it was always 50/50 as to which of us would win the medal. Eddie was also a talented rower and represented the school team and Glasgow Schools. As a gymnast he was awesome. How I envied his ability to walk on his hands! Add the fact that he was intelligent, good-looking and a good fighter and you'll understand why he was the boy we all wanted to be like. He was far too self-critical, though, and even after a winning performance never seemed happy with himself. His tragedy was that he got his girlfriend pregnant, did the honourable thing and left school to get a job, marry the girl and become a father – in that order. I still wonder what happened to him. He could have been a wonderful professional footballer. What a waste!

Apart from Eddie, by 1964 my heroes were Jim Baxter, John Lennon and the young Muhammad Ali. 'The Greatest' first earned my undying admiration when he came over to Britain and defeated the archetypal Londoner, Our 'Enery Cooper. The fight was stopped in the fifth round due to Cooper sustaining bad cuts over his eye. As usual, the English gave more credit to the gallant loser than the future World Champion. By 1964 Ali was scheduled to fight for the World Title against the monstrous figure of the current Champion, the seemingly unbeatable Sonny Liston. How desperate I was for Ali to win the crown. He duly obliged and the legend was born.

This period between 1960 and 1964 was a golden era in Rangers' history. I believe now that I was watching, arguably, the greatest side in the club's history. Over 35 years later I would achieve a life-long ambition by having a book published that celebrated the achievements of that wonderful team. The side still trips off the tongue of fans who saw it: Ritchie; Shearer, Caldow; Greig, McKinnon, Baxter; Henderson, McMillan, Millar, Brand and Wilson. That was a fantastic attacking team. The defence was brilliant, with an utterly reliable 'keeper, two wonderful defensive full-backs and two central-defenders who could tackle, had pace, were competent in the air and could pass the ball. In midfield, although it wasn't called that at the time, we had two silky passers of the ball, Ian McMillan, the 'wee Prime Minister', and the genius that was 'Slim Jim' Baxter. Like thousands of other

Rangers fans, he was my hero. We worshipped that guy. Apart from exquisite skill, he brought fun and glamour to the game. We all wanted to be Slim Jim. He especially endeared himself to us by the way he dominated and humiliated Celtic.

As for the attacking players in that team, they were incomparable. It had two great wingers in Davie Wilson and Willie Henderson. Henderson was the forerunner of Jimmy Johnstone in his ability to dribble at speed and bamboozle defenders. Wilson was a more direct, pacy winger, who had a great goalscoring knack. Both were Scottish internationals. More important than scoring goals, however, was their ability to set them up for the two strikers, Millar and Brand. The 'M and B combination', as it was known, was the most lethal strike force in the country and even nowadays would have a decent claim to have been the best Rangers combination ever. These two complemented each other in style and temperament. Brand was stoic, slender, fast and a goal-poacher supreme, while stocky Millar was fearless, combative and, although not tall, great in the air as well as being immovable on the deck. Together they scored hundreds of goals for Rangers, helped by an almost telepathic understanding that they had developed over their years together in the team.

Obviously I didn't realise how lucky I was then to be watching this magnificent team that won so much. After my first half-season of actually attending Rangers games, I was allowed to go without an adult, going to most home games with my friends. From season 1961–64, I had the time of my life watching Rangers. The following season was a watershed, however, as the club slumped to its worst League position in decades.

The biggest disappointment in that era came in season 1961–62, when Rangers finished second in the League to the greatest Dundee side ever, containing Scottish internationals such as Alan Gilzean, Alex Hamilton and the veteran legend Gordon Smith. Once Champions, this Dundee team even made it to the semi-final of the European Cup. The worst defeat at Ibrox that I saw was when Dundee beat Rangers 5–1 early in that season – and we had played our usual full-strength side, apart from Jimmy Millar. That should have been a warning that we had serious opposition in our quest to retain the title. All I can remember of that defeat was the disbelief that Rangers could be so thoroughly dismantled – and at home. There may also have been a grudging admiration for the skill shown by that fine Dundee side.

The most sensational and memorable part of that season came in June when, to the amazement of everyone in Scottish football, Rangers made their tour of Russia – strictly speaking, the Soviet Union – to play three matches in various parts of that huge country. It looked a foolish undertaking, especially with Baxter unable to accompany them thanks again to the Army needing his services. The silver lining in that cloud turned out to be the emergence of the young John Greig, who would eventually be voted 'The Greatest Ranger' even eclipsing Slim Jim. Also on that tour Willie Henderson would finally be acknowledged as 'Gers first-choice right-winger ahead of internationalist Alex Scott, who would eventually be transferred to Everton, where he would win a Championship medal.

Rangers played three games and came home undefeated, despite the travelling, the hot climate and the poor food available. First up, in the capital, was Lokomotiv Moscow, where a crowd of 21,000 didn't fill the giant Lenin Stadium. If many fans didn't attend, at least the Russian leader, Kruschev, did. The normal Rangers team played and won 3–1, gaining many admirers in the process. From rainy Moscow the team travelled to the almost tropical heat of Tbilisi, the capital of Georgia. The soaring temperatures made the Bulevenski Stadium seem like a giant oven. This time a crowd of 30,000 turned out, complete with fans looking for Rangers players' autographs. Rangers deservedly won this one by 1–0 and moved on to their final match of the tour in the Ukraine. In Kiev they faced the Soviet Champions, Dynamo, and the team's fame had spread. For this match, 60,000 fans turned up. Once again, 'Gers played brilliantly and, but for biased refereeing from the local official, would have won. Rangers took the lead but, in the second half, the home side equalised with a stunning free-kick from 20-odd yards out. In the three-match tour, 'Gers only lost two goals, and both had come from free-kicks.

Impressive as this undefeated tour had been, the most memorable aspect of it came when Rangers arrived home. This was before the development of Glasgow International Airport, so the plane landed at the relatively small Renfrew Airport. An amazing 10,000 fans turned up to welcome their team home. Even more astonishingly, not only did the fans mill around on the tarmac, they managed to get onto the runway areas as well. No wonder the newspapers wrote later of the pilot being scared as he came in to land his plane with people almost lining the runway! It was an unforgettable end to a tour that had enhanced Rangers' reputation on the Continent. I still remember how proud we all were of our team and how much we were looking forward to the following season.

Our optimism proved to be justified as that season turned out to be a case of normal service being resumed when 'Gers won the League and Cup double. Apart from the Scottish Cup Final replay, the game that I remember most was a relatively insignificant League match at Ibrox in December, a week before my birthday.

Rangers thrashed Kilmarnock, which was one of the top sides in the country then, by an amazing 6–1. I had taken my wee brother with me as I was deemed responsible enough at the age of almost 12. It had snowed on and off for most of that day, and with a crowd of 40,000 attending we couldn't get into the covered enclosure, so we stood at the top of the Copland Road terracing, in the open air, with the snow coming down occasionally. Fans were hardy creatures in those days. By half-time my wee brother was moaning constantly that he wanted to go home as he claimed he had gone 'all numb'! Rangers played very well, as the final score would suggest, but by the start of the second half my brother and I were so frozen that we could take it no longer. We opted to leave and head for our gran's house a few hundred yards away. It was so cold that we were near to tears. Never had I been so grateful to enter a warm house. For once I wasn't even bothered when later I heard that Rangers had won 6–1. That day should have been a harbinger of grim things to come, in terms of weather. The early months of the new year saw Britain suffering from the coldest weather experienced in that century. At various times millions went without electricity. In our flat, before the days of central heating, the ice formed on the inside of our bedroom windows. Rangers suffered from a host of postponed games and, in fact, 'Gers didn't play one League match between 2 January and 9 March.

Apart from that experience, all I remember of that season was that Old Firm Scottish Cup Final replay – and I wasn't even there! Still considered too young to go to an Old Firm match, I had to be content with watching highlights of the match on television. The first game, at Hampden, had been watched by over 129,000 spectators. It had been a pretty turgid affair, although Rangers had only been denied a victory because of the brilliance of Celtic's 'keeper, Frank Haffey. That was a phrase that didn't appear too often in sports pages. The replay attracted over 120,000 on the Wednesday evening.

With George McLean injured in the first match, there was a shock recall for 33-year-old veteran midfielder Ian McMillan. It was a bit of luck because 'the wee Prime Minister' produced a dazzling performance that was worthy of his former years. He even managed to outshine Baxter, who also had a great game. Rangers ended up winning by 3–0, with the goals coming from Brand (2) and Wilson, but it was the manner of that victory that thrilled 'Gers fans and sickened their counterparts. Rangers seemed to have every player playing at their peak.

When the third goal went in around 20 minutes from the end, Baxter decided to take the mickey out of the Celtic players. He was at his arrogant best, toying with the opponents, showing supreme confidence as he juggled with the ball or stood on it, keeping possession and casually passing it to teammates. At one point he even sat on the ball while it was in play and dared Celtic players to come and try to take it away from him. None did! Not only was Baxter humiliating the Bhoys, he was doing the same to their fans. Unlike the players, however, the fans didn't need to stick around – and they didn't. Long before the end of the game, the huge 'Celtic End' terracing at Hampden, which could hold around 40,000 fans, was almost deserted. The Rangers fans were in raptures. It was Baxter's finest hour in their eyes. At the final whistle, Baxter even stole the match ball by sticking it up his jersey so that he could give it to Ian McMillan in tribute to the player's magnificent swansong.

It was the following season, 1963–64, that saw various firsts for me taking place. It was also then that I started my collection of Rangers' home programmes. I don't buy a programme for ordinary League games but only if the occasion is of special significance. My collection consists mainly of European matches, Cup semi-finals and Finals, friendlies and testimonials, plus all the home Scotland games. I now have hundreds of programmes kept in binders and categorised. I even have a binder with tickets kept from major games. What an anorak! Coincidentally, that was Rangers' treble-winning season, and I was at Hampden to see the Cups being won…well, almost. I will explain that later. However, my first visit to the national stadium came in May 1963 when I went to my first international match, a friendly between Scotland and Austria – old friends, apparently. Not only was it my first Scottish international, it was Jimmy Millar's as well but, by the end of it neither of us had seen 90 minutes of international football. I was near the front of the Hampden terracing, quite crushed in the big crowd at the Rangers' End on that lovely spring evening as Scotland played brilliantly and led 4–1, with the 'over-robust' visitors not taking their humiliation very well. Since this was the first time I had witnessed foreign opposition in the flesh, I just assumed that they all played like this, rather than like Real Madrid.

By the time two Austrians had been sent off by English ref Jim Finney, things were getting so bad that, seven minutes from the end, the ref abandoned the game due to the 'violent conduct' of the Austrians. What a let-down in my first of many Hampden experiences. Apart from the way Scotland had played, the thing I remember most about that game was being disappointed in Hampden itself. I could see it was bigger than Ibrox, but it was nowhere near as modern or comfortable. Fifty years later, the same could still be said, although the difference in capacity has been drastically reduced.

My first Rangers game at Hampden and first Cup Final came in October of that year when we played Morton in the Final of the League Cup in front of nearly 106,000 fans. Morton was in the old Second Division and was the outstanding side in it, going on to win the title easily while 'Gers were the First Division Champions, destined to retain their title. Rangers won 5–0 in a unique win that saw two cousins, youngsters Jim Forrest and Alex Willoughby, sharing the goals. Forrest got four of them, actually. Jimmy Millar, who had worn that number-nine shirt previously, was first to congratulate the youngster, still only 19, on his display. Forrest and Willoughby had been offered the chance to play for Manchester United but had opted for Rangers. That day must have seemed like the justification they needed for their choice. Amazingly, all the goals were scored in the second half. Finally, I remember my first Cup presentation when Bobby Shearer lifted the trophy in the Main Stand, and we all cheered as if it was the greatest thing that had ever happened.

At the start of that season, my parents considered me old enough, and sensible enough, to go to my first Old Firm game at Ibrox without an adult. The one proviso, though, was that I watch it from the relative safety of the Main Stand, which I'd only been in previously for the Rangers' sports and 'Trials'. Thanks to the excellent cinder running track around the playing field, the Ibrox Athletics Meeting was an annual event, and the biggest names in British athletics usuallly competed. My pals and I used to love going to see household names running, and big crowds were the norm, far bigger than any British athletics meet nowadays. As for the Rangers' 'Trials', this was a pre-season ritual when, instead of playing a friendly against foreign opposition to warm up for the season ahead, Rangers' first, second and third teams all played against each other on the one evening, giving lesser players the chance to kick lumps out of their rivals who were keeping them out of the first team! What I liked about it was that it not only gave young kids a chance to see their heroes but also the up-and-coming players who, in a season or so, might be in the first team.

My first Rangers versus Celtic match, in August, was the return match in our League Cup section that consisted of Rangers, Celtic, Kilmarnock and Queen of the South. 'Gers had already played at Parkhead two weeks earlier and had won 3–0, with Forrest scoring two and George McLean the other. I didn't know it then, but this victory at Ibrox would mean that Rangers would have defeated Celtic by 3–0 on three consecutive occasions. By the end of that treble-winning season, Rangers would have beaten Celtic five times out of fve.

For my first Old Firm game I got to the stand very early. I had to wait nervously for the gates to open. Once inside, I had looked around at very little until the two sets of fans gradually filled up the stadium. In all my matches at Ibrox previous to this, it had been filled mainly with Rangers fans so, by kick-off, it was quite a shock to notice that Celtic fans actually filled half of Ibrox. Nowadays, Celtic fans sit in the Broomloan Stand, but in those days they got that entire terracing plus half the north enclosure opposite me in the Main Stand, half the 'wee' enclosure underneath me and half the Main Stand. At least I was well away from the dividing line that separated the two sets of fans. This segregation had always been practised voluntarily by both sets of fans but in 1960, the Glasgow magistrates made it a formal arrangement in an effort to prevent trouble breaking out. The Old Firm sharing half of the other's stadium continued for quite a few years. I remember sitting in the Main Stand at Parkhead in my first away Old Firm match and thinking what a poor relation it was compared to the magnificent Leitch Stand at Ibrox. For many years I also watched games from The Jungle at Parkhead, level with the 18-yard line, towards the Rangers' End. That was as close as I ever got to Celtic fans, who started at the 'demarcation' line opposite the halfway line on the pitch. As the years went on, gradually, almost imperceptibly, that demarcation line moved towards the 'Rangers' End' so that fewer and fewer 'Gers fans could watch from The Jungle until, eventually, it had been taken over completely by the Celtic fans.

That day at Ibrox, within 10 minutes of kick-off, most of the 70,000 crowd was inside the ground. I remember being utterly fascinated by the absolute bedlam in terms of noise, with Rangers fans singing old favourites such as *Derry's Walls* and *The Sash* while the Celtic fans broke into *Hail! Hail! The Celts are here!* This was before the days when Liverpool fans had started to use *You'll Never Walk Alone* which was then 'stolen' by Celtic fans later on. Even the respectably dressed Rangers fans around me seemed to be getting rather over-excited. At that time, fans didn't wear replica tops to games, but it was still a colourful sight, with one half of the stadium a mass of red, white and blue while the other half was a wall of green and white. There were no banners, 'witty' or otherwise, on display, but I did observe the usual Union Jacks and Irish Tricolours. I know it's a cliché, but it really was as if you could *feel* the tension and the excitement building up just before the teams emerged from the tunnel to the noisiest reception I had ever experienced.

The emotions, the bitter rivalry and the obvious hatred apart, I really enjoyed the game. Rangers won 3–0 again, with goals from Wilson, Brand and Forrest. The first half was actually quite even, with Chalmers thankfully missing a couple of good chances for Celtic. Then seven minutes before half-time, Wilson opened the scoring and Rangers didn't look back. I remember Henderson playing really well and causing the Celtic defenders all sorts of problems, and young Forrest giving Billy McNeill a torrid time. In fact, in the second half, a Baxter pass through the centre had cut open the Celtic defence, and with Forrest bearing in on goal, McNeill had to foul him and concede a penalty. Nowadays he would be ordered off, but not then. Brand efficiently converted, and the game was safe as far as we were concerned. Later another through pass, this time by Greig, found Forrest running on to it beyond the defence to hit a 16-yard shot into the net – just the way I used to do it for my Cubs team!

One of the strangest aspects of the game for me was that when each Rangers goal was scored only half the stadium exploded into an incredible noise of celebration, while the other half was totally silent, as if everyone there had been struck dumb. It is still a phenomenon that occurs nowadays and one that produces an awful feeling in my stomach when Celtic score at Ibrox and the only sound that can be heard is the thousands of Celtic fans celebrating in the Broomloan Stand. It's almost an eerie feeling and one that's inevitable, but you never want it to occur too often.

Celtic's traditional fighting spirit had now gone – at least on the field. However, that was not the case on the terracing. It was then that I realised why my parents had insisted on me sitting in the stand. As Rangers started toying with their opponents, it was too much for some Celtic fans and fighting broke out at the Broomloan end. As was the norm in those days, bottles and cans started to fly and brawling began among Celtic fans. The 'Gers fans were presumably too far away to hit! A huge 'hole' opened up on the terracing as the police waded in to intervene, and by the end of the fray apparently 30 arrests had been made. I must admit to keeping my eyes on this rather than what was happening on the park at the time – it was much more exciting! To think that nowadays all the authorities have to worry about is the 'offensive' songs that both sets of fans sing at each other.

At the end of the match, as I went to wait for my bus home, I remembered to take off my Rangers scarf and put it in my jacket pocket. The trouble at the game had reminded me that some fans don't take defeat well at the hands of their old enemy, and my bus would probably have Rangers and Celtic fans on it, so it was better to take no chances. After those days of the early 60s, there was probably less hooliganism and fighting inside grounds than in the streets around the stadium afterwards. The most dangerous part of an Old Firm game could be getting home safely.

At the end of that season I also experienced my first Scottish Cup Final when I attended the Rangers versus Dundee match in April. It was the biggest crowd I had ever been among – 120,982 people. For some reason I was at the Celtic End of Hampden and stood quite near the front of that terracing. It was typical that all three 'Gers goals were scored at the other end of the park and I only got a close-up of the Dundee goal. A few thousand Dundee fans were in that terracing but standing near the Main Stand, while I was towards the North Stand. There would have been no animosity between the two sets of fans in those days anyway.

It was an enjoyable game. Rangers played well and would have won quite easily but for Dundee's 'keeper, Bert Slater, who defied 'Gers' forwards time and again with brilliant saves. Most observers later declared that it was one of the best Cup Finals in years. Traditionally these matches tend to be damp squibs no matter the teams participating as there is so much at stake that an exciting game is rarely the result. This was the exception, but thanks to Slater it took Rangers until the 71st minute before the deadlock was broken when Millar headed in from a corner. It was so simple after all the fruitless pressure until then. I remember breathing a sigh of relief that a replay had been averted – there was no extra-time in those days!. My relief lasted just one minute because Kenny Cameron equalised from the re-start, and we were back to square one. In one of my Rangers DVDs you can hear a lost-the-plot Arthur Montford commentating on this goal, 'What a game! What a Final! What a match!' It was a swansong too for that great Rangers team of the early 60s, only McMillan and the injured Caldow were missing from the side that had thrilled us for so long.

I should explain about 'almost' seeing the two Cups being won that season. With about four or five minutes left, I decided that a replay was a certainty and left the stadium so that I could get a bus on the first part of my two-bus journey home. I had to walk along Aitkenhead Road to get a bus to Shawlands then another from there to South Nitshill. I was pleasantly surprised to board a half-empty bus almost immediately, and I remember sitting on the top deck at the front looking out at the road ahead. From where I got on the bus it was around a five-minute drive to Mount Florida, where the thousands of Rangers fans were now streaming down the road from the end of Hampden that was opposite where I had been. I couldn't understand why they all looked so happy and were singing and chanting. Then, as many boarded the bus, I discovered the truth. Rangers had scored two goals in the final 90 seconds to win the Cup! My first Scottish Cup Final and I hadn't been there to see the winning goals or the trophy being presented! Subway loyal, eat your heart out!

Once again Jimmy Millar had put Rangers into the lead with another header, following a great dribble from Willie Henderson. Then, practically before the cheering had died down, another brilliant run by Henderson ended with the ball passed between Brand and Wilson, whose shot was parried by Slater only for Brand to net the rebound. It was game over. Bobby Shearer duly lifted the Cup, completing a Rangers treble – and I had missed it. At least I took some consolation from the fact that I had been there all of that season to see 'Gers' progress to that end result. Following Rangers had been an exciting adventure, and the success of that season, in my mind, would continue forever. How wrong could I have been?

CHAPTER TWO

THE NOT-SO-SWINGING 60s AND BEYOND

The following season, 1964–65, turned out to be a pivotal season for Rangers – and Scottish football. In a thrilling last-day League decider between Kilmarnock and Hearts at Tynecastle, Killie had to beat the home side by 2–0 to take the title. In those days it was decided on goal average, not goal difference. Anything less and Hearts would be the champs. Kilmarnock duly managed it, and future 'Gers manager, Willie Waddell, showed unusual emotion as he cavorted around on the pitch, celebrating with his Killie heroes. Nowadays, the Killie manager celebrates escaping relegation.

That season was a disaster for Rangers in the League as they finished fifth, which was almost unheard of in the history of the club. Forty years previously the club had finished sixth – its lowest ever position. 1965 was also almost an interregnum that split the decade in two. For the first half of the 60s Rangers had been more or less all-conquering, but from the season after Killie won the title Stein's Celtic would become the dominant force, winning nine in a row. That was not a great time to be a Rangers fan. None of us would have believed that it would be 1974 before Rangers became Champions again. Part of the reason for that disastrous League standing was injuries to key players, especially Baxter and Henderson, who missed more than half that season. In fact, Baxter would be transferred to Sunderland at the end of the season.

Rangers came second to Celtic no fewer than six times during those nine seasons when Celtic were champions. In some seasons, a fine Rangers team would even come second, having amassed more points than in earlier seasons when the club had won the title!

Season 1967–68 deserves a special mention in this respect. Celtic were the reigning European Champions that season and retained their League title, but this 'Gers side only lost one match (the last one against Aberdeen at Ibrox), winning 28 out of 34, scoring 93 goals and accruing a massive 61 points – yet they still lost out to Celtic by two points! It was halfway through that season that the club sacked manager Scot Symon and installed Davie White, who would only last one full season. In some seasons of this great Celtic run, Rangers would only be one or two points behind the Parkhead team as they retained their title.

Having said that, there was a prolonged stage when Rangers couldn't win anything. In the four seasons from 1966–67 until 1970–71, the club failed to win any of the three domestic trophies. Making up for those dark days when Celtic dominated were such triumphs as the Scottish Cup replay win over Celtic in 1966, the League Cup Final win against them in 1970, thanks to the 16-year-old Derek Johnstone, and the winning of the European Cup-Winners' Cup in Barcelona in 1972.

The beginning of the 70s saw another manager, Davie White, sacked and a new manager in the shape of playing legend Willie Waddell, who tried to revitalise the whole club by going back to traditional values but using modern methods.

There was another first for me in my Rangers-watching career in season 1964–65 – my first European match. 'Gers were in the European Cup and in the first round had been drawn against powerful Yugoslavs Red Star Belgrade. This first leg was at Ibrox in front of a near 80,000 crowd. I remember being in the North Enclosure, almost on the halfway line, to watch an engrossing game that Rangers eventually won 3–1. Even at the end of the match, however, I wasn't euphoric as we all realised that a really tough return tie lay ahead of us, and so it proved as the Yugoslavs won 4–2, thus resulting in a replay as this was before the days of the away goals rule. The replay took place at Highbur.y and 'Gers won 3–1 with goals from Brand and Forrest – identical to the first game at Ibrox.

Next up it was Vienna Rapid. Once again I was at Ibrox for the first leg, which Rangers won by a solitary goal in a game that was a real struggle. The apprehension we all felt about the return leg turned out to be misplaced. In the Prater Stadium, Vienna, Jim Baxter gave one of his greatest displays, teasing and tormenting the hapless and well-beaten Austrians. 'Gers ran out 2–0 winners, and then, with a minute to go, it happened. Skocik tackled Slim Jim and he went down, realising immediately that it was serious. It turned out that his leg had been broken just below the ankle. A player at his peak had been cruelly struck down, and that match turned out to be the zenith of his Rangers' career. He was out until the end of March the following year. In May, he was transferred to Sunderland for a fee of £72,500. I distinctly remember crying myself to sleep that night at the loss of my idol – and I was 14. Rangers' decline set in at the same time.

I remember two highlights from that season. One was the League Cup Final victory in October 1964 when Rangers beat Celtic 2–1, both goals coming from Jim Forrest. Baxter, in dispute with the club over pay, was actually made the captain for that game, and I remember thinking that all would be fine with him for the rest of that season. This time I was crammed in at the rear of the Rangers' End terracing at Hampden. Celtic probably played better than us, but we managed to snatch the goals that came from two defence-splitting passes, firstly from Brand and then Baxter, both of which were coolly converted by young Forrest. Jimmy Johnstone scored a goal to put his team back in the game, but Rangers' defence was immense and held out for a famous victory. As usual, Celtic claimed that they had been hard done by as they had claimed that in the 55th minute the ball had crossed the line before Ritchie had retrieved it. However, all the press reports at the time refuted this. I didn't care. I just remember being so proud, seeing Baxter holding that trophy aloft and then dancing around with his teammates in front of the fans in celebration.

My other highlight of that season came at the start of March 1965 when Rangers played their second-leg quarter-final in the European Cup against the mighty world champions, Inter Milan. Rangers had already lost 3–1 in Milan, and so most 'Gers fans realised that it would be an uphill task to overcome such illustrious opponents – especially with the genius of Baxter still missing, having broken his leg in the previous round. I still can't believe how close we came to forcing yet another play-off match.

This was an all-ticket game and I was going with my cousin, Robert, 'Middy'. He lived in Castlemilk so we met up at Govan Cross to walk up to the stadium. It had been snowing on-and-off all that day and initially that had been a worry. Would the game be postponed? By the time we walked towards Ibrox, though, there was another problem. It had become quite foggy. We tried to estimate the visibility and reckoned it should be alright as it seemed around a couple of hundred yards. Still, there was doubt. So much so that, contrary to tradition, as we went through the turnstiles, we were allowed to keep our tickets, presumably in case of an abandonment. In those days tickets were just one piece, with no tear-off portion. I still have that ticket – a piece of orange card about four inches by two. The price was 7s 6d – about 30-odd pence in today's currency. Robert and I watched the match from the North Enclosure, but, before kick-off, some fans were walking through the crowd asking if anyone would be willing to sell their ticket to them. We declined because we wanted to make sure we would be alright for a replay, should the weather force it, although the snow had been cleared from the pitch and piled at the side of the track. We discovered later that these fans, with any tickets received in that fashion, had gone to the famous blue gates at the foot of the Copland Road terracing and sold them to ticketless fans outside. I reckon the crowd could have been bigger than the official attendance, listed as 78,872.

The whole occasion was wonderful, but the game itself was an anti-climax. The Italians employed their tried-and-tested cattenacio system of defence-in-depth, and 'Gers manfully tried to break them down. It would have been so much easier with Baxter in the team. When Forrest scored, hopes soared because one more goal would give us a play-off. I'll never forget, in that second half, how George McLean's 20-odd yard rocket shot looked net-bound and had us all jumping up in celebration – only to see it crash off the bar and be cleared. It was typical of the Italians' luck in those days. The 1–0 win wasn't enough and we were out. Inter went on to retain the European Cup by beating Benfica in the Final in Milan. To this day, I still maintain that if Baxter hadn't broken his leg in Vienna, Rangers would have knocked the Italians out and who knows? We might just have won that trophy two years before Celtic.

One of the highlights of the mid-1960s was Rangers' Scottish Cup Final replay win against Celtic. The first game, in front of over 126,000, had been pretty much a non-event for an Old Firm match and had ended in a 0–0 draw. Thankfully, the replay was a pulsating match and a victory to savour as Rangers beat more-or-less the same Celtic side that would win the European Cup the following season. I was crammed in at the rear of the Rangers' End at Hampden, right behind the goal in which 'Gers scored that night. Their Danish right-back, Kai Johansen, became the goalscoring hero, but old warhorse Jimmy Millar, playing in midfield was the real hero of the Rangers fans. In a game in which 'Gers had held their own, something special was needed to break the deadlock. It came 20 minutes from the end of the match. A great run up the left saw Willie Johnston put a ball into the box. It was belted out by a defender but only as far as Johansen, running in from the right. He fairly smacked the ball from around 25 yards out, and Ronnie Simpson in the Celtic goal had no chance. At that moment Johansen became 'King Kai' in the eyes of 'Gers fans. He was the first foreigner to score the winning goal in a Scottish Cup Final and the first Scandinavian to win a Scottish Cup-winners' medal.

Rangers fans went crazy. In those days the terracing was open to the skies and was composed of an earth and cinder mixture. When a goal was scored the result was a huge cloud of dust rising to envelop the entire crowd. When we all settled down again after jumping around and hugging each other, I found I was about two yards to the right of where I had been standing and didn't have as good a view as previously, so I had to stand on tip-toe for the rest of the game. Not only was that uncomfortable, but for that final 20 minutes 'Gers took an absolute pounding from Celtic as they tried to equalise, so my stomach was in knots and my nails were bitten as never before. The wait for the final whistle felt like an eternity, and it seemed like only a matter of time before Celtic managed to get that elusive goal. However, Rangers defended well with a backs-to-the-wall performance and managed to see out the game. When that final whistle went I don't think I had ever had such a sense of relief before joy overcame that emotion. As Rangers went up to receive the trophy, another feeling took over – one of pride in a side that had overcome the odds to beat Celtic.

That goal earned Kai Johansen his own special song composed by the fans to honour his achievement. In those days before political correctness, fans of all clubs were much more racist and bigoted. To the tune of an old cowboy song, Johansen's had these lyrics among it: 'Singing Kai yai yippee, the Pope's a f****** hippy, Kai yai yippee, yippee yai!' Nowadays the football authorities threaten punishments against clubs whose fans sing offensive songs. What would they have made of these ones? Back then, songs were the least of fans' troubles while at a game. In Old Firm games especially, fighting could break out in a flash, and fans of the same team would start fighting each other while bottles and cans flew through the air. So much for the 'good old days'.

If that Final win was the highlight of 1966 for me then the lowest point came only a couple of months later. That was when England won the World Cup – an event obviously long since forgotten about. I still firmly believe that Scotland should have been there contesting that tournament. As usual, we blew our chances in a match at Hampden. I remember being in the North Enclosure watching the Scotland versus Poland game, with 'Gers' winger Willie Johnston, at 17 years old, making his international debut. He had been picked by Jock Stein, who was the temporary, stand-in manager for the international side. In front of 107,000 fans, at half-time, the Scots were 1–0 up and playing well, especially Johnston. Then, in the dying minutes, we lost two goals to snatch defeat from the jaws of victory in that vital match. Typical Scotland.

Our next match at Hampden in the campaign was against Italy, and again I was in the North Enclosure with three of my pals, Stewart Watson, Ally McDougall and Graeme Fleming, watching an enthralling match, which was won by a fantastic John Greig goal in the final minute. I still remember how crazy everyone in the 100,000-plus crowd went. When we had all settled down again, my friends were yards away from us as the fans had all moved around in their joyful celebration. We were so proud and excited as we walked to Pollokshaws Road to await our bus home. We went into a chip shop, and while we were waiting the highlights of the match came on their television. How we cheered when Greig's goal was shown. Unfortunately, as always with Scotland, there was to be no fairy-tale ending. We still had to play in Naples in the return match. I remember it was an afternoon kick-off and most of us 'dogged' school to see the game live on television. Typically, Scotland was badly hit by injuries to key players, and Stein had to field a makeshift side that included Liverpool centre-half Ron Yeats at centre-forward. We lost 3–0 and were out of the World Cup taking place across the border. It was a bitter pill to swallow but one that I would find repeated over the next 40 years.

When the World Cup kicked off in England, most Scots were only interested in seeing how long it would take for the English to be knocked out. I had watched some of the early matches, including North Korea beating the mighty Italy and giving the Portuguese a fright. I also remember the hosts struggling in the early stages, usually being pulled through by Bobby Charlton at his peak, while West Germany, with a young guy called Beckenbauer, looked unbeatable. That summer I was going with my aunt and uncle, and my cousins Anne and 'Middy' on holiday to Blackpool. It was great timing to be in England when they won the World Cup. The night before we left for Blackpool, I remember us all watching the Hungary versus Brazil game at Goodison Park live on television in which the Hungarians, with the likes of Albert, Bene and Farkas absolutely destroyed the holders, playing brilliantly against the masters.

The next day we travelled to Blackpool by bus, and I didn't really see much else of the tournament as we were too busy enjoying the many delights Blackpool offered teenagers. I remember being shocked that Brazil had been eliminated and that the Hungarians hadn't sustained their brilliance. We watched the quarter-final between England and Argentina live but in black-and-white. There was a crowd of us watching it in the television lounge of our boarding house. The audience consisted entirely of Scottish holidaymakers. All of us were desperate for the Argentinians to win and were quite confident that they would, bearing in mind England's average displays until then. The anguish was palpable when the English won, thanks to a goal by that archetypal smug Englishman Geoff Hurst and the fact that Argentina's captain and best defender, Rattin, was sent off. None of us could believe that the English had made it to the semi-final. Little did we realise that worse was to come.

Thankfully, on the day of the Final, we were travelling home on the bus so avoided having to see it on television. Meanwhile, Denis Law was apparently out on his golf course trying to do the same! On the bus, nobody even had a transistor radio on. We all avoided hearing any news until we got to the motorway service station at Southwaite. That's when we discovered that the English had actually won the thing. The rest of that trip across the border and up to Glasgow must have been the gloomiest ever. Still, we thought our pain would only last a few months. How wrong we were.

It was around the mid-1960s that I was allowed to go to away games. Naturally, at first, I went to the ones taking place in Glasgow. Apart from Queen's Park, who played at Hampden, there were five Glasgow clubs. I soon visited all their grounds. Parkhead was a shock in a way as it was nowhere near as big or attractive a stadium as Ibrox. It had a dilapidated look about it that surprised me, considering the status of Celtic. The surrounding area also had an impact on me as it was so poverty-stricken and slum-like, and my childhood had been spent in similar surroundings. Parkhead was the hardest venue to get to and a trip to the 'dangerous' East End of Glasgow seemed like a visit to another country. I liked going to Firhill for games against Thistle as we had to get the subway there, which I loved. The subway had a unique smell. I was only once at Cathkin, the home of the now-defunct Third Lanark, but can't remember much about it except that it wasn't far away from Hampden and the pitch surface looked like a bowling green's. As for Clyde's ground, Shawfield Stadium, since it was also a greyhound racing venue the view from a spectator's point of view was poor, the terracing rake being very shallow. All of these grounds made me appreciate just how advanced and comfortable a stadium Ibrox was.

Within a couple of seasons I had travelled further afield in following Rangers. I visited Greenock Morton, Ayr, Kilmarnock, Motherwell, Tynecastle, Easter Road and Dens Park, Dundee. My first away game outside of Glasgow was a trip to Hearts' Tynecastle Stadium. Two friends and I made the journey by rail, using the old 'football special' trains. The only advice I got from my dad was to get off the train at Haymarket station rather than Waverley, the terminus, and, from there, to 'follow the crowd'. This we duly did. Unfortunately the group of 'Gers fans we walked behind were heading straight for a pub on the way to the ground! As they entered, we looked around for other Rangers fans and managed to ask some for directions.

Thankfully it was easy to get to – as long as you avoided a pub crawl on the way. One of my friends who didn't accompany us that day was Graeme Fleming. Graeme was actually a Hearts supporter, a brave thing to be in a school where almost every boy supported the 'Gers. Graeme used to take great delight in winding us all up either before a Hearts' game against 'Gers or, worse, after a Hearts' victory against us. But we all congratulated him once when his team had actually beaten Celtic, thereby helping Rangers. I can still hear him singing the *Hearts' Song* in a voice that wouldn't have got past an *X Factor* audition, and I ony know the words of it thanks to his repeated singing of it down the years:

Hearts, Hearts, glorious Hearts,
It's down at Tynecastle they bide.
The boys in maroon are the talk of the toun
And Auld Reekie is sure to be proud.

We used to tease him about the rhyming of 'bide' and 'proud' and the use of the Scots word 'bide'. Who uses that word nowadays? Graeme was a fragile-looking, John White-type midfielder in our school team and a very popular guy. Whenever I hear Hearts fans singing their song (not that often these days), I always think of him.

Another away day was in February 1967, when my friends and I took the train to Kilmarnock. It wasn't the match or even the trip that was memorable, it was more the unusual occasion. That was the game that was attended by Soviet Prime Minister Alexei Kosygin, who was in the middle of a visit to Scotland. He was second in the Soviet leadership at the time, and he was introduced to the teams on the pitch. He received a rapturous welcome from the 31,000 fans in a jam-packed Ruby Park. You'd have thought that he was related to the Queen judging by the reception he was accorded rather than being the second-most powerful man in an evil dictatorship that was pursuing a cold war against the West. This match, which 'Gers won 2–1, took place only a couple of weeks after their disastrous exit from the Scottish Cup when wee Berwick Rangers beat them 1–0. It was Sandy Jardine's third game for the club, but he would go on to play a total of 674 games for Rangers. Apparently Kosygin had travelled to the game by train from Central Station, Glasgow, just as we had – only not on a 'football special', presumably. Maybe if he had, the Cold War would have ended sooner.

That Scottish Cup first-round defeat by Berwick Rangers at the end of January was one of the lowest points in my life as a fan. It was probably the worst defeat in

Rangers' history, coming as it did from a side from a lower division. Having said that, the defeat at home of Le Guen's Rangers side in the CIS League Cup by lower League St Johnstone in 2006 perhaps runs it close now. I remember coming home and starting to watch *Grandstand* as the old teleprinter results sequence was beginning. When the news of Rangers defeat was shown on the screen I had to look twice and then listen to the presenter confirming the result before I believed it. That humiliating result sent shock waves throughout Scottish football. It was inconceivable. Even after 40-odd years, when the Scottish Cup comes around in January and journalists are looking for a surprise result, they still mention Berwick. It's a pity they don't remember the bigger shock that came when lower division Inverness Caley beat Celtic at Parkhead, costing their manager, John Barnes, his job; or Ross County's defeat of the Hoops in a Scottish Cup semi-final in 2010. If Berwick caused 'Gers fans to suffer, a couple of the players suffered even more. The two strikers that day, the prolific Jim Forrest and the erratic George McLean, were made the scapegoats for the defeat not by the fans but by the Board of Directors. They were never to play for the club again and were transferred as soon as possible. That was a rash decision that would come back to haunt the club later that season when Rangers contested the Final of the European Cup-Winners' Cup – minus their two strikers. To stress this folly, it should be remembered that Jim Forrest scored 145 goals in a mere 163 appearances for 'Gers. What a strike rate!

The one redeeming feature of that season was our great run to the Final of the Cup-Winners' Cup. I was lucky enough to be at all of Rangers' home matches for that adventure. In the first round, we beat Glentoran from Northern Ireland 4–0 in the second leg at Ibrox after a 1–1 draw away in a routine tie. That earned us a match against the German cracks and current holders of the trophy, Borussia Dortmund, with World Cup stars like Held and Emmerich. In a pulsating match at Ibrox in the first leg, Rangers won 2–1, despite a controversial equaliser from the Germans when Held's momentum had taken him off the pitch at the goalline as the play raged on, only for him to come back on at an opportune moment and pass the ball to a teammate, who scored. Incredibly, despite Rangers' protests, the goal was allowed.

In the quarter-final in March, 'Gers were paired with Real Zaragoza. The weather was terrible, and I watched the game from under the cover of the North Enclosure as torrential rain, driven on by a howling gale, buffeted Ibrox. The wind swept the rain straight down the pitch from one goal to the other, so I realised early on that 'Gers' home advantage had been reduced to 45 minutes – the half in which we had the wind and rain at our backs. And so it proved. Rangers went in at the interval 2–0 up but, against the elements, had to defend for almost all of the second half to keep that lead intact. In the return leg in Zaragoza, centre-half Ronnie McKinnon was missing due to a broken nose, which didn't help 'Gers' chances of keeping the Spaniards at bay. Rangers conceded a goal quite early on, but they defended really well for the rest of the match and only lost the crucial second goal from a dubious penalty. The game went into extra-time, where Rangers were awarded a penalty. Unfortunately Dave Smith's effort was saved and the game ended without a winner being scored. Those were the days before some bright spark at UEFA had thought of the idea of a penalty shoot-out to settle such a stalemate. So, how was the tie resolved? The toss of a coin was the favoured method. Captain John Greig was the lone Ranger in the centre circle as he called, correctly, sending 'Gers into the semi-final.

In the semi-final, Glentoran apart, 'Gers met their easiest opponents on that great European run. Bulgarians Slavia Sofia were the opponents, but they were a very predictable, solid, uninspiring side with no star names. I can remember feeling confident that we would make the Final. It turned out to be a closer affair than I had imagined. The first leg was away, and veteran winger Davie Wilson scored the only goal of the game. In the return at Ibrox, our other winger, Willie Henderson, was the only player to hit the back of the net in front of 71,000 fans to send us to the Final.

Our opponents in the Final were the emerging Bayern Munich, which was unlucky. It would be played in Nuremberg, not far from Munich, which was even ore unfortunate. Unluckier still was that the match was to be one week after Celtic had won the European Cup. This was the first time that two clubs from the same city would contest the two major European Finals. Celtic had already done their part. Now it was up to Rangers to uphold the honour of their city. So no pressure there then!

I watched the game live on television, which was still quite an unusual occurrence in those days. Rangers had made life difficult for themselves by binning their two main strikers, Forrest and McLean, after the Berwick debacle in January. Now, in May, everybody was wondering who would score the goals to win this trophy. Scot Symon's solution was to play midfielder Alex Smith and reserve centre-half the big, slow and cumbersome Roger Hynd up front. Despite having two great wingers in Henderson and Willie Johnston in the line-up, chances were few and far between in a largely uneventful match. Unfortunately, 'Gers' best chance fell to Hynd, whose close-range effort was saved. Rangers' chairman John Lawrence later reckoned that this miss cost him a knighthood since Celtic's chairman, Robert Kelly, had received one after their Lisbon triumph. If only Hynd had managed to put it into the net the way he had three weeks earlier when he had scored against Celtic at Ibrox in the 2–2 draw before the Bhoys went to Lisbon to meet their destiny. The 90 minutes ended in a 0–0 draw, and so extra-time was needed.

Eleven minutes into extra-time the Germans got their noses ahead when Roth raced onto a through ball and lashed it over the head of the 'keeper, Norrie Martin. From then on the Germans were content to defend their lead and Rangers just didn't have the energy or the skill to peg the goal back as the game drifted to its inevitable ending. When the final whistle went it was the most disappointing moment of my life. Defeat was bad enough, but Celtic's triumph in Lisbon had made it a million times worse.

It had been a bad season. We had been second to Celtic in the League. We had lost to them in the Final of the League Cup and then had come Berwick and Bayern. If I thought at the time this was bad, though, there was worse to follow the next season. By now a young Alex Ferguson was plying his trade as Rangers' number-nine and was doing quite well. He became a bit of a hero to me with his rumbustious, all-action style, scoring 24 goals in all competitions. Unfortunately it wouldn't last. Season 1967–68 again saw 'Gers second to Celtic in the League, failing to make the Final of either Cup competition but having a decent run in Europe. This time, we were in the Inter-Cities Fairs Cup. We overcame Dynamo Dresden in the first round 3–2 on aggregate. We then eliminated Cologne 4–3 on aggregate before facing the emerging brilliance of Revie's Leeds United in the quarter-final. The first leg that March was at Ibrox, and I was jammed in with 85,000 other Rangers fans to witness a 0–0 draw. 'Gers probably just deserved to win that game but lack of finishing power cost them.

The return at Elland Road saw Leeds run out comfortable 2–0 winners. I was standing in the North Enclosure, one of the crowd of over 43,000 fans who had turned up at Ibrox to watch the match on what then was called 'closed-circuit television'. Huge portable screens were brought into Ibrox for the occasion, and I remember marvelling at the fans who behaved as if the match were taking place right in front of them, singing and shouting, as well as giving the referee the traditional abuse. I felt like yelling, 'It's only a screen. They can't hear you!' But soon I was joining in too. This sort of secondary viewing was supposed to be the future, but it never really caught on, despite a couple of attempts at Ibrox in the 80s with European away games. I zoomed from work once to view the Dynamo Kiev match on the Ibrox screens. I remember watching from the Broomloan Stand and cursing whoever was responsible for the positioning of those screens because the sun was shining right on to them. Since the advent of companies such as Sky, screenings like that will never take place again.

The following season was remarkably similar to the previous one. Once again Rangers came second in the League to Celtic, failed to reach the League Cup Final and were thrashed 4–0 by Celtic in the Final of the Scottish Cup. Two things brightened our landscape: an even better European campaign and the signing of Colin Stein.

Until then, the name Stein had only provoked painful thoughts in the minds of 'Gers fans, but that would change when, at the start of November 1968, Rangers signed Colin Stein from Hibs and, as far as I was concerned, it was love at first sight! This player was manager Davie White's greatest legacy to the club. Stein immediately ousted Alex Ferguson in the 'Gers team and in my affections. I had never replaced Jim Baxter as my Rangers hero, but now Colin Stein made that possible. Stein was bought for £100,000, a record transfer between two Scottish clubs at the time. It would be 1977 before Rangers would spend another £100,000 on one player – Davie Cooper. Stein also eclipsed the 'Gers' record transfer (£65,000), which, ironically, had been for Alex Ferguson, who had arrived at Ibrox in 1967. Rarely can a new player have had such a blistering start at a new club and win over the fans so quickly.

Stein's first game was away to Arbroath, then in the top division. Rangers won 5–1, with the new boy scoring a hat-trick. Next up was his former club, Hibs, at Ibrox. There was a real excitement in the 60,000 crowd, desperate to see what this new striker could do. Rangers walloped Hibs 6–1 with a tremendous display, and Stein scored his second hat-trick. By now the newspapers by now were full of articles debating whether or not Stein could complete a hat-trick of consecutive hat-tricks. 'Gers' next match was away in Dundalk in the Inter-Cities Fairs Cup. Rangers had won the first leg 6–1 so the tie was effectively over. Fans speculated as to whether this would give Stein an edge in trying to score another hat-trick. Unluckily, he failed – just. He had to be content with two goals in a 3–0 win. But what a start to his Ibrox career!

By the end of his first half season, Stein had scored 13 goals in 18 appearances. He also scored four goals in seven European appearances. Until then, I had admired Alex Ferguson as a modern centre-forward but, compared to Stein, he was the poor-man's version. Stein had Fergie's aggression, work-rate and bravery, but he also had so much more. He was two-footed, equally good on the ground as in the air and rampaged and roamed all across the front line. He didn't need others to set goals up for him as he could create chances for himself. In a way, he was like a throw-back to earlier times thanks to his bustling style and the manner in which he could lead the line and bring teammates into the play. He had everything – even a flaw, unfortunately. This was his temperament, which caused him to retaliate when he had been abused just once too often.

In his first season, Stein was a sensation, quickly becoming the idol of the Rangers fans. Everything was going smoothly. Rangers, playing well, had a real chance of winning the title and ending Celtic's dominance. Then, in March, the wheels came off. It was just an ordinary League game at Ibrox against Clyde, and Rangers were playing brilliantly, none more so than Stein, who had scored a hat-trick in what would end up a 6–0 win. I was at the rear of the Broomloan End enjoying every minute of the proceedings and then – disaster! With minutes left Stein had possession and ran across the centre circle with the ball. Clyde defender Eddie Mulheron chased after the elusive forward, trying to kick him from behind with every stride. He must have had four or five swings at Stein with his boot. I couldn't believe that the top ref, Ian Foote, was doing nothing. That's when Stein's temper broke. He stopped, turned round and kicked Mulheron, which resulted in an immediate red card. Stein had to be hauled off the park by Alex Ferguson, so incensed was he by the decision. The 'Gers fans went crazy.

Although that decision hadn't affected the game that day, it had repercussions for the remainder of Rangers' season. When Stein later went up before 'the beaks' to be given his punishment, he suspected, like the fans, that he would incur a ban. They were not wrong. However, nobody expected a six-week suspension. In those days bans were measured in weeks, not games. That suspension meant that Stein missed the last seven matches in the League and the Scottish Cup Final against Celtic. Not surprisingly, Mulheron, the real culprit that day, became a figure of hate for 'Gers fans and even had death threats sent to him. During Stein's ban, Rangers lost two games and drew two. The chairman of the Disciplinary Committee that doled out Stein's incredibly harsh suspension was Sir Robert Kelly, who also happened to be Celtic's chairman. He obviously didn't consider absenting himself from the committee's decision due to having a vested interest in the outcome. During the time of Stein's Draconian ban, Celtic won the title by five points and the Scottish Cup. As a footnote to all this, it could be argued that Stein's ban cost Alex Ferguson his Rangers career. In the 4–0 defeat by Celtic in the Scottish Cup Final, McNeill scored with a trademark header from a corner kick in the first minute. Apparently Ferguson was supposed to be marking his opposite number but had been caught dozing. Losing a goal so early in such a match was a hammer blow, and 'Gers never recovered from it. Fergie became the scapegoat and didn't play for the club again.

Stein was also a Scottish international, eventually earning 21 caps. In a World Cup qualifying game at Hampden against Cyprus, he even scored four goals – still something that no Scot has replicated. Over the following years Stein kept performing for the team and ended up playing 206 games and scoring 97 goals in his two spells with Rangers. He is now rightly in the club's Hall of Fame and remains one of my all-time Rangers heroes.

The other brighter side of that season was our European run again in the Inter-Cities Fairs Cup, but this time we went one round further and got to the semi-final. Here we met Newcastle, and we really should have beaten them. They went on to win the tournament, but they haven't won a top trophy, domestic or otherwise, since. I saw all the home games leading up to the semi and enjoyed our wins against some good teams. In the first round we disposed of Yugoslavs Vojvodina, who had given Celtic a tough time two seasons earlier in their run to Lisbon. We beat them 2–0 in the first leg at Ibrox and knew the return would be no joyride. As it turned out, we lost 1–0 but held out heroically to go through. The next round saw us up against Dundalk from the Republic of Ireland and, as previously mentioned, 'Gers won 6–1 at home before winning 3–0 away, with Colin Stein making his European debut for us.

In the third round Rangers played DWS Amsterdam, beating them away first 2–0 and then 2–1 at Ibrox. We were into the quarter-final in consecutive years. Here the team came up against a really good side in Spanish cracks Athletico Bilbao, managed by former English international Ronnie Allen. In the first leg at Ibrox Rangers won 4–1, having got off to a great start, but then gradually the game lost its edge and pace, and it remained uneventful in the second half until a storming finish in the last five minutes saw Stein and our enigmatic Swedish left-winger Orjan Persson score to give the 'Gers a better chance of progression to the semi-final. This was despite the fact that John Greig had missed a penalty. I remember leaving the stadium elated at the result but anxious about the game to come in Spain. Rangers defended their lead valiantly and, at times, desperately in a rough match that eventually saw fiery winger Willie Johnston sent off for fighting with his full-back opponent. That three-goal cushion was indeed needed as we lost the return 2–0 but reached the semi-final.

The semi-final against Newcastle was a great occasion in the first leg at Ibrox, as Scotland versus England contests always are. Having said that, the Geordie side was full of Scottish and Irish players as well as English. Their captain was Bobby Moncur, who had also played for Scotland. Rangers would be handicapped by the absence of suspended Johnston and the injured McKinnon and Mathieson. Over 75,000 piled into Ibrox to see the joust, and Rangers were all over Newcastle but missed numerous chances or saw great efforts saved by 'keeper McFaul. The worst moment came when 'Gers missed a first-half penalty, taken this time by Andy Penman. That should have sent us to Newcastle with at least a lead to defend. I was very disappointed when I left the ground that evening as I just couldn't see us beating Newcastle on their own patch.

For the return, an estimated 10,000 'Gers fans, optimistic as ever, poured over the border to invade Newcastle. That optimism was intact by half-time, with the score 0–0 in a match that was the reversal of the first one, 'Gers defending most of the time but rarely threatening. Seven minutes into the second half, Newcastle scored through Jim Scott, the brother of former Rangers' winger Alex. Then, 13 minutes from time, the second, killer goal was scored by another Scot, Jackie Sinclair. Trouble broke out in the crowd as fans in the Rangers part of the ground started throwing bottles and cans, causing youngsters to invade to the field. Soon, hundreds of fans were on the park and the game had to be stopped for around 17 minutes before order was restored after fans had fought with police, and the game was played to its conclusion. There was no shame in losing to a good Newcastle side, but the fans' conduct had made it a grim evening for, 'Gers fans everywhere.

It was the following season's European exit that was to cost a Rangers manager his job. Davie White had taken over from Scot Symon and, given time, might have become a really good manager. Time, however, is one thing that Rangers managers seldom get, such are the demands of the club and the fans. White had even brought back former Ibrox idol Jim Baxter, but he was Slim Jim no longer. The years of boozing had taken their toll on him, and he could only show his genius in occasional flashes. Still, many 'Gers fans hoped that such flashes might be enough to help Rangers progress in Europe. In the Cup-Winners' Cup, 'Gers had disposed of Steaua Bucharest in the first round and then were paired with Polish side Gornik Zabrze in the next round.

The first leg in Poland had ended in a 3–1 defeat, although the home side's third goal had only come in the 88th minute. I went to Ibrox for the return thinking that it wasn't a lost cause, that a 2–0 win wasn't beyond us. Baxter and Willie Henderson had been involved in an incident of indiscipline, skipping training at Largs and missing the team bus. However, so desperate was White for a victory, both played against Gornik. I watched from the North Enclosure, and for an hour, like the rest of the 75,000 'Gers fans, I was happy enough. Baxter had opened the scoring in the 18th minute and Rangers were controlling the game. Then the Poles equalised in the 64th minute and the whole mood of Ibrox changed, although another two goals would have forced extra-time. Instead of Rangers netting two, it was the Poles. With only 15 minutes left, Polish superstar Lubanski scored a killer goal with a brilliant solo effort. Then six minutes after that Gornik added a third. The crowd, while admiring the skill of the Poles, turned their wrath on the Rangers manager. At the final whistle chants of 'White must go!' could be heard. They were obviously heard by the Board because the next day White was sacked.

As ever, in times of dire need, the club turned to an experienced, talented 'Rangers man' to turn the situation around. This time it was former Ibrox legend Willie Waddell. A brilliant winger for 'Gers and Scotland in the 40s and 50s, Waddell had won the League with Kilmarnock in 1965 before becoming a football journalist for the *Express*. He seemed the only candidate who might match the personality and skill of Jock Stein at Celtic. I remember feeling tremendous hope that this would be the man to change things at Ibrox for the better.

The determination, grit, skill and love of Rangers that he had shown throughout his career would be called upon now as the club looked for a saviour. Waddell saw his immediate job as one of restoring the image of the club, instilling pride into his players and, once again, making Rangers the most respected club in the country. He promised his staff that he would be hard-working, dedicated and would always put the needs of the club first – and he expected his players to do the same. He would be hard and disciplined but fair. Rangers' traditions would be re-invoked and first-team places would go to players on merit. Youngsters who proved themselves in terms of ability and industry would be rewarded by a first-team position. Although Waddell was seen as similar to Jock Stein, he was more like Scot Symon in terms of reverence for tradition, even if he did understand and utilise more modern methods and tactics.

As the season progressed, Waddell decided which players he could use, which he could rely on and which were past their sell-by date. He also concluded that his players weren't fit enough and instigated double training sessions, which also might have helped him weed out the weak or the unwilling in his quest for success. Among the first of the old guard to go in favour of youth were the likes of Baxter, Davie Provan and Persson. I was sad to see Baxter go but knew it was the correct decision. In a way I wished he had never returned to Ibrox as it had tarnished the boyhood memories I had of my erstwhile idol. Other players would be played in a different position and become much more successful. Sandy Jardine would be converted to right-back and become one of the best in the world in that position. Jardine, along with Willie Johnston, would be given specialist sprint training in order to increase their speed.

The strength of Waddell's personality was usually enough to get things done and get the team training and playing as hard as he desired. Near the end of the season, many of the backroom staff were allowed to leave in order that Waddell could bring in his own appointees. Among them, significantly, was the Hearts' assistant manager, Jock Wallace, who became the first-team coach. The following season it was Wallace who took the training sessions, allowing Waddell to be slightly more removed from his players than Davie White had been. However, they still realised who was boss, and Waddell's team talks and presence at training sessions made the players understand who it was they each had to impress.

The initial months of the Waddell reign were seen as a honeymoon period in which the new manager had the time to ascertain the strengths and weaknesses of the club before formulating his plan of action. However, Waddell knew that results would have to improve from the following season onwards. Jock Wallace's tough training regime was started with the now-infamous Gullane sand dunes becoming a focal point of the players' stamina training and dread. While Wallace increasingly took care of the players' conditioning, Waddell was left to do all the other duties that were part of his remit. They became a new kind of management partnership. Like Struth, Waddell always sought to maintain standards and ensure that the Rangers players had the best of everything when it came to travelling or eating on trips abroad. In return, the players were expected to show the kind of behaviour that upheld the reputation of the club. Woe betide any player who let down the club in any way.

Waddell's need to win a major trophy of some kind was satisfied in his first full season in charge. Based on his own experience as a 15-year-old debutant for Rangers, Waddell always believed that if you were good enough, you were old enough. This philosophy led to him giving youth a chance where possible and culminated in his first Rangers' success. It was in October 1970 that a 16-year-old Derek Johnstone headed the winning goal in the League Cup Final against Celtic, justifying Waddell's faith in the youngster. Unfortunately, that would be Waddell's only success that season. Once again Rangers suffered from inconsistency, leaving them in fourth place in the table this time. They did better in Cup competitions and reached the Final of the Scottish Cup, but it was no fairy-tale end to the season as

Celtic got revenge for their League Cup defeat by winning 2–1 in a replay after Derek Johnstone had scored in the 1–1 draw previously. Despite losing, Rangers' disappointment was reduced by the fact that they qualified for the following season's European Cup-Winners' Cup, a tournament that they would actually win.

Waddell's most telling role while manager came in the wake of the Ibrox Disaster in January 1971, when 66 fans lost their lives. Waddell's dignity, concern and organisational skills all played a big part in steering the club through a most difficult time. He took the weight of responsibility dealing with the media and legal enquiries while ensuring that there was club representation at each victim's funeral or visits to the injured in hospital. It was fortunate that, in its hour of need, Rangers had a great club servant who commanded the public's total respect.

The early 70s saw two of Rangers' greatest triumphs, but sandwiched in between was the club's greatest tragedy. Two of these events occurred in season 1970–71. The first golden memory was that League Cup Final win over Celtic, thanks to the head of the young Derek Johnstone. Even more important was the fact that it signalled the emergence of a striker who would become a Rangers legend and end up in the club's Hall of Fame.

The 1970 League Cup Final was a Rangers triumph in adversity. By October Rangers were already trailing Celtic in the League and would finish a lowly fourth. Celtic had won five in-a-row, as well as five successive League Cups. To make the 'Gers fans even more pessimistic, 'Captain Courageous', John Greig, missed the match due to a bout of 'flu. Manager Waddell and coach Wallace took a chance by giving 16-year-old Derek Johnstone a start, although they wouldn't admit that it was a gamble. Twenty years before Super Ally would repeat one *Roy of the Rovers* dreams after another, Derek Johnstone was doing it. Contrary to what some fans believe, this Final wasn't Johnstone's Rangers' debut. The month previously he had appeared at Ibrox against the humble Cowdenbeath in the League and had scored two goals. Still, for a 16-year-old to be up against the likes of Billy McNeill was a daunting task. You would never have known it. Just before half-time DJ headed the goal that would prove to be the winner.

In the crowd of over 106,000, I watched from my usual place in the North Enclosure at Hampden. This was at the rear, and there were two exits in the Rangers' section. Above each one was a 4ft high concrete wall that you could stand behind and lean on. For the vertically challenged, like me, this was a god-send because, if you arrived early enough to get behind the exit that was below you, you had an uninterrupted view of the pitch and nobody could stand in front of you. But you had to be *really* early. From this vantage point I had the perfect view of the goal. To the right, on my side of the park, Willie Johnston turned back near the touchline and swung in a great cross with his left foot. Johnstone rose between McNeill and fellow Lisbon Lion Jim Craig to bullet the ball into the net. How we celebrated. Here was I, a 19-year-old, watching the dream while Johnstone, three years younger, was actually living it. Now all we had to do was negotiate the second half to win the trophy. Amazingly, Rangers did this quite comfortably, and when the final whistle went the Bears celebrated the winning of the Cup – and the emergence of a legend-in-the-making.

At the end of that season a crowd of over 120,000 saw the Scottish Cup Final, which I attended as well. Johnstone scored Rangers' equaliser at the other end of Hampden against Celtic again to salvage the match and cause a replay. Unfortunately, circumstances forced Rangers to give another, less gifted, youngster his debut that evening. Imagine being given your first match at the end of a season in a Cup Final. I remember when his name, Jim Denny, was read out over the tannoy. All the 'Gers fans looked at each other and said, 'Who?' We had never heard of him. The debutant went on to suffer a nightmare of a match and went on to become a nonentity!

I was at Ibrox to see the young Johnstone score his first goal for the club against Cowdenbeath and I was there when he scored his final goal, which came in February 1985 in a 2–0 win against Morton. Big DJ enjoyed two spells at Rangers, playing at centre-half for much of his career, but he still ended up scoring 210 goals in 546 games for the club. Unfortunately, thanks to his antics as a football pundit on Radio Clyde, many Rangers fans dismiss him nowadays, but it should never be forgotten that he was a legend. It was a miscarriage of justice that when the fans were voting for their greatest Rangers team of all time, Mark Hateley was voted in ahead of Johnstone to accompany McCoist. A strike combination of Super Ally and DJ would have been a sight to behold.

After that League Cup Final triumph came tragedy. On 2 January 1971, 66 Rangers fans lost their lives in what is now known as the Ibrox Disaster. That is the most terrible thing that has happened in my 50 years of following Rangers. It's been well documented now but the accident came at the end of the traditional Ne'er Day Old Firm match that ended in a 1–1 draw. In front of a crowd of 85,000, Celtic's Jimmy Johnstone had scored in the 89th minute before Colin Stein equalised in the 90th. Contrary to the myth at the time, these late goals played no part in the disaster. The accident actually took place minutes after the final whistle and the cause has never been verified, but the most likely reason seems to be that a fan stumbled going down Stairway 13 and that had a knock-on effect where hundreds fell, unable to do anything about it due to the tremendous weight of numbers pouring down the stairs. I knew what it was like to be among such a flood because on quite a few occasions, at Ibrox and Hampden, I had almost lost a shoe as the crowd surged down the exit stairs. That day at Ibrox most of the fans died due to suffocation or crushing.

But I survived it.

I survived it because I was not there.

I was not there thanks to my girlfriend at the time, Linda Hyndman.

However melodramatic it might seem, I always like to think that Linda saved my life. She took me to a New Year's party put on by one of her girlfriends, we had a great time and a number of us stayed the night. On 2 January, when we got up, I took Linda back to her home, which wasn't far away. Due to a scarcity of buses, I ended up walking the three miles back home. I had been intending to go to the Old Firm game later on, but, being hung-over and exhausted from my walk, I decided not to bother.

If I had gone, I would have been leaving by Stairway 13. If I didn't leave a minute or two before the final whistle to avoid the rush, I always waited for a few minutes after the end of the game to let the worst pass. The chances are that, had I gone, I would have been on Stairway 13 at the time of the accident. Most would call that fate.

A couple of years later, when I had become a teacher back at my old school, I actually taught two of Linda's younger sisters. Also, her mum, who was a lovely woman, was the cleaner in charge of the men's staffroom, so I was able to have a chat to her every so often. Linda eventually married, emigrated to Canada and has lived in Vancouver for over 30 years. Her two sons are Canadian but have grown up as Rangers fans and still get up at unearthly hours to watch 'Gers' games live on television. They're just another part of the far-flung Rangers family.

If the Ibrox Disaster was Rangers' greatest tragedy then winning the European Cup-Winners' Cup in 1972 was its greatest triumph. I was at every home match in our path to Barcelona, and what an exciting time that was. The amazing aspect of our run was that we played good sides all the way through and only won our home matches by a single goal, apart from the semi-final against the mighty Bayern when we won by two. We beat teams from France, Portugal, Italy, Germany and USSR. Apart from when we played Sporting Lisbon in round two, we had the advantage of playing the first leg away in every round and only Sporting beat us (4–3) All the other away games finished 1–1, which was a testament to Rangers' great defence.

The most enjoyable match was our semi-final win over Bayern Munich at Ibrox. It took us to another European Final, we got revenge for our 1967 Final defeat at their hands and, last but not least, the Germans were a great side full of internationals such as Beckenbauer, Maier, Muller and Hoeness. I watched that game from my usual vantage point. Despite the absence of the injured Greig, an 80,000 crowd was full of expectation before the start, thanks to 'Gers having scored an away goal in the drawn game in Munich. Within minutes of the kick-off, that expectation had turned to unbelievable ecstasy. In the opening minute Rangers went ahead. Jardine made a typical run up the right, cut in and unleashed a shot that curled into the far corner of Maier's goal. It was hard to decide if the Germans were more disbelieving than the fans. Even better was to come though. In the 23rd minute, young Derek Parlane, Greig's replacement, slammed in a second goal and everyone inside Ibrox knew that the game was won.

On that same evening, while 80,000 watched 'Gers, across the city 75,000 Celtic fans were watching their side take on Inter Milan in the semi-final of the European Cup in a re-run of their 1967 Final – just as we were doing against Bayern. This time, however, the results were reversed. Rangers triumphed, but Celtic went out. That was the icing on the cake as far as Rangers fans were concerned. Celtic's first game in Italy had ended in a 0–0 draw and so had the return at Parkhead, so it was to be decided on penalties. There was absolute joy when we heard via our transistor radios that Celts' 'Dixie' Deans had missed his penalty to eliminate our rivals. In the Old Firm environment there's nothing nicer than schadenfreude! It would be Rangers taking centre stage on its own when it came to the Final against Dynamo Moscow.

Being in my final year at university, I was an impoverished student and couldn't afford to make the trip to Barcelona for the Final, although about 20,000 Rangers fans did. Making it even worse, the Final wasn't being televised live. This was because Scotland was playing Wales in a home international game at Hampden and, in those primitive times, the SFA wouldn't allow a live broadcast in case it affected the attendance at Hampden. However, the entire Rangers game would be shown later in a delayed transmission set-up. I was in the North Enclosure watching Scotland beat Wales but listening on my 'tranny' to the live radio broadcast from Barcelona. As Rangers scored goal after goal, those with radios kept everyone informed of what was happening out in Spain. I remember that most of the fans surrounding us seemed to be 'Gers fans, and so we were in a great frame of mind despite watching the dross in front of us at Hampden, although Scotland eventually won 1–0 thanks to a Lorimer goal. Maybe the Scots players had also heard how well Rangers were doing.

At 3–0 and coasting we were all in a joyful mood, but when Moscow Dynamo scored near the hour mark, Rangers found themselves defending in depth and clinging on for dear life. Most of us focused more on our radios than on the Hampden pitch as we became more and more anxious. Thankfully, a second Dynamo goal wasn't scored until three minutes from the end, but even those last few minutes were agony as we all wondered if, yet again, we were going to throw away a famous victory. Thankfully, 'Gers held out and the celebrations could begin. I wondered if the Scotland players thought we were cheering them at that point. I was eager to get home and see Rangers' greatest triumph on television. I think I would have walked the 10 miles home just to see it.

In the aftermath of the match fighting took place when Franco's Fascist Guarda Civil started battering into the celebrating Rangers fans. The policemen using batons and extreme violence merely provoked, rather than frightened, the Scottish fans, who seldom take kindly to an injustice of any kind. This resulted in the Barcelona 'riot', as the hacks immediately dubbed it. At the end of the match in Lisbon in 1967, Celtic fans had invaded the pitch to celebrate in exactly the same manner. However, they hadn't been faced with the same type of brutal policing methods, and thus no trouble had occurred. It still annoys me that Rangers fans get a bad press for the events of that evening.

The following day, the victorious team flew back to be met by the Lord Provost of Glasgow, John Mains. Then it was on to Ibrox, where the Cup was paraded in front of over 20,000 Rangers fans in the teeming May rain. I was there to see the celebrations. Compared to sunny Spain, this was a grey occasion, thanks to the weather but also the fact that the 'Gers team all stood on the back of a coal lorry bedecked in Union Jacks and red, white and blue with John Greig holding the trophy aloft. Apparently it was such short notice to arrange the parade that this vehicle was all the club could come up with. The fans nevertheless sang their hearts out and chanted their refrains as the truck did its lap of honour twice around the running track at the stadium. Many of the fans had just returned from Barcelona and were still wearing their souvenir sombreros which were handy for the rain. Meanwhile, 'Gers' midfielder, Alex McDonald, on the back of the truck, still wore his sunburn!

Even more annoying than the adverse publicity the club received for the events at the Nou Camp was the punishment dished out by UEFA to Rangers. The club received a two-year ban from European competition following the events in

Barcelona. Manager Waddell prepared an appeal and personally delivered it to UEFA so he succeeded in having it reduced to one year but it still rankled that we didn't get the chance to defend our trophy. At least one good thing emerged from the debacle of our ban, though. The following season a new European trophy came into existence, thanks to Willie Waddell and a Dutch newspaper. With no European football available to Rangers, an unofficial European Super Cup was instigated in which the winners of the European Cup would play the winners of the Cup-Winners' Cup. It was an idea that captured the imagination, and the contest has taken place every year (with some changes) since January 1973 when Rangers played Ajax of Amsterdam over two legs. The first leg was at Ibrox and, for some reason I watched this game from the wee enclosure. A 60,000 crowd watched 'Gers lose 3–1 to a brilliant Ajax side, with the likes of Cruyff strutting his stuff. I remember thinking, while watching the match, that this was a totally different kind of football we were being privileged to watch. At the end the Rangers fans gave the European champions a standing ovation. We did slightly better in Amsterdam by only losing 3–2, but we could all see that Rangers were a million miles away from a side such as the great Ajax. On the other hand, this new venture had shown Rangers to be pioneers yet again.

Before this game was played, I had a real shock in the September of that season when my hero, Colin Stein, was transferred to Coventry. Manager Jock Wallace also got rid of Willie Johnston. The two goalscoring heroes of Barcelona were gone months after that triumph. The manager had decided that he didn't need such stars in his set-up. He considered them 'too big for their boots', although he didn't say so publicly. Wallace would end up winning two trebles in the 70s. Stein deserved to be part of that. He was the only Rangers player who had come anywhere near to replacing Jim Baxter in my affections. However, I did not cry myself to sleep when Stein left as I had done with Baxter – after all, I was 21 at the time!

In 1973, to commemorate the club's centenary, it transformed the old North Enclosure into the Centenary Stand. The other commemorative event that year was the friendly in August against our old adversaries and traditional counterparts from England, Arsenal. As a reward for the fans' support and loyalty, the club made the admission prices the same as those 100 years earlier. I got my ticket for the new stand for sixpence. For younger readers, that is about 5p in today's currency. It was no wonder that 71,000 fans turned up. Pity 'Gers lost 2–1.

The Centenary Stand was a big disappointment to me. It sounded much grander than it actually was. As was usual in those times, Rangers' management took the cheap option. The covered enclosure was the same with just bench-type seating added. The benches were wooden and backless, and they had two lines and a number in the centre painted on them to indicate the area that the fan was allotted as his 'seat'. By that time I had watched Rangers games for years from the North Enclosure and I wasn't going to be put off by that. I became an aficionado of the Centenary Stand. For every home game, I dutifully took up my seat right on the halfway line, near the rear of the stand, as long as I was inside the stadium early enough to pick my seat.

This was one of many 'improvements' I have witnessed over the years of going to Ibrox. In the early 60s the most dramatic change was when the terracing was concreted. We thought that this was a luxury! The floodlights were next to go. When I started attending games, the Ibrox floodlights were situated under the front of the roofs of the Main Stand and the North Enclosure, unlike most grounds then that had huge pylons stuck in the middle of their terracing. In the late 60s, the old lights were removed and mini pylons with much more modern, more powerful lamps were positioned on top of those roofs. We were told at the time that these lights were the most powerful ones in the world and were necessary for the televising of matches that was becoming more professional and, eventually, would be in colour. Ironically, since the construction of the 'new' Ibrox, the floodlights have reverted to under the front of the Main Stand, now called the Bill Struth Main Stand and the Govan Stand, where I sit to this day.

Watching games in the Centenary Stand, when it had been the North Enclosure only became possible when I had become old enough and tall enough to see events from there. Until then, I always stood near the rear of the terracing, normally where the crowd was a bit sparser. In the 60s, apart from the Main Stand and the wee enclosure, Ibrox was a continuous stretch of terracing. Fans, if they desired, could walk from behind one goal to the other end at half-time. This could be done at most grounds but not Hampden because the North Enclosure there was separated from the rest of the stadium by a huge steel fence. At Ibrox there was no such obstacle, so this was what we did. If, during the first half, we were standing at the back of the Copland Road end watching 'Gers shoot into the goal right in front of us, we would walk round to the Broomloan end at half-time so that we could see them attacking the goal right in front of us again. It was great. You could either go down the staircases and walk all the way round, underneath and behind the terracing, or, if the crowd wasn't too dense, merely move through the fans without leaving the terracing. All that changed with the advent of the Centenary Stand.

Two fences were erected that ran down the length of the terracing to separate the fans on the terracing and those enjoying the 'comfort' of the new stand – and paying extra for the privilege. You could enter the Centenary Stand via specially allocated turnstiles at Cairnlea Drive, with a walkway cordoned off once inside the ground, or from the other end by going through the turnstiles at the Broomloan end, walking round behind the terracing and paying in at new turnstiles at that end of the stand, almost underneath it. The club also had the foresight to build turnstiles at the rear of the actual terracing, at each end, so that if fans changed their mind and decided to move from the mostly uncovered terracing to the shelter of the stand they could do so by paying at that point of entry.

Despite improved cover, Ibrox was still exposed to the heavens. The entire Broomloan end was uncovered, but in the late 60s a roof was put over the Copland end. This was another grave disappointment to me. I was expecting it to cover the entire terracing, the Rangers' End. However, when it was unveiled it covered maybe about a third of the fans at that end. Even Hampden managed to do this properly when the SFA decided to cover the Rangers' End there. Its roof covered the whole of that huge terracing. If you were lucky enough to be under the cover of the new roof at the Copland end, it seemed very cosy when the rain was thundering down on the roof above you, and a bonus was the way the noise of the crowd was amplified and directed towards the pitch.

After the Disaster of 1971, safety improvements were made to the rear of each terracing. Just in front of each stairway, a big concrete wall was constructed. This was to prevent fans surging directly from the terracing to the stairs at the final whistle. The wall meant that the stream of fans was filtered at each end of the wall, providing a narrower channel by which to access the staircase.

This particular era ended with yet another memorable Rangers' triumph, which saw the club win the 1973 Centenary Scottish Cup Final by beating Celtic 3–2 at Hampden. This was a momentous match for various reasons. It was the SFA's Centenary Final and was attended by a member of the royal family – Princess Alexandra– for the first time. 'Gers' opponents were Celtic, who had just pipped them for the League title by one point. No wonder over 122,000 fans packed into Hampden.

This Final was a feast of football, fit for a king, never mind a princess. A typical full-blooded Old Firm contest, the play raged from end to end and took various twists and turns throughout the 90 minutes. For once, I was in the North Enclosure and didn't have to stand on tip-toe to view a see-saw match. Kenny Dalglish put the

Celts ahead when he thundered a shot into the net from just inside the box. However, after pressure at both ends, it was Rangers who got the next goal, equalising before half-time.

Left-back Willie Mathieson sent a pass up the left side for Alex McDonald to collect. The midfielder somehow bustled his way past a defender before getting to the goalline, where he sent over a dangerous cross that was met by the head of Derek Parlane about eight yards out in the centre. The striker's downward header into the corner gave the 'keeper no chance. In the second half Rangers seized the initiative and went 2–1 up thanks to the pace of Alfie Conn. Winger Quinton Young, in his own half, sent a long pass through the middle. The ball was missed by Johnstone and his marker, but Conn pounced on it. He outstripped veteran Billy McNeill as he raced towards the Celtic box, eluding a last-gasp, despairing tackle by the Celtic captain. As a defender closed in on him and the 'keeper came out of his goal, Conn slid the ball past them and into the net.

From then on the game ebbed and flowed, with Celtic desperate to get the equaliser. Eventually it came about, thanks to a George Connelly penalty. There could be no disputing the award as a Deans shot was entering the net only to be palmed away by a desperate John Greig on the line. If the current rules had been in place, Greig would also have been sent off. At that point it was touch-and-go as to which side would get the winner, but when it came, the scorer was the player least likely to have been nominated by the fans as the match-winner.

Way out on the left, Tommy McLean took an in-swerving free-kick. As ever, he flighted the ball perfectly to the spot where the rising Derek Johnstone out-jumped his marker to head the ball for what should have been the winning goal. Fate, however, took a hand and the ball bounced off the left-hand post. Not only that, but it trundled across the goal line before hitting off the other post. Thankfully, as it came out, it was a Ranger who was on hand to put it into the net, but it was not one of the usual suspects. This time it was defender Tom Forsyth, of all people, who had followed the cross in and, seemingly with great difficulty, managed to scrape the ball into the goal from all of six inches with his studs. The way Forsyth ran off in celebration you could have been forgiven for thinking that he'd blasted the ball in from 30 yards. It must rank as the shortest Cup-winning goal in history – but big Tam didn't care. I only saw his wild celebration later on television because at the time we were going absolutely bonkers as we celebrated. Everybody knew, even then, that he'd won the trophy for Rangers. For the first time ever, the world's oldest trophy was handed over by a princess to the King of Ibrox.

CHAPTER THREE

THE GOLDEN SEVENTIES

The mid-to-late 70s, which saw the end of Jock Stein's dominance, became a happier time for the club, with the winning of the Championship in 1974 (the year I married my first wife) after a 10-year gap, and two trebles in the following three seasons under Jock Wallace, who'd been promoted from coach under Waddell. However, it would be two seasons before Wallace managed to achieve what every Rangers manager was expected to – the League Championship. So dominant had the Celtic sides been, winning nine titles in a row, that the format of the League was to be changed after season 1974–75. Thus, this would be the last season of the old First Division before the advent of the new Premier Division, designed to encourage fiercer competition. I must admit I was glad to see the back of the likes of Cowdenbeath, Dumbarton, Airdrie and Ayr. The irony was that Wallace's Rangers stopped Stein's run of consecutive titles without the aid of a new format. Further irony came from the fact that the once-discarded and now re-signed Colin Stein scored the goal at Easter Road in the 1–1 draw that brought the Championship back to Ibrox for the first time in 10 years. Wallace had now shaped a squad of players in his own image that could succeed where so many in the recent past had failed.

The following season Rangers created yet another record as the first club to win the new Premier Division. Not only that, but it became a treble-winning season. A blank season next year could be explained by the dreaded injury curse to key players such as Tom Forsyth before Wallace repeated his treble feat in 1977–78, having added three skilful players to his team that had won the treble in 1975–76: Russell, Smith and Cooper. The fact that two trebles in three seasons had only ever been achieved once before – by a Jock Stein Celtic side – puts Wallace's success into perspective. Jock Wallace was at the height of his powers, whereas the other Jock was basically sacked as the Celtic manager, having been replaced by Billy McNeill.

Season 1974–75 actually started on a downer for me due to the fact that, Barcelona ban excepted, Rangers had failed to qualify for European competition for the first time in my 'Gers-watching life. However, to outweigh that, they had won the Championship for the first time since 1964, the year that was the end of an era – although I didn't realise that at the time. Dereks, Parlane and Johnstone led our goalscoring charts but it was my old hero, Colin Stein, who headed the vital goal in a 1–1 draw at Easter Road that clinched the title. I was thus doubly happy. By then I was teaching back at my old school, Crookston Castle, and had my English classroom covered in photos of 'Gers heroes. It would probably be a sacking offence nowadays. The pupils appreciated the wall displays, which sat side by side with ones on English literature, but some of the staff weren't so keen. Guys who were Thistle or St Johnstone fans, or who were just anti-Rangers, now had to listen to me telling them how great a team I was now watching. It only got better as Rangers would win the treble in 1976 and 1978, thus making our men's staffroom a much happier place for all the Rangers fans. I was lucky that, in December 1979, I was promoted to a school in Bearsden called Boclair Academy because from 1980–86 was positively the worst era in Rangers' history. It was so bad that, for the only time in my life, I gave up on the club – albeit temporarily. But more of that later.

Season 1975–76 saw Rangers create another first – the first club to win the inaugural Premier Division. Not only that, but we won our third treble. The club has completed the elusive treble seven times now, and I have witnessed every one bar that first one in the 40s. Also, as I write, the club has had 12 managers since the 19th century, and I have been a fan while 10 of them were the boss at Ibrox. I really am getting pretty ancient!

On the way to the Championship, Rangers beat Celtic by six points. In the head-to-head matches with their old rivals, 'Gers won the two home games and drew the two away ones. We also beat Celtic in the Final of the League Cup to take the first leg of the treble. The new 10-club League set-up, with teams playing against each other four times, didn't seem to be any more competitive than the original one. Still, we weren't agonising about it as Rangers had won the last of the old division's titles and the first of the new one. I must admit that the one thing I really enjoyed about the innovation was the fact that 'Gers had those two extra matches against

Celtic. This is only a good thing, however, when your half of the Old Firm is in the ascendency.

In October 1975 I was among the poor 58,000 crowd (although Hampden, by then, had a reduced capacity) to see Rangers beat Celtic in the League Cup Final by an Alex McDonald goal. The best part of the experience came after the match when, as usual, Celtic's officials had something to complain about. Regarding the actual game, they were annoyed at the tackling of 'Gers' brilliant defender, Tom Forsyth, who had become my new hero. Apparently, they thought that big Tam had been too tough when tackling the likes of wallflowers such as McGrain and Dalglish. Jock Wallace defended his player afterwards, realising that it was very seldom that the opposing manager singled out individual players to criticise. In the absence of Jock Stein, who had been injured in a car crash, assistant manager, Sean Fallon did the ritual moaning on behalf of his club. He even complained about the ref, Bill Anderson – but only afterwards. His complaint was that the top seven officials had been ignored for the prestigious Final. Fallon obviously thought that any one of the seven on the FIFA international list would have been better than the less experienced referee. With the traditional sour grapes, Fallon also claimed the Final was the worst he could remember. The game had been a nervy, tousy, pretty boring affair, but the result was all that counted as I watched from my usual spot.

The Scottish Cup Final in May 1976 saw us complete the treble with a win against Hearts, but the most memorable game of the tournament came in the semi-final when Rangers had to come from behind to win 3–2. I will never forget that Hampden evening when Derek Johnstone showed us what a talisman he had become for 'Gers. We knew that it would be no easy task to overcome Motherwell to reach the Final. This 'Well team would end up fourth in the League and had already knocked Celtic out of the Cup thanks to an incredible 3–2 win at Parkhead, having been 2–0 down at half-time. Rangers didn't have to be warned that their opponents would be formidable. The way the match started suggested as much.

Motherwell took command from the beginning and Rangers just couldn't seem to get going, showing none of their usual rhythm or fluidity. Motherwell were defending brilliantly and their tactic of hitting Rangers on the break with crisp, precise movements was working perfectly, one of their strengths being the pace of strikers Pettigrew and Graham. By the end of the first half it was obvious that they had out-thought and out-fought Rangers, and they were two goals up. Eight minutes from half-time, McLaren had given 'Well the lead, and, if that wasn't bad enough, a minute from the interval whistle Pettigrew added a second by rushing away from the 'Gers defence and chipping the ball over the diving McCloy before running on to it to slide it into the empty net.

At the start of the second half it looked like Rangers had the proverbial mountain to climb. In fact, for most of the half it must have seemed like Everest – until they were rescued by their brilliant striker, Derek Johnstone. The Lanarkshire side managed to hold onto its lead until the last quarter of the match and, by that time, most fans had installed them as favourites to win the trophy, never mind this tie. Then Rangers were thrown a lifeline by referee, J.R.P. Gordon, who awarded them a penalty-kick.

The penalty came about when Jackson, deep in his own half and near the left touchline, punted a ball up the left channel for Johnstone to chase. He outpaced a defender just before the ball entered the 'Well penalty box, near the left-hand side. By now the 'keeper, Rennie, had come out, diving at the feet of DJ, but, making no contact with the ball, he sent the big striker tumbling forward. It happened right in front of me, so I knew it was a penalty. Despite the protests from Motherwell's players and fans, television evidence showed that the ref had got it right. It had been a foul and it had occurred inside the area. Alex Miller calmly stepped up and stroked the ball into the net.

The equaliser was created by an unexpected source – 'keeper Peter McCloy. One of the Girvan Lighthouse's famous mammoth kicks soared into the night sky and bounced into the opposition's penalty box, with Derek Johnstone once again chasing it. He out-jumped the 'keeper and nodded the ball into goal. It was so simple but also effective.

By now the tide had turned in 'Gers' favour, and the confidence could be seen draining away from the Motherwell players. With only two minutes left Jardine punted a free-kick into the heart of the 'Well penalty box from the halfway line. As it landed, it was missed by Parlane and two defenders, but Johnstone, running in behind them, got to it before the 'keeper, chested it down and away from him and gleefully tapped it into the net from a yard out. In my opinion, this game was one of Derek Johnstone's finest.

Rangers had snatched victory in the dying moments of a supreme tie. At the end I felt joy and relief but mainly pride that this side had shown such 'character', as big Jock was fond of saying. This win had been achieved by spirit rather than consummate skill. It was that kind of Rangers spirit that would see the side win the Final and complete the treble.

The Final itself, in front of over 85,000 fans, was a bit of an anticlimax. It wasn't such an enthralling match and Rangers won the Cup comfortably. Some might claim that it was actually won before three o'clock because the referee started the game before it was officially three, and Rangers scored in the opening minute thanks to a Johnstone header. Actually, it took all of 45 seconds for DJ to score – amazingly, not quite as fast as the winner he had scored at Tannadice the week before to clinch the title. That one had only taken 22 seconds, and his manager, Wallace, hadn't even seen it as he had been taking up his seat in the dug-out. Thousands of fans were still trying to get into Hampden when the goal had been scored. This was in the days before every big game at Hampden was an all-ticket affair. Apparently, it took some fans half an hour to get into the stadium, and even then they claimed they couldn't see the pitch so they left. The post-match debate was about how to improve things for the fans in future big matches at Hampden, with the suggestion that all big games should be all-ticket.

DJ's header was very similar to his first one at Hampden in that famous League Cup Final win against Celtic when, at the Rangers' End, he met a cross from the right and headed powerfully into the net. I reckoned that this header was even better than the one that made him famous. Alex McDonald added another before half-time, and the Cup was basically won. For good measure, though, Johnstone added a third in the second half after a great run by Bobby McKean who would tragically die within a couple of years. Hearts got a consolation goal but 'Gers ran out 3–1 winners to secure the club's third treble.

The following season was a terrible disappointment. The team went from heroes to zeroes as it won nothing. Much of this could be attributed to the fact that our best defender, Tom Forsyth, was injured for around a third of the season. Rangers lost eight League games, a rarity until then. Other key players suffered injuries as well, and the balance, rhythm of the team just wasn't there. Still, the astute Wallace added three important players to the same core who had won the previous treble for the start of the next season: Davie Cooper, Bobby Russell and Gordon Smith. It was an incredible success; Rangers won its second treble in three seasons.

Rangers won the League, but only two points separated them from second-placed Aberdeen. Celtic didn't even qualify for Europe having ended up in fifth place. That gave us great pleasure again, but in the 80s our roles would be reversed. Once again we beat Celtic to win the League Cup in front of just over 60,000 fans. It was an uneventful match (or as uneventful as any Old Firm Final can be), a bruising, physical encounter. The newcomers to 'Gers' Final, Davie Cooper and

Gordon Smith, bagged the goals in a 2–1 win. The third newcomer, Bobby Russell, also got a medal, although injury prevented him from playing in the Final. Big-hearted Sandy Jardine gave him his medal as Russell had played in every game in the League Cup apart from that Final. That exemplified the team spirit that the squad possessed.

Later, in the Scottish Cup Final, 'Gers won 2–1 against Aberdeen, the team that was easily the biggest danger to Rangers all that season. The victory, through goals either side of half-time by McDonald and Johnstone, was far more comfortable than the score suggests. Bobby Russell didn't miss this Final and was the Man of the Match. The fans, like me, who were there will always remember it for the Aberdeen goal, not because it was the most spectacular ever seen at Hampden but because it was so bizarre. Five minutes from the end, McMaster passed to Ritchie inside the box, but the Don sclaffed his shot and it went spinning up into the air. 'Keeper Peter McCloy believed that the ball was sailing well over his bar and so jumped on to the bar and dangled from it. While he was doing this, the ball seemed to dip and go under the bar into the net. McCloy, hanging happily, must have been the last man in Hampden to realise that a goal had actually been scored! He must have wanted a hole to open up so that he could have jumped into it and covered up his embarrassment.

The week before this Final, 'Gers had clinched the League Championship for a record 37th time by beating Motherwell 2–0 at Ibrox to pip Aberdeen to the title. The Dons had actually won three of the four League games against us, beating us 3–1, 3–0 and 4–0, so the title could have been snatched away on that final day. However, against 'Well, two goals in the first 20 minutes from a Jackson header and Gordon Smith settled the matter and it was simply a case of the 'Gers fans awaiting the final whistle to celebrate their title triumph. One week later, with the treble completed, everything looked rosy in the Ibrox garden. But then came a bombshell.

The manager who had just won his second treble in three seasons, resigned just a couple of weeks after the Cup Final. Jock Wallace, at the peak of his powers, caught everyone on the hop with his sudden departure. He moved to Leicester City, then a Second Division club. To his eternal credit, Wallace never did explain why he had left Ibrox. He could have made a fortune by selling his story to the newspapers but he didn't. He always kept the matter private until his dying day. Of course, that led to much speculation: it was a personality clash with Waddell, the general manager; it was his salary; he didn't feel he had got the recognition he had deserved; he wasn't being allowed to buy players he wanted. The list could go on, but the fact is that nobody was ever told. All the fans realised, however, that it must have been something serious for a True Blue like Wallace to leave the club at his most triumphant moment.

If Wallace leaving was a shock, maybe the immediate appointment of captain John Greig as his replacement wasn't. With the elevation of Greig to the manager's chair, everything still looked to be on track. At the end of that season Rangers, under Greig, were effectively five minutes away from succeeding in back-to-back trebles until a late goal at Celtic Park allowed Celtic to snatch the title, and the Ibrox club had to be content with winning the two Cup competitions. From then on, however, it was all downhill, with only the odd League Cup or Scottish Cup win to pacify the fans, who were getting more disgruntled as the years wore on.

The League Cup was retained in March, when 'Gers beat Aberdeen 2–1 thanks to McDonald and Jackson goals. Then, during a 16-day period in May, Rangers had to play Hibs three times in the Scottish Cup Final. The first two games ended in dire 0–0 draws before 'Gers won the second replay 3–2. The crowd, with each successive game, got smaller and smaller, starting at over 50,000 and ending with over 30,000. I am proud to say that I stuck it out. I attended each of those three drab, boring games. Having suffered, I wanted at least to be there to see us lift the trophy. It was only a consolation, though, as seven days earlier we had lost our League title – and to Celtic at that.

That evening against Celtic was one of the worst experiences that I have ever had watching Rangers. The match was at Parkhead, and I was crammed in at the Rangers' End, near the back of the terracing. All 'Gers needed was a draw and the title would have been ours. Rangers led by 1–0 at half-time, and when Celtic's winger Doyle was sent off early in the second half, all the Bears around me were convinced that we had won the League. I should have learned by then never to count your chickens. Encouraged by their fans, Celtic fought back and eventually went 2–1 up. However, before we had time to despair, Bobby Russell equalised.

Then, in the dying minutes, a cross from the right was turned into the Rangers' net by Colin Jackson in an own-goal. I knew then that the title had gone. Like other fans, I started making my way down the stairs towards the exit. As I was doing this, while watching the action on the pitch, Murdo MacLeod hit a characteristic screamer that almost burst the Rangers' net. That was the signal for all the 'Gers fans to make for the exits. I have never felt so sickened in all my 'Gers'-watching life. It took a long time to get over that experience.

Little did I realise that this season was to be the high watermark of Greig's managerial career at Ibrox. Greig's early work was commendable, but his biggest problem was that he couldn't replace himself on the field. Add the fact that many of his players were ageing and that it must have been tricky to go straight from the dressing-room to the manager's office, and you can see that his task was an uphill one.

The two Cups apart, the best aspect of Greig's first season as manager was his surprising tactical nous and success in the European Cup. Rangers eliminated Juventus in the first round after a brilliant 2–0 win in the second leg at a three-sided Ibrox, where the Copland Road end had been demolished and was a building site for the first of the three new stands to be built in successive seasons. This win was followed by PSV Eindhoven in the next round, which will live in the memory for the 3–2 win in the second leg in Holland after a 0–0 draw at home. By then Rangers had made it to the quarter-final, and fans were starting to believe that we could even make it all the way. It was not to be. We drew Cologne in that round, lost 1–0 away and in the second leg at home could only manage 1–1. It was a shame that our form had dipped just before the quarter-final because Nottingham Forest beat Cologne in the semi and went on to win the trophy. I still firmly believe that it could have been us.

None of these, however, was the most momentous event in my life that season. On Monday 20 November 1978 my son, Stewart, was born. 'Gers helped me celebrate the following Saturday by winning 3–0 at Ibrox against Morton. I remember the Monday, though, better than that Saturday. I had driven home from school to Battlefield, and as I parked the car in front of my tenement building at around half four, I heard my wife, who had watching out for my arrival, knocking on the window of our second-storey flat. I looked up and knew something was wrong, so I raced up the stairs. I was capable of doing that in those days! On arriving at the front door, I was told that the baby was coming. It was a case of a quick turnaround, helping my wife down to the car with her suitcase, and zooming to the Southern General Hospital in Govan.

When we arrived I took my wife to the maternity department, and a nurse put her in a wheelchair to whisk her away to a ward. I sat in a small waiting-room, nervous and worried. After about five minutes a nurse came to take me to my wife. I was so happy. I felt great to be a father. As I followed her I remember thinking, 'Well, that was quick! What's all this about it taking hours and hours for a baby to be delivered?' Imagine my shock when I was taken into a small room where my wife was just lying on a bed, having been examined before being taken up to the actual maternity ward. Stewart didn't arrive until just before midnight, over six hours later. While my wife was in labour and I sat beside her for all those hours, it was murder. There is nothing you can do and, as the labour intensifies, you can't even speak to each other. It's a boring but worrying experience for the father, although it is much worse, of course, for the mother.

Once Stewart had been born I was asked to leave the delivery room while the medical staff checked out mother and baby. I took the opportunity to go and find a pay phone (no mobiles in those days) to tell my mum and my mother-in-law the great news. I was so excited and thrilled that my hand was shaking, and I could hardly get the coins into the money slot of the phone. After that, I was given a bit more time with my family before leaving for home.

I was so overjoyed that all the way home to Battlefield that I was singing out loud to myself. Little did I realise that singing was not something I'd be doing often at Ibrox over the forthcoming years. I got to bed at half one but woke up at half eight in time to phone the school office and tell them that I would be absent that day as I was going to register the birth.

By the mid-to-late 70s, I was a teacher, was married, had a car and lived in Battlefield, a six or seven-minute walk away from Hampden, at the Mount Florida end, the Rangers' End, which was really handy at times. My dad and cousin Middy were coming with me to all Rangers' home matches. I had deserted my vantage point in the Centenary Stand to sit opposite in the Main Stand. I did this because one day, while sitting in my usual place, it occurred to me that I was paying extra to sit there, on a wooden bench, but, for a little more money, I could be sitting in the Main Stand. The Main Stand had been designed and built in 1928 by that doyen of football ground designers, Archibald Leitch. At that time it was the last word in safety, comfort and luxury, but even in the 1970s it was a fantastic stand and is probably still the best one in Britain.

In those days Rangers only had a couple of thousand season-ticket holders and only Old Firm games and 'big' matches were all-ticket affairs. Apart from games against Celtic, home crowds varied from 20,000 – 40,000. You could pay into any part of the stadium at the turnstiles. It was no problem getting into the Main Stand as long as you arrived early enough – and my dad and I did. My cousin would make his own way there and arrive well after us, but we could always keep his seat by leaving an empty space between us until he arrived. We always sat in the same seats anyway, provided we had arrived at our usual time. They were great, right on the halfway line, behind the low wooden partition that separated the ordinary punter from the directors and guests in the Directors' Box.

From these seats we watched the new Ibrox emerge from 1978 until 1981, when the old terracings were demolished and three identical new stands built in their place. It was fascinating watching the site prepared and then the steel girder work being erected so that we could start to see what the eventual shape of the new construction would be. In fact, in that era, sometimes it was good to be able to look at something other than the field of play, so dire was the product on offer. When the first, the Copland Stand, was complete, it was a spectacular sight. A 'goalpost' design meant that the fans in the stand would have no supporting columns to obstruct their viewing of a match. They would also be sitting much nearer to the pitch than the previous terracing had been. It was a colourful sight as the seats had been divided into vertical sections with different colours: blue, red, yellow, orange and brown. For once, thought fans, Rangers had not taken the cheap option but had built something that would stand the test of time and provide the ultimate in safety and comfort for the fans. The successive two stands would be identical and the credit was given to Willie Waddell, whose vision had made it all happen. It was said that this new stadium was the real tribute to those who had lost their lives in the Ibrox Disaster of 1971.

CHAPTER FOUR

ROCK BOTTOM EIGHTIES

Once the new stands had been completed in 1981, we moved back across to where we had always watched our 'Gers' games, and the Govan Stand is where I have been ever since. Although the stand had been in use from the start of that season, the official opening took place on 22 December when Rangers played Liverpool, with King Kenny and all, as the papers used to say. Liverpool won 2–0, but Rangers gave them a game and the near capacity crowd loved it despite the chilly night. I remember that I took my cine camera with me and surreptitiously filmed some of the action,which was strictly forbidden. A cine film cartridge only lasted four minutes, so I had to start filming only when I thought something was going to happen on the field. This is not an easy thing to achieve when you're looking at the park through a viewfinder and trying not to be seen by the stewards who are supposed to prevent any filming of a game. I still have those 'highlights', and they aren't much worse than the old *Scotsport* ones used to be.

In the pre-Souness days, most games were pay-at-the-gate so, like the Main Stand, we got there early enough to pick our seats. We were always in the Govan Rear, right on the halfway line about halfway up. It was the best view you could get at Ibrox, in my opinion. On the odd occasion we even went right to the back of the Govan, the very last row, on the halfway line. What a view! Pity the games, all too often, didn't match it.

The December before that Liverpool match, my daughter, Heather, had been born, and at least that brightened life up, even if, all too often, Rangers couldn't. Showing no concern for her parents, Heather was born on a Sunday, thereby denying me another day off my work! Again, we went to the Southern General hospital after leaving Stewart in the care of my parents. We arrived in the morning, and this time I did know what to expect. It didn't seem so long this time, and Heather was born in the afternoon. Imagine my worry when I was told that there had been a problem with the new baby. In the course of the birth, she had torn a muscle in her upper arm. When I saw her in her cot, she had that arm pinned to the mattress at a particular angle so that the injury could be given a chance to heal. For weeks, if not months, the poor soul had to be pinned in such a way. Thankfully, it caused no permanent damage.

The early 80s was my worst period for watching Rangers. Greig, as manager, still had some old stalwarts such as McCloy, Jardine, Jackson, Forsyth, McLean, Russell, Johnstone and Cooper, but they were becoming more injury-prone and were ageing. Unfortunately, the additions to the squad made by Greig and later Wallace were not of the same quality in most cases. Until the appointment of Souness in 1986, it was players of the standard of Colin McAdam, Jim Bett, Ian Redford, Robert Pritz, Ally Dawson, Gregor Steven, Craig Paterson and Dave McKinnon that 'Gers fans had to watch – and these ones were the better ones. I can think of ones who appeared as nonentities and who left as the same. So many of them were disappointments. A frequent comment on Colin McAdam, bought from Thistle and a centre-half converted to centre-forward, was that Celtic, in signing his brother, Tom, had got the better deal. When I heard that Greig had gone to Sweden and signed a midfielder, I was delighted – and then I saw what he'd brought back. Robert Pritz was indeed Swedish, but I had expected a blonde-haired, Viking-like, formidable, tough player. I couldn't believe it when what ran out was a wee, fat and unimposing lump.

One honourable exception in this list of sub-standard Rangers was the big central-defender from Northern Ireland, John McClelland, bought from the mighty Mansfield Town. He was a shining light in the darkness of the early 80s. He inspired others, was cool, always gave everything for the cause, could read the game and tackled well. I always felt sorry for him as most of his teammates just weren't in his class. He eventually became the club captain and only left later due to a dispute about his salary, heading for Watford, of all clubs, who offered him far superior terms. The Rangers' management should have hung their heads in shame at letting such a player go when he did. I hope that eventually he will be elected to the club's Hall of Fame.

If this period saw turmoil off the pitch with the rebuilding of Ibrox, it was the same story on the park as one Rangers side after another failed to win the League.

Not only were they failing to achieve that, they weren't even finishing runners-up, as the side of the late 60s had at least managed. In the worst sustained spell in the club's history, from season 1979–80 until 1985–86, Rangers finished in fifth, third, third, fourth, fourth, fourth and fifth positions. This was unheard of, and the fans were finding it difficult to accept. The fans weren't even pacified by the occasional Cup victory although in May 1981 I was at Hampden to watch one of Rangers' best-ever Scottish Cup Final wins in the replay against Dundee United that became known as 'Cooper's Final'.

For once I sat in the old North Stand, and what a view I had of the proceedings below me. The first game had been dire, and Rangers had even missed a last-minute penalty that led to the replay. Cooper, Johnstone and young John McDonald were all recalled to the side for the replay, and how it paid off. Cooper was magical, destroying Dundee on his own with great dribbling and passing skills. In a comprehensive 4–1 win, McDonald scored twice, courtesy of Cooper brilliance, then Russell netted from a Cooper free-kick. Cooper himself had started the rout by scoring the first.

With my house in Battlefield being so close, I got home in time to see the highlights of the game on television. I was really looking forward to seeing those great goals again. All the streets around were full of the parked cars of 'Gers fans at the match. However, being a more middle-class area, there were no urchins wanting to watch the fans' cars. It felt even better to stroll home and see the other fans all scrambling for their cars to make a quick getaway while I merely had to walk to my tenement. Nowadays when I go to Hampden, I am one of those fans rushing to their car in those same streets.

By 1982 we had to move to a bigger house, and so we moved to Cardonald, which is only a couple of miles from Ibrox. It was the nearest I'd lived to the stadium since childhood. Over the preceding years, teachers' salaries, as usual, had lost their value in relation to the cost of living, and inflation under Thatcher's Tories meant another period of strike action was looming. I was very hard up, and in fact, it was so bad at one point that I decided not to go to a match to save money. When I couldn't resist the lure of Ibrox, even in those darkest times on the pitch, I figured out the cheapest way to go to the match. I walked the two miles to the stadium to save petrol or a bus fare then paid to go into the wee enclosure, the only standing area left at Ibrox and so the cheapest. I can't remember the game but I do remember it was yet another dire affair, and I cursed myself for going as I walked the disconsolate two miles home again.

Other Cup Finals during those grim years saw us lose more than we won. In the Scottish Cup Finals we beat Dundee United, in the aforementioned match but lost to Celtic and Fergie's champions, Aberdeen, twice (once in extra-time). However, we fared better in the League Cup Finals, only losing once, to Celtic, but winning against Dundee United twice and Celtic once. The 3–2 win against Celtic saw Ally McCoist score a hat-trick and finally become accepted by the Rangers fans after a nightmare start to his career at Ibrox. I watched this Final from the Main Stand at Hampden, one of the few times I ever sat in it.

It was a pulsating match. McCoist scored just before half-time with a penalty, and when he scored again with 61 minutes on the clock it looked like the Cup was going to Ibrox. A typical howitzer of a punt from 'keeper McCloy bounced just outside the Celtic area. Sandy Clark, tussling with Aitken, nudged the ball to his right, and McCoist was there to send it into the net. I was very relaxed at that point – although I should have known better. Celtic mounted a come-back and scored through McClair with only 23 minutes left. It still looked like 'Gers would hang on until the final minute, though, until ref Bob Valentine awarded Celtic a penalty, this time conceded by McCoist. They scored and it went into extra-time.

Just before the end of the first period of extra-time, 'Gers got another penalty when Super Ally was fouled by Aitken. McCoist took the kick but Bonner dived and saved it. Fortunately for McCoist, the ball rebounded straight back to him and he slammed it into the net to complete his hat-trick. As was usual in those days, Celtic players didn't take this defeat well and were aggrieved with the ref, who had booked eight players, although only three had been Celts. At the end, while waiting for the presentation ceremony, they even hounded the ref with their protests. This just made it even more enjoyable for 'Gers fans as we waited to see captain John McClelland lift the trophy.

If that Final was a triumph for McCoist, the following season saw his lowest point as a 'Gers player. In a Scottish Cup tie at Ibrox against Dundee, Rangers were toiling in a match that would eventually be won 1–0 by Dundee. Even worse, McCoist was missing chance after chance to put Rangers into the next round. Even I could have taken some of the opportunities. Eventually, the frustration and anger of the Rangers fans boiled over, and the entire Copland Stand sang, 'Ally, Ally, get tae f***'. It says a lot for McCoist's temperament that he overcame that sort of venom and went on to become a legend.

Unfortunately, John Greig couldn't take the abuse he was getting any longer. Rather like Davie White before him, the Ibrox job came too soon. Nobody could fault him for taking the job as it had probably been his ultimate ambition, but circumstances conspired to thwart his success. His stewardship of the club unluckily coincided with the rise of Aberdeen and Dundee United, thanks to Alex Ferguson and Jim McLean, not to mention a regeneration of a Billy McNeill-led Celtic. At the start of his final season in charge, Greig had signed the future legend Ally McCoist, but his disappointing start did nothing to help the disastrous beginning to the new season. However, the signing of McCoist turned out to be Greig's most valuable legacy to the club he loved.

By the end of October 1983 Rangers had already given up on the Championship, having managed to collect a meagre seven points from the first nine matches. A home defeat by a Jock Wallace Motherwell side was the last straw for the loyal fans, who made their feelings known after that match. Greig had always put the interests of Rangers first, and on 28 October 1983 he decided to resign and let another manager try to turn the fortunes of the club around.

Although I had always loved John Greig as a 'Gers captain, and he had been at the club for as long as I had been going, I must admit that when he resigned I was relieved and looking forward to seeing who would replace him. He had been given plenty of time to get things right but had failed, so it was time to move on. The two hottest managers at the time were my former 'Gers' hero, Alex Ferguson of Aberdeen, and Jim McLean at Dundee United. I was genuinely thrilled at the prospect of Fergie taking over. I couldn't see him turning down his old club, even though he was already a legend at Aberdeen. When he stayed at Pittodrie and Jim McLean was approached I consoled myself with the thought that at least we were getting the next best thing. The papers were claiming that McLean had accepted the position, but, seemingly at the last minute, he had a change of heart and declined to move. This was devastating for me as it made me realise just how low Rangers' stock had fallen when the two best managers in Scotland could refuse what was once the top job in the country, and one that doesn't come along too often.

As when White was sacked, the club turned to a tried-and-trusted 'Rangers man' who would initially steady the ship in the turbulent waters that it found itself floundering in. This saw the return of Jock Wallace. By then Big Jock had become the Motherwell manager, but he jumped at the chance to return to Ibrox. At that point he was the first man to manage Rangers twice. The fans welcomed him back as one of their own and, when he saluted them before his first match back at Ibrox, he did a little jig and gesture as the 'Gers fans sang the traditional ditties. However, it would take much more than the traditional Rangers' values to rescue the club this time. Wallace would be up against two young, innovative, modern managers who feared no club. Wallace might instil discipline, organisation and greater fitness during his regime, but it would not be enough. The old saying in football about 'never going back' turned out to be just as true for this colossus as any mere mortal.

Two League Cups, beating Celtic in 1983–84 and United the following season, were Wallace's only triumphs in his second spell as manager. Indeed, he only lasted two and a half seasons before a ruthless new chairman, David Holmes, sacked him and started the Rangers' revolution by appointing Graeme Souness as player-manager, the first in the club's history.

By the time Wallace had taken over from Greig, my son, Stewart, had started accompanying my dad and I to games at Ibrox. He was just coming up for six years old and was desperate to go to matches. Remembering how long it had taken me to make my first appearance at Ibrox, I decided to take him to see if he would sit for 90 minutes and take in all that was happening. Not that there was a lot of ecitement in those days. I must admit to a feeling of pride as the three of us sat there in the Govan, three generations of MacCallums supporting the 'Gers. That sense of pride maybe changed to guilt after a couple of seasons of watching the dross on view, though. I had started at the top, watching maybe the greatest 'Gers team of all time, but here was poor Stewart starting with possibly the worst sides in Rangers' history. I almost felt like reporting myself to the RSPCC. He hardly saw a match where 'Gers played well and won. Mostly it was grim and disappointing viewing. At least his frequent trips to the toilets and food kiosks alleviated the boredom at times. For practically all of my life going to Ibrox I have refrained from buying either fare or drink from the kiosks under the stands. The exorbitant prices and basic food have always put me off. However, when I started taking Stewart to games, all of a sudden my match expenses underwent a dramatic increase. A youngster will eat anything at a football stadium – especially if they aren't paying! Nowadays, I really sympathise with fans who have a couple of kids accompanying them to matches. The cost per match must be horrendous.

In 1984 another change came to Rangers and most other clubs – the advent of shirt sponsorship. I hated the idea of desecrating the Rangers shirt with an advert or slogan. It just seemed so tacky. On the other hand I saw the advantage of having a new and constant revenue stream – although in those days, fans didn't really think of such matters, especially compared with the interest in a club's finances these days. In other countries, this type of sponsorship was a straightforward practice. A company gave a club money in return for the chance to advertise its product or name on the team's shirt. However, in Scotland, the Old Firm was the greatest source of advertising, and with the bitter rivalry between Rangers and Celtic there was a problem for any company wishing to sponsor a club's shirt: can you do it without alienating the other half of the Old Firm's supporters and thus risk losing customers? The solution was to find a company willing to put its name on the shirts of both Rangers and Celtic.

A Scottish double-glazing company C.R. Smith had the honour of being the first to sponsor the shirts of the Old Firm. This made me even more disappointed because I was against the idea in the first place, but I expected the shirt to display at least a world-famous brand like Coca-Cola, not a fairly local company. This form of raising funds was successful, and through the years various companies have sponsored the Rangers shirt. In 1987 McEwan's Lager replaced C.R. Smith and stayed on the shirt for the longest period – 12 years. Then it was media giant of the time, NTL, for four years, Carling from 2003–10 and now Tennent's. It is interesting, though perhaps inevitable, that three of our five sponsors have been drinks companies. I still hate to see the Rangers shirt spoiled by the name of a company, although I do realise that now, more than ever, the club needs the money it accrues.

By the start of season 1985–86 my dad had stopped going to Ibrox with us. It was around September of that year that my mum told me she was worried about him. He wasn't his usual smiling, laid-back self, and he hardly spoke. The two of them used to come out to Erskine, where we now lived, every other week and go out to the bowling club on a Saturday night with my aunt and uncle, who also lived in Erskine. One Sunday my mum asked me if I would take my dad down to the local pub for a drink and see if I could get him to open up. That hour or so was excruciating. We had a couple of drinks, but I did virtually all the talking. He hardly said a thing, although he listened and smiled at things I said. When I reported back to mum, all I could say was that I could see there was a problem and that a visit to the doctor was called for.

Over the next couple of months Dad had various tests and saw various consultants, and by the end of November he was a patient in the Southern General Hospital. It was in December that we were told he had inoperable cancer. For the next six months it became a case of visiting him in the Southern or at home, once he had been allowed back just before Christmas, and then eventually at the hospice in the north of the city. In all that time he never spoke one word to anyone. The doctors told us that there was no physical reason why he couldn't speak. It was just a case of him not wanting to. Like that day in the pub with me, he would just listen and smile and look interested, but the visitor would have to do all the talking. If I saw him in hospital on my own, as I sometimes did, I would have to talk non-stop for an hour. No problem there, some folk might say, but it is really painful when you don't get a reply from the person you are talking to. It's hard enough at the best of times keeping a conversation going with someone who is in hospital, but when they don't speak it's a million times worse. And that is what it was like for six months until my dad died.

In April 1986 I made an evening visit to the Southern on my own. I had plenty to say and could tell him that Rangers had just signed Graeme Souness as their player-manager. I don't think I imagined it, but his smile seemed bigger than usual while I was relating the momentous events of that day. I was so excited. I think I was probably even more delighted at the prospect of having Souness in the Rangers' midfield as having him manage the club. One of my biggest regrets is that my dad died at the end of May, so he didn't see the transformation that Rangers was about to undergo. The appointment of Souness was when I started going back to Ibrox.

In Wallace's final season two events stick out in my memory: the death of Jock Stein and the fact that for the only time in my life I gave up on Rangers. The League games following the tragic death of Scotland manager Jock Stein in Wales while in charge of a World Cup qualifying match, were marked for tributes of one minute's silence at every match. Rangers were playing Clydebank at the old Kilbowie ground, and my dad and I were there that day. Rangers won 1–0, but the most memorable aspect of the match was the minute's silence. The crowd of nearly 10,000, the majority of it Rangers fans, stood and observed an impeccable silence. It was a very moving occasion as the Rangers fans remembered the Big Man. I think it was the great football historian and broadcaster Bob Crampsey who stated that it was the greatest tribute Stein could have had. The fact that these 'Gers fans showed their respect for a man who had caused them so much pain as Celtic's successful manager through the years said it all.

When John Greig had resigned and Wallace had been installed as the new manager, I admitted to being sceptical about the appointment. I was willing to give the guy a chance, but I didn't really think he could overcome the talented sides that Ferguson and McLean had put together on the east coast. And there was always Celtic to contend with. And so it proved. Despite the League Cup wins there seemed to be no improvement in the League. By season 1985–86 I could see no light at the end of what had been a very dark and long tunnel.

On 2 November over a dozen matches into the League programme, I decided that I had had enough. At that point Rangers had played 13, won only six, drawn three and lost four games. The fare on display was absolutely dire. Poor play is something that can be endured if the team is at least 'winning ugly' but this 'Gers side wasn't even managing that. I like to think that I am a principled person, and I can be determined, or stubborn, as some would say. I made up my mind after the terrible 0–0 draw against Clydebank on 2 November watched by under 17,000 fans at Ibrox, that I would not go back to Ibrox until Jock Wallace had gone – and I stuck to that, although I must admit it did pain me.

My abstinence wasn't easy, especially after the following week when 'Gers walloped Celtic 3–0 at Ibrox. It was sod's law that I stopped going and Rangers had its best result of that season! In those pre-Sky television days, even Old Firm matches were not shown live, so I had to content myself with listening to the Old Firm game on radio. I don't like listening to matches on radio as the commentator always makes every move sound as if it's dangerous and a goal inevitable, but when you see the action later it was nothing of the sort. It's too nerve-wracking an experience for me. I was elated that Rangers had thrashed Celtic, disappointed that I had missed being there but still determined not to let that one result tempt me to renege on my promise to myself. I was correct to abide by my decision because nothing really changed, and by the end of that season the Rangers League record read played 36, won 13, drawn nine, lost 14. Few 'Gers teams in history have lost more games than they had won. Those results ensured that the club ended up in fifth place in the table.

For the remainder of that season I kept to my word. On 7 April Jock Wallace and the club 'parted company', as the cliché says. In other words the manager jumped before he was pushed. I immediately decided to return to Ibrox at the first opportunity. Having said that, 'Gers only had four matches after the Wallace departure and only the final game was at home. Three of the final four games were against the teams in the bottom four of the table. Rangers lost 2–1 away to both Clydebank and then St Mirren before securing a 1–1 draw at Pittodrie. The final game of the season was at Ibrox against Motherwell, and Rangers needed a win to ensure European participation the following season. Even with the prospect of the new manager taking up his duties the next season and the stakes being high regarding that European place, a crowd of only 21,500 turned up. But at least I was one of them again. It felt great to be back. Thanks to McPherson and McCoist goals, Rangers won 2–0, and the first target set by Souness had been achieved. Bigger and better things were to come.

It was just as well the new Souness-led Rangers would be there in 1986 to cheer me up because it was in the July of that year that my first wife left me and the two children for another man. She went on an Orange Walk with some friends – and never walked back. I was determined that I would keep my two kids, who were aged five and seven at the time, and I told her so in no uncertain terms when she had phoned me to tell me that she was leaving me. One of the hardest things I've ever had to do in my life was to sit the two kids down and tell them that their mum wouldn't be coming home, just a month after I'd had to tell them that their grandad had died.

Fortunately, after the death of my dad, my mum had been allocated a house in Erskine, only five minutes walk away from mine. My initial worries about how I could juggle being a teacher with taking care of two small kids were somewhat alleviated. I had the whole of the school summer holiday to get myself organised and accustomed to taking care of the kids, and when school restarted I took them round to my mum's house before going to my work. My mum would go round to my house in the afternoon so that the kids would be able to come straight home from school and she could leave when I returned from school. It's funny the way things worked out. I really do believe in fate now.

CHAPTER FIVE

HAPPY DAYS ARE HERE AGAIN!

The appointment of Graeme Souness as Rangers' player-manager astonished all of Scottish football. Souness had had no previous connection with the club, had spent all his professional career outside of Scotland and had no managerial experience. Despite all of this, it was seen as something of a coup for chief executive David Holmes to have lured the man from Sampdoria for a fee of £300,000. 'Gers might have been getting a novice manager but, in his dual role, they were getting a classy and experienced midfield player. Many believed that even if the boss's hat didn't fit Souness, his ability on the field would pay dividends for the club. I had never particularly liked the guy as a player, but I recognised that Rangers was getting something special and, if he was going to be backed by the finances of the majority shareholder, Lawrence Malborough, grandson of former chairman John Lawrence, then it was an exciting prospect as far as I was concerned.

Optimism increased with the news that Dundee United's experienced and much-admired coach, Walter Smith, would become Souness' assistant manager. Since Souness had little knowledge of the current Scottish game, this was seen as a vital move in ensuring that he would settle into his new job with as few errors as possible being committed. Smith, with his wealth of coaching experience, would also be able to deal with the day-to-day training of the players. One of the words commonly used to sum up Souness at that time was 'winner'. He had enjoyed a trophy-laden career at Liverpool, winning all there was to win, including the European Cup, and, on the field, his desire to succeed showed itself in his crunching tackles and ability to drive his side on. Nobody doubted that the same commitment would be shown in his new role as manager.

Once he had got into his stride as manager, other words would be used to complement that of 'winner' when people were trying to describe his managerial style. Professional, committed, determined, authoritarian, stubborn, abrasive and confrontational were the most frequently used ones. The players at Ibrox quickly learned that if you didn't do things Souness's way, then you wouldn't be around for very long. Having been appointed just before the end of the season, Souness and Smith had the chance to appraise the players they'd be taking charge of and decide who would be discarded. With the financial backing of Lawrence Malborough, it quickly became evident that Souness would be spending money – big money in those days – to perform major surgery on the underachieving team.

Souness's intentions were revealed early on when, after signing largely unknown striker Colin West from Watford for £175,000, he secured the services of England goalkeeper Chris Woods from Norwich for £600,000, then a record for a 'keeper. As if that wasn't enough, he still had the biggest surprise up his sleeve, and surprising football people seemed to delight Souness. The acquisition of England captain and centre-half Terry Butcher from Ipswich for £725,000 astonished every Scots fan and shocked most English ones. It seemed barely credible that such a high-profile English player, fresh from the World Cup in Mexico, would desert England to ply his trade in Scotland. I had never rated Butcher as highly as the fans in England had but the fact that we had got a player that Manchester United had wanted made it a thrilling acquisition. It was to be the start of Souness's policy of signing good quality players from wherever they played. At a stroke, he had reversed the century-old trend of the best Scots players leaving to 'better' themselves in England. The prestige of Souness, the fact that he had moved to Scotland to play as well as manage, the possibility of European football, the tremendous stadium and the high wages were all factors that lured English players to Ibrox in Souness's early days there.

Souness, like any manager who knows his stuff, realised that a new spine of the side would have to be created and that the defence, especially, would have to be strengthened. The arrival of Woods, Butcher and West was the first piece in his jigsaw. He offered £650,000 to Dundee United for their young Scots defender Richard Gough, whom Souness had played with during the World Cup in Mexico months before, but United refused to sell the player to Rangers and eventually he was sold to Spurs. That season, in December, Souness would sign another experienced England defender in Graeme Roberts, from Spurs, but Gough would not be forgotten. Roberts' first game was at Ibrox on 27 December 1986. The fans loved him from the start due to his grit, energy, enthusiasm and fierce tackling, and his debut was sensational. Here was a guy who seemed to be playing for the jersey already. His tenacity even created a goal in the 2–0 win that kept Rangers at the top of the table. I remember feeling euphoric that Butcher, already a hero at Ibrox, had a partner who might become his equal.

As his rookie season started, Souness had cause to feel pleased with the way things had gone. He had secured most of the signings he'd wanted and prepared his players well. However, if he hadn't realised it before, he soon appreciated that every match Rangers play is like a Cup Final for the opposition. Furthermore, Souness's image and his big spending had fostered an even more resentful feeling among some players and managers that meant teams would be getting stuck into 'Gers as never before. This all kicked off in the opening League game at Easter Road when a tousy affair had seen Hibs take the lead and a frustrated Souness lash out at George McCluskey. A huge melee took place in the centre circle, and, at the end of it, Souness was sent off for his role in sparking off the trouble in the first place. The new Ranger had learned a valuable lesson.

Nevertheless, as Souness developed and his team started to gel, the future looked bright at Ibrox. By October he had won his first trophy by defeating Celtic in the Skol League Cup Final. I saw that game with Stewart from the wee enclosure at Hampden. They were the only tickets I could get. Right against the wall at the front, we had a terrible view in general but a great one of the two winning Rangers goals. The first was Ian Durrant's and the winner was from a Davie Cooper penalty right in front of us. When we got the traditional end-of-season video, you could actually see the two of us in the crowd celebrating.

By Christmas Rangers were the League leaders, and we were enjoying a style of football we hadn't experienced in years. Having been in the Main Stand at the first Old Firm game at Ibrox under Souness, which 'Gers won 1–0 thanks to a brilliant Cooper pass and Durrant finish, I was desperate to be at the traditional Ne'er Day match. I queued up outside Ibrox for hours to get tickets, only to be told that they had sold out. I missed Souness's finest hour as a 'Gers player when he destroyed Celtic in that game on 1 January. Fleck and McCoist might have scored the two goals to win that match, but Souness was at his arrogant best as he controlled the midfield and sprayed passes all over the park while the snow fell on the stadium.

The game wasn't live on television, but I remember listening to it on my car radio while I drove to visit relatives. I could hardly wait for the highlights to be shown that evening. Missing that game made up my mind. I was going to buy a season ticket the following year so that it wouldn't happen again. When I applied for tickets for myself and my son, Stewart, I asked for the Govan Stand Rear. In the close season when my tickets arrived, we had two great seats, midway between the 18-yard line at the Copland end and the halfway line, as well as being halfway up towards the back of the stand. I still sit there to this day.

Rangers had been so good defensively that a record 12 consecutive clean sheets had been kept by 'keeper Chris Woods until January, when a shock 1–0 Scottish Cup exit at the hands of Hamilton, bottom of the Premier League, broke the sequence. That was one of the biggest travesties I have ever experienced in football. 'Gers murdered them that day, but one slip up by McPherson gave them the winning goal, and, despite bombarding the opposition goal, we just couldn't put it in the net. I even had the misfortune to watch the ball slide between the posts in front of me as I was in the rear of the Copland Stand for that match, having been unable to get a ticket for the Govan Stand. Getting tickets during Souness's debut season was proving to be difficult, especially when, for years before this, you could pay at the turnstiles and go anywhere you wanted to sit. That season we sat in the Main Stand at times, the Govan and even the Broomloan. By the end of that season the average home gate had gone from 25,000 to over 36,000.

That Cup result was the most disappointing one in the manager's first season, but he kept faith with his players and trusted them to keep up their good work in the League – which they did. In the penultimate League game of the season, at Pittodrie, Rangers only needed a draw to clinch their first Championship in nine years. Unfortunately, the manager wasn't on the field to see this happen as he'd been sent off again in the first half. Fittingly, it was a fierce Terry Butcher header that had put 'Gers into the lead and enabled them to hold on for a draw, despite having been reduced to 10 men. How the Rangers fans celebrated when they invaded the Pittodrie pitch and congratulated the players – something that would be unthinkable nowadays.

In his first season in management, Souness had regained the title and won the League Cup as well as introducing quality players and instilling a new mood among the players who'd already been at the club when he'd arrived. The fans had been impressed, as shown by the fact that the average home gate had risen dramatically from the previous season.

Off the field, too, Rangers had started to create policies and sponsorship deals that would increase revenue in order to fund the type of signings that Souness would be aspiring to in the future. Despite such a great start to his managerial career, the next season would let Souness experience the downside of management. Despite acquiring the long-sought-after Richard Gough, Souness's defensive plans were ruined when skipper Terry Butcher broke his leg in November, and 'Gers eventually slumped to third place in the League. Souness had to be content with merely winning the Skol Cup again.

The most enjoyable experience in that disappointing season was when 'Gers beat Aberdeen in the Final of the Skol League Cup. Nearly 72,000 saw the game end in a 3–3 draw after extra-time. Stewart and I were right at the back of the Rangers' End at Hampden, just above one of the exits, and we had a brilliant view of what turned out to be one of the greatest games I have ever attended. It was an open game with both sides attacking each other with relish. The fortunes of each team swung back and forward with practically every attack. 'Gers' three goals came from a magnificent Cooper free-kick, then great inter-passing following a throw-in revolving around Ian Durrant, who finished the move off, and a relatively dull goal from Robert Fleck, uncle of the present Ranger John Fleck. Cooper's goal may have been the best, but Durrant's display will live in the memory.

Before that, most fans recognised that this was a special young player, one brought into the side by previous manager Jock Wallace. After this match we knew that we had witnessed a world-class display from a Ranger who could be our talisman for years to come. An energetic, skilful, goalscoring midfield man, Durrant was every manager's dream. He was a lovely passer of the ball, covered every blade of grass like a colt, with his boundless energy and enthusiasm, and had the knack of running ahead of his forwards to get into goalscoring positions. He did all of these that day at Hampden, and his boyish enthusiasm shone through – especially when it came to the penalties.

A penalty shoot-out was a relatively new way of deciding stalemate games in those days. When it came down to that to decide who would win the Skol Cup, we were so lucky that the penalties took place at our end of Hampden. The tension and excitement was palpable. One penalty after another was netted, and we grew more anxious with each until it came to Dons' fifth one when Welshman Peter Nicholas stepped up – and missed. How fitting that the fate of his team should rest with Ian Durrant, who was to take the penalty that won the Cup. He ran up and confidently slammed the ball home as if he was out playing with his friends in a bounce game. We jumped around hugging each other, believing that this was one of the great victories. Meanwhile, down on the pitch, Durrant and Ally McCoist were like little kids, prancing around, hugging each other too. After all, they were Rangers fans, just like us. We all thought Durrant was destined to become one of the immortals after that day.

Durrant didn't quite reach that status, however, although he is now a member of the club's Hall of Fame. The following season, in October 1988, at Pittodrie,

Aberdeen's Neil Simpson stamped on Durrant's knee and changed the course of his career. As he was carried off, nobody could have known that Durrant would miss virtually the next three seasons after undergoing various operations in America to repair his shattered knee to enable him to play top flight football again. Durrant did make a comeback, score more goals and win more medals, even playing 13 times for Scotland, but his early promise was never quite fulfilled, although he always remained a hero in the eyes of the Rangers fans.

From his initial moves, Souness's exciting signing policy continued unabated, and along with Richard Gough, quality, experienced Englishmen would arrive in the form of Ray Wilkins, Trevor Francis and Mark Walters, as well as Scots such as John Brown. These would be supplemented in his third season by Gary Stevens, Ian Ferguson, Kevin Drinkell and Trevor Steven. This season would see Souness's strongest Rangers side yet regain the Championship and retain the Skol Cup for the third consecutive year. A stunning 5–1 win against old foes Celtic was perhaps the highlight of this season for many Rangers fans. That was one of those games that will live in my memory forever. As each goal went in, the 'Gers fans wanted more. My one disappointment was that we didn't at least equal Celtic's 7–1 against us in 1957. When Mark Walters scored the fifth goal to make it 5–1, I looked at the scoreboard and the clock showed that there was still half an hour left. Unfortunately, we didn't add to our tally that day, but it was still one of the great 'Gers displays.

I was so pleased that I recorded the *Scotsport* highlights of the match, took the tape into my school on the Monday and, at lunch-time, wheeled the English department's tv and video trolley to the staffroom, where the 'Gers fans on the staff and I could enjoy Celtic's humiliation over again, at least twice. Even the solitary Dons fan seemed to enjoy the experience, although the few Celtic fans there just had to grin and bear it. I can still hear Gerry McNee's commentary as the fifth goal was just about to be scored: 'And there's Aitken, in a fankle…' That was when big Roy was falling over just inside the box and fouling McCoist watching Mark Walters run on to the loose ball and slam it into the net.

At the start of his stewardship of Rangers, Souness had been of the opinion that a win against Celtic was the same as against any other side, merely gaining two points in the League. By the 5–1 match, however, Souness had come to appreciate the fans' point of view that beating the other half of the Old Firm wasn't just another victory. 5–1 against your old rivals doesn't happen too often. I would have to wait until the Advocaat era to experience another one.

It was in the November of this season that one of the most dramatic changes in Rangers' history took place. A relatively unknown businessman called David Murray, who was a friend of Souness, bought Lawrence Malborough's majority shareholding in Rangers for a mere £6 million. Due to relocating his business interests to Nevada, Marlborough needed to offload the family shares, and Murray was alerted to this by Souness. It still annoys me when Murray gets the sole credit for 'revolutionising' the club by people like Derek Johnstone who should know better. By the time Murray became the virtual owner, Rangers had already been 'turned around' by Marlborough and the chairman, David Holmes. The club was successful on the park and was winning trophies, and attendances were climbing year on year. The stadium was virtually complete, although later on Murray would oversee the seating of the Enclosure and the addition of the Club Deck. There is no doubt that Murray brought even more success to Rangers throughout his years and provided various managers with the funds needed to maintain that eminence. This, however, was building up financial problems in the distant future. Murray's initial season was the start of the nine-in-a-row years, a period that was my most enjoyable in the 50 years I have been going to Ibrox.

At the end of Murray's first season, Rangers had regained the League title and retained the Skol League Cup, beating Aberdeen yet again. Only a 1–0 defeat in the Scottish Cup Final at the hands of Celtic denied the club that elusive treble. Apart from the annoyance that it had been Celtic who denied us the victory, I was upset at how the result had come about. Celtic, the club that claims it never gets any decisions from referees, this time benefited from two in what had been a poor match. Of the first, there is no dubiety as television proved afterwards. The ball went out for a Rangers throw-in, but Aitken of Celtic grabbed the ball first and took the throw. As the ball eventually reached the edge of the 'Gers' penalty area, right-back Gary Stevens was there to pass it back to 'keeper Chris Woods. This happened right in front of me as I was sitting in the Main Stand, level with the 18-yard line. Unfortunately, for once, the ever-reliable Stevens made a hash of it and miscued his pass-back, leaving it short, allowing Celtic's Joe Miller to run onto the ball and slip it past Woods and into the net.

Near the end, a second decision cost Rangers dearly when an equalising goal was chalked off. Again, this was right in front of me, and when the cross into the box was headed in by Terry Butcher we all jumped up to celebrate before being thoroughly deflated by the referee disallowing it. Afterwards it was claimed that Butcher had 'leaned on' a defender while rising for the cross but if you watch it again, it was the type of joust that goes on all the time in the box and is hardly ever penalised. I really felt we had been robbed that day – of the Cup and of the treble. Celtic fans were jubilant at the end. They were even more overjoyed at the thought of seemingly having re-signed their 'golden Bhoy' striker Maurice Johnston from Nantes. Boy, were they in for a shock!

The following season, his fourth season with the club, Souness had his biggest surprise yet for Scottish football fans – apart from his resignation near the end of the following season. Just before the season started, he shocked just about everybody by signing former Celt Maurice Johnston, who appeared to have signed a contract to rejoin his old club. Discovering that the deal was far from done, Souness moved quickly to lure Johnston to Ibrox from his French club, Nantes. What made the whole affair more astonishing to Scottish football fans was the fact that, in signing Johnston from under the noses of Celtic, Souness would be breaking with Rangers' unofficial sectarian policy of not knowingly signing Catholic players. Johnston would become Rangers' first high-profile Catholic player of the modern era, causing more angst among Celtic fans than 'Gers ones in the process. Souness had stated from the beginning that he would sign players on merit alone, regardless of colour or creed and here he was putting that policy into stunning effect.

I was at home when my brother, Ian, phoned from his work to tell me the news. At first I didn't believe him, so incredible did it seem. But he quickly convinced me it was true. I switched on my television to see the Scottish news, which was running with this as its lead story. I was jubilant. Not only had Souness rid the club of the sectarian stick with which its enemies continually beat it but he had signed a classy striker to accompany McCoist and, as a bonus, had riled Celtic fans. It was one of the most pleasant shocks I have ever experienced as a Rangers fan.

This signing paid off handsomely as Johnston scored 19 goals in competitive matches in his first season and seemed to complement the striking prowess of Ally McCoist, long the goalscoring hero of Ibrox. Johnston's goals, especially those against Celtic, saw him accepted quickly by the 'Gers fans, and the future for the striking duo of McCoist and Johnston looked bright. I can still see his first goal against Celtic at Ibrox. It couldn't have been scripted any better. With the score 0–0 in the last minute, a low cross into the Celtic box was half-cleared to the edge of the penalty area where Johnston controlled it before whacking it low into the corner of the goal. It was only later that I saw his wild celebration on television because we were too busy going crazy at the time, jumping around in the Govan, knowing that it just couldn't get any better than that. That season, I was proud of my fellow 'Gers' fans when I saw how readily and quickly they had accepted Mo Johnston. The few idiots, encouraged by the media to burn their season tickets outside Ibrox on the announcement of his signing, turned out to be that – just a few. The vast majority of Rangers fans welcomed Souness's bold signing and showed it even before he scored his first goal in a 1–0 win against Aberdeen at Ibrox in his fourth League game for the club. Johnston went on to score 15 League goals that season – one more than McCoist.

Then, the following season, Souness signed Mark Hateley from Monaco and everything changed. Souness' stubborn streak was emphasised when he decided to pair Hateley with Johnston, leaving McCoist on the bench, to the disgruntlement of the fans. Despite pressure from the supporters and sportswriters to reinstate McCoist, the manager kept faith with Hateley, who took quite a while to settle in at Ibrox and win over the fans. Most couldn't see that the big Englishman was the first pick and the only decision left was whether it would be Johnston or McCoist to partner him. Few appreciated that it wasn't Hateley who was keeping their hero out of the side.

In what turned out to be Souness's last season with the club, the Skol Cup was won again, with Rangers beating Celtic in the Final by 2–1, while the League title was retained on the final thrilling day of the season. By then, however, Souness had gone. With Rangers leading the table from Aberdeen and only four games left, Souness shocked everybody by announcing that he'd decided to take the vacant manager's post at his former club, Liverpool. He wanted to see out the League campaign but chairman, David Murray decided that it would be better if he left immediately to let the club concentrate on winning the title. Murray stated that he thought his friend and manager was making the biggest mistake of his career by going to Liverpool and that he'd regret his decision, but he wouldn't stand in his way.

The Souness years had been so successful, with all sorts of big-name English international players joining the club, as well as foreigners, that the fans (myself included) looked for a high-profile, non-Scottish manager to be appointed as his replacement. Most reasoned that this was the type of person needed to lure more big names to the club. Managers of the calibre of Terry Venables were being quoted in the press, so it was something of a shock and, to me, a disappointment, when the new boss was announced as the current assistant manager, Walter Smith, who had always kept a low profile when it came to the perception of the fans. I thought that even his name was boring. I feared that everything that had been built up would be ruined. How wrong I was.

Walter Smith was quickly appointed manager and when the penultimate match saw Rangers lose 3–0 at Motherwell, it suddenly meant that Rangers had to beat Aberdeen at Ibrox on the final day of the season to win the Championship. That match was one of the most memorable in my 'Gers-watching life. Unlike the fans of most clubs, Rangers fans, in the course of their lives, have had numerous great days to remember but, even for 'Gers fans, this match that decided the League that season will always be one of their fondest memories. It was a wonderful climax to what had been a season full of ups-and-downs. In the first half of the season, skipper Terry Butcher had been transferred after a fall-out with Graeme Souness. Then the brilliant replacement defender, Oleg Kuznetsov from Dynamo Kiev, was crocked in only his second game for the club and would be out with his cruciate ligament injury for the next year. To top it all, leading the table from Aberdeen, with only four games left, Rangers lost their charismatic manager.

On a hot, sunny day, Ibrox was full to bursting, with only a small contingent of Aberdeen fans interrupting the sea of red, white and blue. The atmosphere was tense, electric and expectant. Those who had been at the Kiev match a few years before thought that the mood was exactly the same as it had been then, with the huge Rangers crowd ready to urge the side on to a famous victory.

Having lost their manager, many fans thought that the home side could be up against it and that the momentum had switched to Aberdeen. To make matters worse, injuries were taking their toll on Rangers. Captain Richard Gough's inspirational presence would be missing, and true blues like stalwart John Brown could only play thanks to pain-killing injections. Indeed, before the end of the game, Brown's Achilles tendon would have snapped, young Tom Cowan would have suffered a broken leg and a clearly unfit Ally McCoist would have had to come off the bench to contribute in the latter stages of the game. It was a case of the walking wounded gritting their teeth, showing the true Rangers spirit and hobbling off with the spoils.

Early in the game a Gary Stevens cross was slung into the Aberdeen box and Mark Hateley leapt up for it with typical power and determination, crashing to the ground with the young Dons 'keeper, Michael Watt. Many later surmised that this had been an intentional ploy to test the 'keeper's mettle and let him worry about what was in store for him throughout the rest of the match. If so, it would pay off before half-time.

The first real chance of the game fell to Dons' midfielder Van de Ven, who broke through the middle with only 'keeper Chris Woods to beat. Tension perhaps got the better of the player and, instead of netting, his weak shot went straight into the arms of the 'Gers 'keeper. It was a miss that the Aberdeen players would rue an hour or so later. The game thundered on without any other real opportunities being created. Then, near the interval, came the moment that would be the start of Mark Hateley's legendary status.

For once, Mark Walters had found himself way out on the left-hand touchline, 30-something yards from goal. He curved a wicked, pacy cross into the heart of the Dons' box where Hateley, rising above Alex McLeish and the 'keeper, bulleted the ball into the net. Ibrox went berserk, as did most of the Rangers players. They had taken the initiative and were now in the driving seat in the Championship race, and they could only throw it away. With the fervent backing of the Ibrox crowd, that wasn't likely to happen.

Another Hateley goal in the second half seemed to put the final nail in the Aberdeen coffin. In a sweeping move, a Mo Johnston shot was parried by the 'keeper, but, as it bounced away from his diving body, there was Hateley, like any good striker, following up the shot to clip it into the Dons' goal and virtually bury the visitors. As you would expect, Aberdeen had to throw caution to the wind and go all-out to get a goal that would give them some hope of snatching a draw. Normally, this would lead to the opposition creating chances as they became exposed. However, by now, most of the 'Gers players were dead on their feet. Those who had begun the game injured were struggling to keep going, others had been injured during the match, and those who were fit had expended all their energy trying to compensate for the injured.

Although the last 10 minutes were a struggle, the side fought for each other and managed to prevent Aberdeen from making any real chances that might have given them some hope and allowed them to put more pressure on the Ibrox side. During that spell I was as nervous as I have ever been at a game at Ibrox, believing that if Aberdeen could snatch one goal, a frantic, last-gasp effort might see them grab another to give them the title. When the final whistle was blown to signal that Rangers had retained their title, it was a mixture of relief and joy that enveloped Ibrox Stadium. New manager Walter Smith paraded the trophy with his players, some of whom hirpled around and one, 'Bomber' Brown, enjoyed the moment on crutches – a graphic reminder of the blood, sweat and tears that had literally gone into winning that season's Championship.

Two goals in that game created a new 'Gers' hero in Mark Hateley and, although Smith was now the manager, every fan knew that it had been Souness's Championship, his fourth in five seasons.

Burndyke Street, as it is now. Our tenement was where the trees are on the left of the photograph. The rear of the Govan Stand can be seen in the background, in front of the high flats.

My dad's local across from the flat we lived in as kids.

Copland Road, with the University tower on the horizon.

The dry dock across from my old tenement as it is today, with modern buildings on the other side of the river.

Ibrox Stadium. My gran's Wine Alley was at top-right corner of frame.

Hampden Park. I lived to the right of the high flats on right side of frame.

The programme for the first Cup-Winners' Cup Final.

The programme for my first League Cup Final.

My ticket for the Inter Milan match in 1965, one of my prized possessions.

The programme for an Inter Milan match in the 1960s.

A Cup-Winners' Cup Final programme.

The programme for my first European match, Rangers versus Red Star Belgrade.

The programme for my first Scottish Cup Final from 1964.

In the manager's office at Ibrox.

'Encouraging the team' from the dug-out on an Ibrox Tour.

A commemorative flag for the world record 50 titles.

My painted head for the 2003 Scottish Cup Final against Dundee.

My brick in the Klos Panel.

The Klos Panel at the end of the Govan Stand.

The four books I've had published on Rangers.

A book signing in Waterstones, Glasgow for my *Hall of Fame* book.

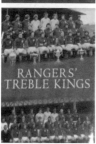

The 2008 UEFA Cup Final programme.

The 2008 UEFA Final display in the trophy room at Ibrox.

The 2008 UEFA Final Referee's Report.

The 2008 UEFA Final Team Lines.

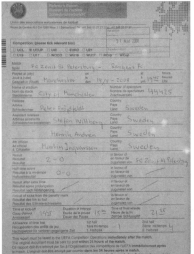

The fans enjoy the sunshine in Manchester on the afternoon of the UEFA Cup Final.

My son-in-law, Robert, and I in Albert Square before the UEFA Cup Final.

Half an hour to kick-off at the City of Manchester Stadium.

'Gers fans in the City of Manchester Stadium.

The UEFA Cup Final. My seat was behind the foreign media men.

The UEFA Cup Final prior to kick-off as 'Gers fans crank up the volume.

Motherwell form a guard of honour on the last day of season 2009–10.

The team emerges for the presentation of the 2009–10 Championship trophy.

Celebrating the 2009–10 title win at Ibrox.

The 2009–10 Championship trophy presented at the end of the Motherwell game.

Outside Hampden for the 2009–10 Co-op Final against St Mirren.

'Gers fans' display at the Rangers' End of Hampden during the 2009–10 Co-op Final.

The view from my Hampden debenture seat during the 2009–10 Co-op Final.

Rangers won the 2009–10 Co-op Final against St Mirren despite being reduced to nine men.

Souness's departure had shocked Rangers fans as well as most others in Scottish football but, in retrospect, perhaps it shouldn't have been seen as such a stunning course of action. As well as having personal problems in his family life, Souness had incurred the wrath of the SFA, its administrators and discipline committee members on more than one occasion, and it was surmised that he felt he was up against it in his dealings with authority. He had also had many confrontations with members of the press and frequently sought out individual reporters when he felt aggrieved at articles they'd written. He had even had a run-in with Aggie, the tea lady at St Johnstone! The bitterness of the whole Old Firm sectarian aspect had also depressed him, not to mention being continually under the microscope in such a small football environment. The lure of restoring the fortunes of the Anfield club no doubt also had a big impact on his decision to leave Rangers.

I, like most Rangers fans, on the whole, wished him well. He had turned around the fortunes of the club when at its lowest ebb and proceeded to give us the time of our lives. How could we have known that things would get even better with Walter Smith at the tiller of HMS Rangers?

CHAPTER SIX

THE WALTER SMITH YEARS

The sudden departure of Graeme Souness may have shocked Scottish football but, for many people, the speedy appointment of Walter Smith as his successor was equally shocking. After almost five years of big-money signings and glamour, many thought that a big-name manager was what chairman David Murray would be looking for, so the promotion of the assistant manager was certainly a surprise. However, those in the know realised that this was a shrewd move from the chairman.

Before joining Rangers, Smith, a 'Gers fan since boyhood, was recognised as a top-class coach and throughout the five-year reign of Souness it had been Smith who had had a hands-on remit, taking the day-to-day training. The players appreciated him and respected him already. They knew his qualities and that he was capable of stepping into Souness's shoes. Smith had been the perfect foil to Souness in that he was a calming influence, a serious-minded, rational, cool character as opposed to his volcanic boss. Having said that, the players also knew that Smith, while being less confrontational than Souness, was a disciplinarian and no easy touch, soft-spoken though he was.

One of the biggest doubts surrounding the appointment of Smith was whether or not he would have the same influence when it came to attracting the non-Scottish players with big reputations to the club. The other doubt was whether he'd have the same control and dominance over established international players without having had the kind of playing pedigree that Souness had been admired for. Both these doubts were quickly swept aside when it became obvious that Smith had the total respect of all the squad and, in time, could still sign top-class players from outwith Scotland.

When Smith began preparing for his first season in charge, his immediate problem stemmed from rules rather than players. The UEFA three-foreigner only rule in European matches had become a big handicap for Rangers because at that point they had 12 international players on the books. Smith realised that he'd have to try to decrease the number of foreigners in his squad to compete in Europe while not weakening the side domestically. If only three non-Scots were allowed, then they had to be key men and outfield players, so goalkeeper Chris Woods was the first casualty as Scottish 'keeper Andy Goram replaced him. Other Scots who joined were David Robertson and Stuart McCall, both international players. Unfortunately, despite efforts to cope with the three foreigner rule, Sparta Prague eliminated Rangers from the European Cup in the first round that season on the away goals rule.

Nevertheless, despite failure in Europe, Smith's first season in 1991–92 was a successful one, winning the double, a feat Graeme Souness hadn't been able to manage. Victory over Airdrie in the Scottish Cup Final brought the Cup back to Ibrox for the first time since 1981. The only rain on my parade regarding that feat was that I wasn't at Hampden to see it achieved as I couldn't get a ticket. Compensating for that, though, was the victory over Celtic in the semi-final, when Rangers played for most of the match with 10 men, showing the team spirit and skill that Smith's team was infused with. That was one of my greatest experiences watching Rangers. I was at the now-seated Rangers' End of Hampden, too near the front for my liking but glad to be there at least. Within six minutes, in driving rain and wind, 'Gers' left-back David Robertson was unjustly sent off in my opinion. Celtic's Joe Miller, halfway inside Rangers' half, pushed the ball ahead of him as Robertson had raced in to tackle. The result was that he ran straight into the Ranger and tumbled over dramatically. The referee did not take the dreadful conditions into consideration and sent off Robertson. Even if it had been a deliberate block, it should only have merited a yellow card. Most 'Gers fans thought that it hadn't even been a deliberate foul, let alone a sending-off offence. We couldn't believe that we were going to have to play Celtic for 84 minutes with only 10 men.

In the first half McCoist scored a trademark goal out of nothing that proved to be the winner, but after that it was 'keeper Andy Goram especially who ensured that Rangers kept their lead. This was 'The Goalie' at his best. Time and again he defied the Celtic forwards, and their midfielders, like McStay and Collins, despite some great attempts at goal, just couldn't beat Goram. As 'Gers' 10 men hung on, the last 15 minutes were the most nervous I had been since the Kai Johansen Final, but when the whistle was blown the relief, elation and pride that was felt by the Rangers supporters was evident.

Despite doing the double of League and Scottish Cup, my most important moment that season was when 'Gers beat Hearts 1–0 at Tynecastle in early September in the quarter-final of the League Cup. A brilliant McCoist volley won the tie, but I remember this match for other reasons. While 'Gers were playing in Edinburgh that night, I was having my first date with my second wife-to-be, Jessica. While I was with her, I totally forgot about the Rangers game for once, and I only discovered we had won when I got home and watched the recorded highlights. I must have known it was love even then! The following year, 'Gers' treble season, we got married and one of her grown-up daughters thought I was a hero. At least, that's what I took her to mean when she said that I 'must be very brave to marry mum.' Eighteen years later we are still married and Rangers have won umpteen trophies in that time. You might not know what is around the corner in your personal life, but you can usually depend on Rangers winning trophies.

That season was also significant for seeing a welcome increase in the capacity of Ibrox by the addition of the Club Deck. After one and a half years of work, the new Club Deck was opened in 1991. Partly funded by a debenture scheme, the work had cost £20 million and added 7,169 seats to Ibrox's capacity. Because Archibald Leitch's Main Stand was now a listed building, the new tier had to be constructed without damage to the existing stand. The original stand had a temporary roof put over it while work went on above it so that life could go on as normal for those fans who preferred to sit in the Main Stand.

To gain planning permission for the Club Deck, Rangers had to convert their training ground, The Albion, 100 yards away from the stadium, into a car park. Before it had become the club's training ground, The Albion had been a greyhound racing track, only a couple of hundred yards away from another one, The White City. I well remember both greyhound tracks from my childhood. Govanites must have been real gamblers in those days! I found it fascinating to watch the construction of the Club Deck from my vantage point opposite in the Govan Rear. It was exciting to see the structure take shape, and we all wondered what the huge, individual X-shaped girder work pieces were as they lay on top of the concrete stepping. As it turned out, these were eventually all joined together to form the supports from which the roof would be suspended. They were hoisted onto the massive steel supports at either end of the construction by two specially hired cranes, which apparently were the largest in the world. The expense and time it took turned out to be worth it; the new tier certainly enhanced the appearance of the Leitch stand and Ibrox overall.

At the same time, to the annoyance of the East Enclosure aficianados, the only remaining standing area at the stadium, the Enclosure, was converted into an all-seater stand, thus three tiers of seating now stood where once there had been only one.

Season 1991–92 paved the way for Smith's most successful one the following year. Season 1992–93 saw a 'Gers side at its peak. Not only would Rangers win its fifth title in a row but the treble would be achieved for the first time since 1978 under Jock Wallace. It would be the fourth treble I had experienced as a fan. Not only that, but Rangers would sustain their best run in the European Cup since the semi-final appearance in 1960, completing a run of 10 games unbeaten. Just as impressive was the side's 44-match unbeaten run in all competitions.

The most impressive result, and most memorable, was Rangers' elimination of English Champions, Leeds, with victories home and away, to qualify for the newly-created Champions League. Unfortunately, the one extra goal they needed in a 1–1 draw at Marseille to qualify for the Final eluded them, and the fans had to be content with glorious failure in the innovative premier competition. The prolific scoring partnership of McCoist and Hateley played in neither of the Marseilles matches as one was missing from each match. Considering the form both players had been in throughout that season, this might have made all the difference. Apart from just failing to make it to the inaugural Champions League Final, the other disappointing aspect of that tournament from a personal point of view was that I missed the Marseilles game at Ibrox.

It took place in November and, as any teacher will tell you, that is deep in parents' evening territory. The calendar for school events, and especially parents' evenings was always given out to teachers at the end of the previous term. These dates were sacrosanct, and nobody could foresee which big midweek matches, if any, might clash with the evenings to be spent on duty, telling parents about the 'strengths and weaknesses' of their offspring. Unfortunately for me, that Marseilles game clashed with a parents' evening and I had to sit listening to anxious parents trying to keep my mind off the game. If only they had realised how anxious I was. It was a terrible night in terms of the weather and torrential rain had been bucketing down for hours. By the time I left the meeting, I was splashing through the puddles in the car park to drive home, listening to the commentary of the game on the car radio.

I had barely driven away when Rangers scored. I was elated, especially listening to the commentator waxing lyrical. Then, a minute or so later, he said something that made me realise that the goal hadn't even put us in the lead but was merely an equaliser. When I got home, I watched my recording of the entire match and realised then that the 2–2 was a great result in the circumstances. That thrilling draw, with headers from McSwegan and Hateley, was one of 'Gers' greatest comebacks in Europe – and I had missed it. To avoid similar occurrences, after that evening I spoke to the deputy head, George Scanlon, who was in charge of composing the school calendar, and gave him a rough idea of when possible future midweek matches in Europe might take place so that he could try to avoid scheduling a parents' evening on those dates. I never missed another Champions League game at Ibrox, although I did have to watch the live TV coverage of an away UEFA Cup tie against Borussia Dortmund in the English staffroom after work while waiting to take part in yet another parents' evening at 7 o'clock. That game finished 2–0 to the Germans as they scored in injury time to send the game into extra-time and then penalties which, naturally, being German, they won.

In that Champions League campaign, it was the two matches against English Champions Leeds United that will live in the memory – the first, at Ibrox, not because of a great performance but because of the grit and heart of the 'Gers side to come from losing a first-minute goal and turn it around before half-time. When Rangers drew Leeds United to see which side would qualify for the newly created Champions League, the tie was immediately tagged with the cliché 'The Battle of Britain'. However, in order to avoid any possible battle between the rival fans, both clubs decided to implement a ban on travelling supporters. The Leeds side was full of star names including Cantona, Strachan, McAllister, Speed and Batty to name a few. Leeds, having knocked out German Champions Stuttgart in the previous round, were expected by the English media to dismiss Rangers with ease.

Within the first minute of the first leg at Ibrox, the journalists' views were probably reinforced when a Strachan corner, headed out, was met on the edge of the box by Scottish captain Gary McAllister, who volleyed the ball perfectly, going high behind Andy Goram. Ibrox was eerily silent. However, by the time the ball was on the centre-spot the crowd had found its voice again and roared 'Gers on to recover from our disastrous start.

Rangers battled back and gradually took control of the match. It was a dour game with few chances created by either side, and tension seemed to affect the players' performances. However, by half-time, the home side had turned the match around to go up the Ibrox tunnel leading 2–1, thanks to an own-goal by Leeds 'keeper Lukic and a goal poked into the net by Ally McCoist. The second half was largely a non-event, with both sides' defences on top and the creative players being cancelled out. Thus a 2–1 win made it look as if 'Gers would have to be at their best in the second match to survive. I was proud, though, of the Rangers' spirit that had been shown, and I knew that, with this group of players, no cause could ever be considered lost.

By the time of the return leg, the Leeds manager Howard Wilkinson, his players and especially the English sportswriters were supremely confident, if not arrogant, about Leeds' prospects of overturning the one-goal deficit, thanks to that away goal of McAllister's. The Rangers players were aware of the opposition's attitude and were fired up to show everybody in England that not only was Scottish football better than they realised but that Rangers were a good team, in no way inferior to Leeds.

A first-minute shock was in store again but this time for the Leeds fans. A Goram kick-out was nodded on a couple of yards by Durrant to Hateley, just outside the Leeds' box. The big Englishman, without hesitating, swivelled and lofted a brilliant shot over Lukic into the Leeds goal to stun everybody. Within a minute, Rangers had cancelled out the crucial Leeds away goal and had taken the heat out of the tie. Naturally the Leeds' reaction was to attack in numbers and with a ferocity that reminded 'Gers fans that this tie wasn't won yet. Thankfully, defenders like Gough and John Brown stood firm, and when Leeds occasionally did create a chance, Goram was at his defiant best between the posts.

The second half continued in the same vein until a wonderful Rangers counter-attack all but finished off the English Champions. A Leeds attack was broken up by John Brown, just inside his box. He tapped the ball to Ferguson, who moved it forward to Hateley. Hateley's clever back-heel found Durrant moving forward. Taking the ball on a few yards, the midfielder prodded the ball forward to Hateley, who'd continued his run upfield. He immediately took it out to the left wing and kept running. From 30 yards out, he looked up, saw McCoist making a run at the back post unnoticed, and curled a precision cross over to him. McCoist's brilliant diving header went in at the far post with the 'keeper and defender powerless to prevent it. The joy on the faces of the Rangers players showed that they knew they'd won the tie.

Leeds continued to battle, as all English sides do, but they knew it was in vain. It was simply a matter of pride. Minutes from the end they finally breached the Rangers defence and scored a consolation goal. But the glory went to Rangers, who had just beaten, deservedly, the English Champions home and away and earned new respect for the club. Watching the match on television, listening to English commentator Brian Moore mournfully describing the Leeds defeat, just made this experience all the more satisfying.

Domestically it was a wonderful season, with Aberdeen being defeated in the Final of both Cups and yet another title being retained. Again, I couldn't get a ticket for the Scottish Cup Final, played at Parkhead due to the reconstruction of Hampden, and had to watch the match on television. At least by then such games were allowed to be shown live. Rangers beat their old rivals far more comfortably than the 2–1 score-line suggested – the same score by which 'Gers had defeated the Dons in the League Cup Final the previous October. The one black spot had been the broken leg suffered by ace McCoist after he'd won the Golden Boot award for being Europe's top scorer for the second time, no less. Super Ally missed out on another Scottish Cup Final and ended his glittering career with only the one medal in that competition, won against Airdrie the previous season.

Normally Rangers completing the treble would be the highlight of any year for me, but in 1993 that was overshadowed by my personal highlight some weeks later when I married Jessica at Bearsden Registry Office. We have been happily married ever since – and 'Gers have done two trebles since then.

Unfortunately, instead of going from strength to strength the following season, it was a relatively disappointing one in that injuries and exhaustion from the previous season's success seemed to take their toll on the squad of players. One of my strangest-ever experiences in watching Rangers came near the end of that League season. At the end of April, in the final Old Firm game of that season, 'Gers played their old rivals at Ibrox in unique circumstances. For the only time I have ever heard of, there was to be no Celtic fans present. Chairman David Murray had decided that Celtic would be given no tickets for this match as the Celtic fans had vandalised seats in the Broomloan Stand just once too often. With their club refusing to compensate Rangers for the damage, the last resort for Murray was to ban away fans.

It was an odd experience watching an Old Firm game with only 'Gers fans at the match. I never thought I'd say this, but I really missed not having our old enemies taking up one end of Ibrox. It proved to me just how much we need each other. We have to be able to shout abuse at each other and vent our feelings. It was a pretty dour game with not much to shout about anyway, so maybe that didn't help the atmosphere. Maybe due to the circumstances and a feeling of grievance, plucky Celtic played better than us. Things got even worse when a brilliant John Collins free-kick put the visitors ahead. Thankfully, before the end, 'Gers' Ukrainian star Mikhailichenko equalised with a deflected shot from the edge of the box, and our blushes were spared. Miko, as he became known, was an incredibly skilful player but also incredibly laid-back, even lazy. Walter Smith once said of him, 'He has great economy of movement.' Movement or not, he saved us that day, but I never want to play Celtic minus their fans ever again. It just wasn't as much fun.

The League Cup and the Championship were retained, while in the Scottish Cup Final a jaded-looking 'Gers side went down 1–0 to Dundee United, thereby losing its chance to become the first team in history to win back-to-back trebles. In hindsight, I should have expected the worst. Although 'Gers only won the title by three points from Aberdeen, the League had actually been won well before the Cup Final. In the month leading up to the Final, Rangers had lost three and drawn two of their last five League matches – not the sort of form that you want in the run up to a Final. Form cannot be switched on like a tap.

I was at Hampden that day near the front of the Rangers' End, and it was one of the lows in my 'Gers-supporting life. We might have realised that it wasn't going to be our day when McCoist had to be replaced even before the game had kicked off as he had hurt himself in the warm-up. Also, with Goram injured for most of that season, our 'keeper was Ally Maxwell. The solitary goal that denied us that consecutive treble came when there was a misunderstanding with a pass-back between David McPherson and the 'keeper, which allowed the loose ball to be netted by Craig Brewster to win Dundee United the Scottish Cup for the first time, having lost their previous six Finals. This fact didn't cheer me up in any way. That was the second time I had seen us blow the treble by losing 1–0 in the Scottish Cup Final. I suppose that's why it is such a difficult feat to accomplish.

The League Cup Final win against Hibs that season was one of my highlights. Again, this game was played at Parkhead due to reconstruction at Hampden. I had a ticket for the Jungle, while my son, Stewart, had a ticket for the Celtic End, at the Gallowgate end. I saw him safely inside the ground and then walked round to my part of the dilapidated stadium. We would meet up again after the game.

This match was memorable for a few reasons. Firstly, winning the Cup created a new record of Rangers winning six consecutive domestic trophies. This would become seven by the end of the season when the Championship was retained. Fans will also remember the game for two great 'Gers goals and for yet another McCoist moment. Super Ally was on the bench for this Final due to the fact that he still lacked match fitness in his recovery from a broken leg sustained six months previously while playing for Scotland in Portugal. McCoist was itching to play in the game but knew that the manager had made the right decision, keeping him in reserve should he be needed.

On a mild, sunny day that belied the fact that it was near the end of October, a crowd of 48,000 watched Rangers dominate the game from the beginning without being able to convert their superiority into goals. Then, 10 minutes into the second half, the breakthrough came thanks to the talent of a rejuvenated Ian Durrant. The flowing move started in Rangers' half with the ball being passed to Ian Ferguson, just inside the centre circle. He did a quick one-two with Durrant then ran forward before passing it to him again. Durrant made one of his trademark runs right through the centre towards the Hibs defence then slipped the ball to the right to Hateley and continued onwards. Hateley's cute return pass found Durrant running on to the ball at the 18-yard line. As he tried to control it and run, the ball bobbled up, but this, in fact, helped the Ranger because as Jim Leighton ran off his goalline, Durrant showed his coolness by simply chipping the ball over him.

Most thought that the match as a contest would be over, but Hibs weren't ready to give up yet. Minutes later, out of nothing, they had equalised. Deep in his own half, right-back Gary Stevens took a pass from Gough and rather carelessly attempted a passback to 'keeper Ally Maxwell. As the ball bounced up inside the area, Hibs striker Keith Wright intercepted it before it could be gathered by the 'Gers 'keeper. Wright then ran past Maxwell to the left and fired a hopeful cross in front of the Rangers goal. Unfortunately, Davie McPherson, running back towards goal to cover his 'keeper, turned the ball into his own net.

This goal sparked renewed pressure from Rangers in an effort to regain the lead as soon as possible. Cue the entrance of the hero. McCoist's whole career had seemed to be a real-life football fairy tale, and his entry then on the field was to provide yet another chapter of it. A top striker, struck down by a terrible injury, makes the comeback of a lifetime and scores the winning goal to win the Cup. It sounds like the stuff of fiction, but that's what happened.

A long throw-in from David Robertson out on the left made it into the Hibs penalty box. Hateley and Trevor Steven jumped with defender Kevin Tweed for it, but the ball glanced off the defender's head and continued towards the penalty spot. There McCoist, surrounded by three defenders, chested the ball down and, with his back to goal, did a bicycle kick over his shoulder and shot the ball past the helpless Jim Leighton into the corner of the net. The resulted in delirious celebrations from Super Ally, his teammates and all the 'Gers fans in the stadium. They all knew that

McCoist had done it again and had won the Cup for them. The real Roy of the Rovers was indeed back. Being in the Jungle, celebrating Richard Gough lifting that trophy was one of the great days.

In the coming seasons, Rangers' success would continue and more brilliant players would be seen in the blue jersey. Perhaps one of the best was the Dane Brian Laudrup, who arrived in the summer of 1994. Not only was he thrilling and entertaining to watch, he was also so effective, creating and scoring so many goals for the team. The following season Laudrup was joined by a superstar of a different kind in Paul Gascoigne, the English international, whose brilliant performances helped Rangers to win the club's eighth title in a row as well as the Scottish Cup. To show the esteem in which Brian Laudrup is held by Rangers fans you need only remember that he is the only foreign player to have been voted into the Greatest Ever Rangers team. Before arriving at Ibrox, Laudrup had played in his native Denmark, Germany and Italy, so he was an experienced campaigner, but the fee of £2.5 million paid to Fiorentina was to become one of the greatest bargains in 'Gers' history as the Dane went on to play the best football of his career at Ibrox. That season was to be a bitter-sweet one for me personally.

To describe Laudrup as a tremendous left-winger is simply inadequate. He was so much more than that. A natural athlete, he was hard-working and dedicated plus he had all those qualities in a forward that simply terrify defenders. Pace, terrific acceleration and sublime ball control coupled with vision made him a nightmare to play against and a joy for Rangers fans to watch. Having said this, at almost 6ft tall, he wasn't in the mould of the traditional Rangers 'tanner ba' winger. He was the sophisticated, modern version of it. With Laudrup in the side, 'Gers fans thought that it was possible for their team to beat anybody. Not only was he a productive player, setting up chances for his teammates with quality crosses and cut-backs, and scoring fantastic goals himself, but he was an entertainer. The fans just loved watching him run at the opposition and bamboozling defenders with his skill and speed. A mazy dribble from Laudrup was something to live in the memory indeed.

His ability to twist and turn might have been a great asset but so was his coolness under pressure. Even in the penalty area it always looked as if his control and intelligence gave him that extra edge in finding space or a colleague to pass to. When he raced infield, waltzing past one defender after another, it must have been a sobering sight to the opposition, knowing that, at any time, he could unleash a powerful shot that would be unstoppable. No wonder he ended up with 82 caps for Denmark.

In an Ibrox career of many highs, perhaps two especially should be identified. Laudrup's most memorable performance must be the Scottish Cup Final of 1996 at Hampden when, almost single-handedly, he destroyed Hearts. Not only did he score two of the five goals that day but he also set up the others that constituted Gordon Durie's hat-trick. Normally a hat-trick in a Final would see that player named man of the match, but in that game it was the genius of Laudrup that had lit up the old stadium. The words 'Laudrup's Final' would bring back happy memories to any Rangers fan in years to come. I was near the front of the Rangers' End at Hampden, but at least I had a great view of the four second-half goals going into the net right in front of me. As a kid, I used to sit on the wall at the front of the terracing and now, in my 40s, thanks to the luck of the draw in getting a ticket, I was sitting near the front again.

If that match saw Laudrup's greatest performance, then his most memorable and important goal would be seen the following season at Tannadice when it was a goal from Laudrup's head, rather than either talented foot, that would ensure that Rangers would win their ninth consecutive Championship. Headers had been one of Laudrup's few weaknesses, but he bulleted that one in as if he were Mark Hateley. That goal might have been the most significant in his Ibrox career, but there were so many others.

Laudrup was a curse to Celtic in his time with Rangers, scoring quite a few memorable goals in League matches at Ibrox, Parkhead and in the League and Scottish Cup at Hampden. As Celtic's O'Neill discovered one night at Parkhead, one slip against the man could be costly. With the score at 0–0, O'Neill slipped as he tried to control the ball in the centre of the park, just inside his own half. Laudrup pounced on it and raced away from the defence, straight up the middle. Then, from 18 yards out, he smashed the ball into the net for the goal that would win the points that night.

Right from his first match, Brian Laudrup was a sensation at Ibrox. A long, driving run in the final minute at Ibrox against Motherwell in the first League game of the season saw him set up a dramatic winning goal for Duncan Ferguson, resulting in a win 2–1 for 'Gers. We all knew that Walter Smith had found an absolute gem. Unfortunately, I missed a few matches in his debut season – due to dying!

Remember, remember the fifth of November. I certainly did that year. I had been at Ibrox to see 'Gers beat Thistle by 3–0 with Laudrup, who had had a great game, netting a great final goal. I had really enjoyed the performance of the team and was in a contented mood, looking forward to the remainder of a promising season, even one that would be lacking European football since 'Gers had been knocked out of the Champions League qualifiers in August thanks to AEK Athens. That season hadn't started at all well. In the space of seven days in August, 'Gers lost three games at home – to AEK in the Champions League, to Celtic in the League and to Falkirk in the League Cup. Thankfully, we recovered well from these setbacks, and by that Thistle game at the start of November we were looking good again.

However, that Saturday, in bed around midnight, I couldn't sleep and had what I thought were indigestion pains. I took a couple of Rennies to alleviate this but it made no difference. After an hour or so I took another couple but still no change. My wife was worried and kept asking how I was feeling. I kept telling her it was just a bad case of indigestion. It was only when my left arm went numb that I agreed to let her call our GP. My doctor came out to my house and examined me. He immediately recognised the symptoms of a heart attack and phoned for an ambulance. Soon I was on my way to the Southern General Hospital. I remember being in the ambulance and having a drip inserted, then arriving at the hospital and being taken to a ward but not much else. I remember a couple days when family and friends visited me – but I don't remember dying.

Apparently, at the end of my first week in the hospital I went to the bathroom to brush my teeth and collapsed. I say 'apparently' because I have no recollection whatsoever of any of this but have been told by others since. I suffered a cardiac arrest and was very lucky that I was discovered by a doctor and the emergency procedures applied immediately. I've been told that it was touch-and-go. My wife was phoned by the hospital and told to get there as quickly as possible as I might not survive for long. You can imagine her feelings as she was driven to the hospital. Once she had arrived I was doing better, but they had no idea what the arrest might have done to my brain and so the doctors prepared her for the worst when I might come back to consciousness. I might wake up and have no memories of all those great Rangers' moments I'd experienced in 30-odd years!

Over the next week I gradually recovered – with no apparent brain damage. Seemingly for days, I repeated myself when talking to visitors and obviously wasn't as lucid as my normal self. My family thought some of the things I said and did while not in my 'right mind' were unintentionally hilarious. Just a week or so before my heart attack we had gone to the cinema to see the film hit of the year, *Forrest Gump*, and apparently I kept asking my visitors if they had seen it, over and over, causing much amusement. In view of what had just happened perhaps a quote from that film is particularly apt: 'Life is like a box of chocolates, you never know what you're gonna get.'

The human mind is a wonderful thing. Mine obviously protected me from what had happened because even to this day I don't remember any of this. I've been describing what I was told by other people. Another two weeks in hospital saw me well enough to be discharged, with an appointment for future tests to find out just what my health situation was. Eventually tests showed that I needed a bypass operation and I was absent from school until that could take place in the following September. That was as much a shock to me as anything because in over 20 years of teaching, if you added up all the days I'd been absent, it probably would have amounted to single figures. Apart from work, my holiday was affected as we had booked to go to Andros in Greece but had to cancel. On the other hand, I temporarily had no more essays to mark or lessons to plan. Yippee!

Until this point in my life I had never believed the old saying that every cloud has a silver lining, but it might just be true. With no school work to occupy my time, or mind, I finally had the opportunity to do something I'd wanted to do for years – write a book about Rangers. This wasn't to be just any book about any 'Gers side. It was to be a tribute to the great Rangers side of the early 60s that had ruled supreme when I first started going to Ibrox. I decided on the title even before I had written a single sentence: *The Best of the Blues*. I spent my time writing and researching, looking at videos of that era, reading the newspaper reports of the time stored in the microfiche system in the Glasgow Room of the Mitchell Library, and then having it all typed out by my ever-obliging wife. I'm almost ashamed to admit it, but in those days we didn't even own a PC.

Once I'd finished the manuscript, I sent it to publishers in the hope that they would like it enough to publish. Mainstream Publishing expressed an interest but declined to publish, mainly because the book didn't have the backing of the club. With a bit of luck, I arranged this through one of Rangers' commercial managers, Paul Geddes, who read the manuscript and liked it. I also knew that the book needed something extra, like interviews with some of the players of that era. The problem was that I had no way of getting in touch with those former stars. Then, in December 1999, at a League game against Hearts at Ibrox, Sandy Jardine presented some former players to the crowd to celebrate the 100th anniversary of Rangers being at the present Ibrox. Among them were many of the guys that I would have loved to interview. The thought occurred to me right then that Jardine was the person I should contact and see if he would put me in touch with the stars I needed to question.

Later, Sandy Jardine gave me contact details and I got in touch with most of the former players who agreed to be interviewed in person, like Jimmy Millar, or over the phone, like my hero, Jim Baxter. I was so pleased that I managed that interview with Baxter because he died just before my book, which I dedicated to him, was eventually published. The book came out in 2001 and has sold over 2,000 copies – and it probably wouldn't have happened if I hadn't had my heart attack.

The only annoying thing about having a book published is that usually it takes so long between being told it will be published and it actually appearing in the bookshops. You get the initial thrill of the news it has been accepted and then nothing for months and months until you have to write an author's mini autobiography and the blurb for the publisher, suggest advertising outlets and finally do the proof-reading. That's when you realise it's almost ready. When that first book was published and I received the author's free copies, I felt so proud, as if I'd really achieved something. You don't make much money out of such a project, but, for me, it was all about paying tribute to that team of the early 60s and knowing that thousands of other Rangers fans would be able to read that book, hopefully bringing back some great memories for the older ones, like me. It was an even better feeling when I actually saw the book on sale in bookshops, especially the Rangers' shop at Ibrox. I had the same feelings with my subsequent three books although, when I think about it, I'd like to believe that, throughout my life, I'd achieved more as a teacher, and in some small way maybe I helped kids on the way to their dreams.

After I'd left hospital, it was a couple of months before I was allowed to go back to Ibrox. Not being able to go reminded me of when I was nine and desperate to go to see Rangers but having to wait until my parents allowed me. At the end of my first week home from hospital, I watched the 'Gers versus Dundee United game live from Tannadice. In what should have been a tricky game, Rangers played brilliantly, especially Laudrup, and won 3–0. The Great Dane and Dutch winger Peter Huistra had scored two fantastic goals, but I can still see the third goal, scored by Durrant. Laudrup must have run 40 yards with the ball, beating a couple of opponents, and then just outside the box he threaded an unbelievable pass between three defenders right into the path of Ian Durrant, who had made a lung-bursting supporting run. The midfielder turned the clock back by slotting the perfect pass first-time past the helpless 'keeper and celebrated like a 17-year-old again. What a tonic that was for me. Forget the beta blockers!

Once I did get back to my seat in the Govan, I must admit I did try to be calmer when watching the matches, but, at times, it was difficult as Laudrup was one of the most exciting players we had seen in years. The team, on the whole, seemed inspired by Laudrup and played some great stuff. We won the League easily that season by 15 points from Motherwell but were knocked out of both Cups early on. Maybe it was just as well. Too much excitement might just have killed me.

The following season – 1995–96 – brought further progress for both Rangers and myself. I was eventually to have my bypass operation and Rangers would receive a new beating heart in the form of Paul Gascoigne. Brian Laudrup had joined Rangers as pretty much an unknown quantity to 'Gers fans, but when Gazza breezed into Ibrox, Rangers fans knew they were getting a genuine superstar. In terms of shock value, Rangers signing Gazza was on a par with the signing of Mo Johnston – but for different reasons. Here was a genuine English icon joining the club from an Italian side when he probably could have gone home to practically any club in England. Paul Gascoigne was great news for the fans, for the media and for hairdressers. When he was mobbed at the main door at Ibrox, he was sporting a bleached-blond hairstyle, and within days thousands of kids had copied their new idol. But it wasn't only teenagers who were excited – grown men were positively desperate to see the legend in action.

This action came in pre-season with the club's International Challenge Trophy, which saw 'Gers first beat Steaua Bucharest and then Sampdoria, with Gazza strutting his stuff in both matches. Gascoigne scored in the first match against the Romanians and then celebrated by miming the playing of a flute. What an uproar that caused the following day! The media were all over the story like a rash, with close-up photos. Most fans didn't even notice it at the time, so busy were we celebrating. How provocative for the Englishman to pretend to be playing an Orange band flute at Ibrox in front of a crowd exclusively made up of 'Gers fans. The criticism he received was just a taste of what was to come, but the Rangers fans loved him for it. Welcome to Scotland, Gazza!

By September Gazza was well into his stride as a Rangers' icon, but I was well out of mine. My bypass operation was to take place in the Western Infirmary on 28 September. I remember the exact date because I went into the hospital the day before my operation, and it was on that evening that 'Gers were playing their second Champions League game of their campaign against Borussia Dortmund at Ibrox. I had already bought my package of three tickets and so had to give mine away. Meanwhile I had to content myself with watching the match in the patients' TV room. On the whole, I was reasonably pleased with 'Gers' 2–2 draw that night, and at least the game took my mind off my forthcoming operation for a couple of hours. By morning I had things other than football on my mind as my operation was before lunch-time.

Two things stay in my mind about the operation. I remember being wheeled down to the theatre and being left lying on the trolley in a corridor, staring at the ceiling, unattended, wondering if I'd been forgotten about. I also remember when the anaesthetist tried to give me an injection to knock me out and couldn't find a vein, another medic had to have a go while I was thinking, 'If they can't even render me unconscious, what chance do I have of the heart op going to plan?'

The fact that I'm writing this 15 years later should tell you that the operation was a complete success. However, when I had had my cardiac arrest, my heart muscle in the left ventricle had been irreparably damaged, and so the bypass didn't make a new man of me, as happens normally with such ops. I still have to take various pills to control the function of my heart, but at least I'm alive – and I have seen Rangers win numerous trophies and even appear in a European Final since the year I died.

While I was in hospital, one of my great radio-listening experiences (and there hasn't been many) was listening to Rangers beat Celtic 2–0 at Parkhead in the first Old Firm League game of that season. 'Gers had already beaten Celtic 1–0 at Parkhead in the quarter-final of the League Cup only 11 days earlier, so consecutive away wins was a special event. When I left hospital and saw the second Rangers goal scored by Gazza, I was enthralled by the guy. In the second half, with Celtic pressing in the Rangers' area, Gazza was back in his own box helping out. The ball was suddenly cleared upfield, right to the centre circle. A quick pass to the right wing, another into the centre, and, miraculously, there was Gazza, unmarked, running clear to get to the ball and sweep it past the Celtic 'keeper. He must have run the length of the pitch in a few seconds with no opponent able to keep up with him. It was absolute genius. But that was typical of the man. He scored some of the greatest goals I have ever seen.

Gascoigne's first season at Ibrox was absolutely wonderful, and it saw the club win its eighth League Championship in a row as well as the Scottish Cup. I really believed, for the first time perhaps, that nine-in-a-row was possible. With Gazza and Laudrup in the side, as well as the now veteran McCoist, Goram, Gough, Durie, McCall and Durrant, how could we have possibly have failed? With these players, the League ended with our away record being one game better off than our home one. Gazza's season was an amazing rollercoaster ride. He had fantastic performances, brilliant goals, many assists, yellow cards and, always headlines – good and bad. In December we beat Hibs 7–0 at Ibrox and Durie scored four goals, but the man-of-the-match was Gazza. It was in that match that he received a yellow card for handing the ref's yellow card back to him after he had dropped it but obviously had done it in too cheeky a fashion for the ref's liking. He also scored a brilliant goal after going on a mazy run from the halfway line, beating one Hibs player after another, about five in all, driving into the Hibs box and guiding his shot home so deftly. I can count on one hand the 'Gers players I've seen through the years who were capable of such sublime skill and power. But that wasn't even his finest hour.

Gazza's best moment came in the penultimate game of the League season at Ibrox, when 'Gers beat Aberdeen to win their eighth successive title. Once again Paul Gascoigne delivered when the fans needed him to, netting a stunning hat-trick. In this crunch match, Rangers were a goal down before Gazza took on the Dons' defence single-handedly to equalise before half-time. A penalty and another stunning goal gave Rangers the necessary victory and eight-in-a-row. His second goal, to give Rangers the lead, will never be forgotten by fans who were there that day. Collecting the ball deep in his own half, Gazza went on one of those characteristic, lung-bursting runs of his. Straight through the centre of the Dons' defence he ran, shaking off one opponent after another before passing a shot into the corner of the net. He was voted Man of the Match that day and later Player of the Year by the Scottish sportswriters. No wonder he was carried shoulder-high by his teammates at the end of the game. His delight at winning the title was there for all to see after the team had been presented with the Championship trophy, and how the 'Gers fans loved him! Feelings of ecstacy surged through me as I stood in the Govan, thankful that Walter Smith had had the foresight to sign such a gem of a player.

As if not to be out done by Gazza, a couple of weeks later it was Brian Laudrup who took centre stage with a sublime performance in the Scottish Cup Final against Hearts. Poor Gordon Durie – once again he scored a hat-trick but this Final will forever be known as 'Laudrup's Final'. As if to show that there was still more than one superstar in the 'Gers side, Brian Laudrup was the player who showed the magic that had made him a hero of the Rangers fans.

A tough game had been expected, but it became one of the most one-sided in recent Scottish Cup Final history as Rangers players dazzled Hearts in the Hampden sunshine. That was one of the most enjoyable Cup Finals I have ever attended. I was sitting near the front of the Rangers' End and so luckily had a great view of the final four second-half goals scored by the 'Gers. The first goal that put Rangers on the road to victory came from the Laudrup/Durie combination that was to destroy Hearts that day. A ball headed out of defence found Laudrup in the centre circle. The Dane hooked the ball forward to Durie, who instantly headed it back to Laudrup as he ran towards him. Laudrup then nodded it deftly to the right for Durie, who had peeled away and kept his run going. Looking up, Durie then chipped the ball over the Hearts defence for it to be collected by Laudrup, who moved into the area with it and smacked a right-foot shot past the 'keeper. It was a goal fit to win any Cup, but there were four more to come.

Despite having the majority of the game, Rangers couldn't increase their lead in the first half, so when they came out after half-time their priority was to grab a second goal that would finish the match. When it came it was courtesy of Hearts' French 'keeper, Giles Rousset. Out on the right Laudrup twisted and turned, bamboozling a couple of defenders before sending in a low cross. It wasn't a great cross, being too near the 'keeper, but, amazingly, instead of gathering a simple ball, the 'keeper, in trying to scoop it up, let it go between his legs and into the net.

Soon after, the match looked over when Stuart McCall sent a pass to Durie near the centre circle. He swept the ball out to the left, where Laudrup raced onto it, without checking his stride, and from 10 yards outside the box he put over a pacy, knee-high cross that Durie volleyed in, having got across his marker. After this, Hearts scored a goal but never really threatened a comeback, and once again Rangers increased their lead to three when, in his own half, McCall fed the ball to Robertson on the left. The left-back passed inside to Laudrup, who got past Hearts' McManus as the defender tried to grapple him to the ground. Now bearing down on goal as the last defender came towards him, Laudrup slipped the ball to the right in front of Durie for the striker to run it past the stranded 'keeper and prod the ball home.

It wasn't long before Durie completed his hat-trick. A kick out was headed by Durie from the centre circle, just inside the Hearts' half. It was perfectly angled for Laudrup lurking out on the right. As the Dane ran up the right, Durie continued his run straight down the middle, unmarked. We were all screaming for the cross to be delivered and, at the perfect moment, Laudrup floated an exquisite ball into the centre, right in front of Durie, who merely nodded the ball into the net without even having to adjust his stride. Gordon Durie scored a rare Cup Final hat-trick but still wasn't the Man of the Match. That honour belonged to the Great Dane who had shown his complete range of skills throughout the game, scored two goals and made the other three. Not a bad day's work. Even Gazza must have admired it.

In his four seasons at Ibrox, Laudrup won the sportswriters' Player of the Year award twice, in 1995 and 1997. In the other two seasons he was plagued by niggling injuries that caused him to miss quite a few matches. The season between his two awards saw the accolade going to his teammate, Paul Gascoigne, whose performances had been stunning, so Laudrup had no need to feel disappointed. At the end of his third season Laudrup changed his mind about leaving Rangers to go to Ajax and stayed for another season, but even the brilliant Dane couldn't inspire a jaded Rangers side to capture the longed-for 10-in-a-row. At the end of that season he signed for Chelsea but left behind some golden memories of one of the most skilful players ever to have worn the blue jersey.

During this period Ibrox underwent further transformation. In 1995 the original, multi-coloured seating in the stands that had consisted of blue, red, yellow, orange and brown sections disappeared to be replaced by blue seats only, becoming a 'Blue Heaven' for the 'Gers fans. I must admit that I missed that multi-coloured seating, but the all-blue scheme was more apt, I suppose. Then, in 1996, the corners at Ibrox were at last filled in to make the stadium even more imposing and intimidating. The gaps between the Govan Stand and its adjoining Broomloan and Copland Stands were transformed by seating with huge Sony JumboTron television screens sited above the seated area. These were supposed to be used for broadcasting away matches back to Ibrox (which happened twice, I think) and for showing the action from games while they were being played in the stadium, as well as an advertising outlet. The capacity of the stadium was now just over 50,000.

Despite glittering domestic success, progress in the Champions League still eluded Rangers, with the club failing to survive the initial group stage. Nevertheless, the greatest moment in the club's history was just around the corner. In season 1996–97 Rangers completed the seemingly impossible nine-in-a-row Championships. Smith must be given great credit for the way he kept his side going under the type of pressure that no Scottish side had ever had to suffer in the past. Everybody knew that if Rangers failed to win that ninth title, it would seem for many that all those others didn't matter at all. Equalling Celtic's record was that important. Despite some nail-biting moments at various points in the season, Smith's Rangers succeeded, and the greatest run in the club's history was completed, ensuring the manager's place in the Rangers' folklore.

That season was one long bout of nail-biting for 'Gers fans. The most significant game came in the middle of March when 'Gers faced Celtic for the last time that season and at Parkhead. Most believed it was Celtic's final chance to stop nine-in-a-row. Rangers had already beaten their old rivals three times out of three in the League, but everybody knew that this would be a titanic match. With the rain pouring down on Parkhead, the Rangers players took the field on one of the most momentous days ever. After 29 games played, Rangers were five points ahead of their ancient rivals, the only side that could stop nine-in-a-row. Everybody concerned knew that a win for Rangers would virtually decide the destination of that season's League flag. Beforehand, assistant manager Archie Knox had told star Brian Laudrup that this was the most important match in the club's history – and he wasn't being melodramatic. Even the Dane realised that without having to be told.

The team's preparations in the lead-up to the game didn't augur well. As had happened so many times previously, Rangers had been badly affected by injury. Walter Smith confided that, at one point, out of a total staff of 58, an incredible 34 were unavailable to play. Andy Goram, a talisman for the side at Parkhead in the past was out through injury. Even worse, his deputy, Theo Snelders was also injured, and so, in such an emergency, Welshman Andy Dibble had to be brought to the club on loan. To make matters worse, captain Richard Gough was struggling with injury and, in any other circumstances, wouldn't have played, but so crucial was this game and so desperate was the situation Rangers found themselves in that Gough just had to play.

If the team's defence had been weakened then so had the attack as it lacked Gascoigne, a match-winner, and striker Gordon Durie, who had been rushed to hospital with appendicitis. This inspired Walter Smith to pull a masterstroke. He brought back charismatic striker Mark Hateley from Queen's Park Rangers, where he had gone the previous season, hoping that his presence would inspire the team and improve its chances of success. It was almost as if the big Englishman had been signed for this one game and that it was his destiny.

If all this didn't have the Rangers fans feeling rather nervous before the game, then the memory of a 2–0 defeat from Celtic in the Scottish Cup the week before at the same venue was sure to do it. The Celtic players who had knocked Rangers out must have felt confident in repeating the feat. This, plus the fact that it was their last chance to prevent nine-in-a-row, meant that the home side would be fired up for the match. They would also want to avoid losing their fourth Old Firm League game that season.

The first half saw a tousy, nervous affair with both teams looking frightened of losing, so high were the stakes. A Hateley looping header had threatened at one end before Andy Dibble had to dive at the feet of Cadete to block the striker's shot for a corner. Then Jorg Albertz took a free-kick from deep inside his own half, on the left touchline. The ball sailed towards the Celtic box. Hateley out-jumped Annoni, but both missed the ball as it bounced to the edge of the area. Defender Alan Stubbs, harassed by Durrant, mis-headed the ball backwards, allowing Durrant to run onto it and, as 'keeper Kerr came off his line, lob it over him. The ball bounced a yard from the goalline and Brian Laudrup just got ahead of Malky McKay to bundle it into the net despite the flailing hands of Kerr, who'd got back to his goal.

The nearest the home side came to equalising was when a free-kick 22 yards out was flicked up into the air for De Canio to volley towards the Rangers goal. The ball, however, crashed off the bar with Dibble looking beaten. As the teams went in at the interval, there was no doubt, though, that Rangers were in the driving seat.

The second half was similar to the first, with even half-chances few and far between. Then, in the 67th minute, came a flashpoint that could have changed the course of the game. Laudrup, boring through the middle, was chopped down by Malky McKay. While supporting the Dane's run, Hateley had been tripped. As Laudrup lay on the ground, Jackie McNamara kicked the ball from a few feet away, and hit it off Laudrup's head. As an enraged Laudrup jumped up, a melee started that even involved Celts 'keeper, Kerr, who had run out of the penalty area to get involved with an annoyed Hateley. The end result was that Mark Hateley got his marching orders from referee Hugh Dallas. However, disastrous as this could have been, Rangers escaped when McKay was sent off some minutes later and the numbers were evened up.

Near the end Rangers almost tied the game up thanks to an amazing run by Swedish defender Joachim Björklund who seldom ventured into the opposition half. Having dispossessed a Celt deep in the Rangers half, on the left touchline, 'Jocky' must have had a nosebleed as he galloped up the park, right into the Celtic penalty area. At the perfect moment he laid the ball off to Albertz on the six-yard line, but, as the German turned and was about to shoot, a sliding tackle partially blocked his shot and it went tamely to the Celtic 'keeper.

When the final whistle went, the emotions of the 'Gers players and fans couldn't be contained. Unfortunately, neither could Celtic's. Volatile striker Paulo De Canio had to be manhandled to grapple him away from Ian Ferguson, whom he seemingly wanted to fight. The Italian wouldn't give up and continued shouting and gesturing towards the Ranger, apparently signalling that he wanted to break his leg. As the 'Gers players went to the tunnel they were pelted by coins from Celtic fans in the Main Stand but, thankfully, didn't hang around to pick them up as souvenirs of the match that had virtually ensured the magical nine-in-a-row.

On 5 May Rangers fans packed Ibrox to celebrate nine-in-a-row by beating Motherwell in the third-last game of the season and the final one at home. Motherwell turned out to be party-poopers by winning 2–0. Like the other 50,000

Rangers fans, I was stunned. This hadn't been in the script. Suddenly we were going to have to beat either Dundee United or Hearts away to make the dream come true. That midweek the Rangers players rose to the occasion, and, from a Charlie Miller cross on the left, Brian Laudrup headed the solitary goal to win the match and create history. This game wasn't even live on television, but I was so happy I didn't mind waiting until later on to see the recorded highlights and enjoy an unforgettable occasion. Before that I had to keep tuning in to my radio to check that everything was still on course.

The majority of Rangers fans still got their chance to celebrate nine-in-a-row the following Saturday when 'Gers were playing at Tynecastle. Rangers had set up a transmission on the big screens at Ibrox so that the fans could watch the final League game of the season, and then afterwards the team was to be flown by helicopter back to Ibrox to receive the Championship trophy. Rangers lost 3–1 and a youngster called Barry Ferguson actually played well, but nobody was really bothered about the match. We were all just awaiting the arrival of the team home. I was sitting in the Main Stand near the front, ready to salute our heroes. Although it was May the rain was bucketing down, but nothing, absolutely nothing, could rain on our parade that day. Walter Smith and the players came out and lifted the trophy and received their medals. Walter made a modest speech and the crowd was in raptures. It was also great to see so many young fans there that day. I really thought that they would experience the same success that I had while watching the club. It didn't quite work out that way.

Another highlight of that season was the League Cup Final against Hearts, which we won 4–3 in a thrilling game. With Hampden yet again out of action, the match was played at Parkhead, and I was lucky enough to get a ticket for the rear of the Rangers' End. Poor Hearts! In the previous Final between the two clubs six months previously, it had been Brian Laudrup who had destroyed them. This time, it was to be 'Gers' other genius – Paul Gascoigne. Having said that, this victory probably meant more to Ally McCoist than any other Rangers player: his two goals would see him equal a 'Gers' record of over 30 years standing, and his tally for League Cup games would match Jim Forrest's. Super Ally would also be collecting a ninth winners' medal for this competition.

Rangers started the game with an attacking whirlwind. The first goal came from Brian Laudrup, cutting in from the right past a couple of defenders before threading a pass to McCoist on the 18-yard line. Without hesitation, he smacked the ball low, just inside the right-hand post. What a view of it I had from my seat high above the action.

More 'Gers' celebrations occurred soon after this when Albertz slung over a corner-kick from the left. The high, out-swinging ball was headed back across the area by Gordan Petric to Moore on the six-yard line. His goal-ward header was nodded into the net from a couple of yards by McCoist, who had nipped in ahead of the 'keeper. The match looked all over with most of it still to be played. However, perhaps with memories of their previous humiliation, Hearts were not for surrendering. They fought back, aided by the fact that some Rangers players had obviously thought that the game had been won and had started showboating and playing rather too casually. A Fulton goal before half-time might have been the wake-up call some 'Gers players had needed. McCoist, furious, had his own method. Near the interval he raced halfway up the field to give Gazza a push on the back followed by what looked like a choice mouthful.

Apparently, in the dressing room the arguments raged between various teammates, annoyed that a commanding lead had been allowed to be reduced. Soon after the restart, the situation worsened when a suspiciously offside-looking John Robertson goal tied the game. At halftime, the wayward genius Paul Gascoigne had strolled into the VIP lounge and downed a double whisky before running out for the second half. Jock Wallace, famously, had once rubbed whisky onto the heads of 'Gers players before a big Final in order to invigorate them, but obviously Gazza thought that a waste and used the spirit in a more traditional way.

Nevertheless, it worked. In the final 20 minutes it was Gazza whose talent rescued Rangers to secure the trophy. From just inside the Hearts' half, he took a pass and started to run directly at the opposition defence, straight up the middle. The defenders, knowing what he was capable of, backed off. Unfortunately for them, they backed off too far, and from 22 yards out Gazza stroked his shot into the bottom corner of the net. His ability and coolness had allowed him to pass the ball into the goal.

A few minutes later and Gazza had done it again. This time he received the ball out near the left touchline and, beating two opponents, cut inside. His run took him to just outside the box, where he completed an exquisite wall pass with Charlie Miller, whose touch had opened up the goal for Gazza, sending him into the penalty area. Once again the Geordie genius simply passed the ball into the goal before the despairing tackles of the Hearts defenders could get to him. Gascoigne had won the game for Rangers but what had inspired him? Had it been McCoist – or that glass of the water of life?

A late Weir consolation goal proved no threat to Rangers' lead, and when the whistle was blown, the celebrations started with Paul Gascoigne, no doubt, being at the centre of them – this time quaffing the obligatory champagne. He had certainly earned it, but probably no player was happier than Ally McCoist.

Unfortunately, the following season was a huge disappointment as departures from Ibrox and injuries to those left meant that the team's effectiveness was reduced. The fact that Walter Smith had intimated that he would resign at the end of that season was seen as another possible reason for the failure of some of the players at the club. The task of achieving 10-in-a-row was also made more difficult by the resurgence of Celtic under a new manager, Wim Jansen. Smith had continued buying star foreign players such as Amoruso, Thern, Porrini and Negri, but the new side failed to make its mark in Europe or to hang onto the League Championship, which, near the end of the season, was there for the taking. The selling of Gascoigne before the end of that season was a disastrous mistake in my eyes. Defeat in the Scottish Cup Final to Hearts completed a most disappointing final season for Smith as manager. By then, everybody knew who his successor was to be – Dick Advocaat, the manager of PSV Eindhoven.

Typical of that season, the enigma of Italian striker Marco Negri was a frustration for 'Gers fans. He looked set to beat all kinds of McCoist-like goalscoring records in his first season, having scored over 30 goals by the turn of the year. His visible lack of delight or a celebration of any kind when he scored was a puzzle to the 'Gers fans. Moody Marco, we all thought. He was hit on the eye in an accident playing squash with Sergio Porrini, and that was what put him out of the team initially, but, in effect, he hardly kicked another ball for the club amid rumours of discontent behind the scenes. It was a shame because he did look like a proper poacher, capable of scoring at least 30 goals every season. He had the ability but not the mentality to play for Rangers. The absence of Negri's goals and, latterly, Gazza was a factor in failing to make it 10-in-a-row. My daughter, Heather, had no doubts though, otherwise she wouldn't have had 10-in-a-row printed on the back of her home top. That might be a collector's item these days.

It still rankles me that we failed in our bid for 10-in-a-row. We blew it with two 1–0 defeats in our last four games – at Pittodrie and then at home to Kilmarnock. That defeat really sickened me as much as any defeat I've ever experienced in my 50 years of watching Rangers. To lose the title by a mere two points devastated me, especially since I believed we genuinely had a better team than Celtic that season. Despite the ultimate disappointment, there were some tremendous memories.

Richard Gough (brought back from America for one last season) scored with a thundering header at Ibrox to beat Celtic 1–0. Then there was 'Gers' 2–0 win against Celtic at Ibrox in April, a week after we had knocked them out of the Scottish Cup semi-final by 2–1, at 'neutral' Parkhead. All four goals scored by 'Gers in those two games were magnificent. I can still see them now. I was lucky enough to have got a ticket for the Cup semi-final, played at Parkhead due to Hampden's redevelopment. Since it was to be treated as a neutral venue both clubs got half the stadium, which was a reminder of 'the good old days' when I had started going to such matches. I was sitting at the rear of the Rangers' End where McCoist and Albertz scored the two goals in the second half to put 'Gers into the Final before a late goal by Celtic made the score more respectable.

I can still see those two goals. The first was a brilliant Albertz cross from the left that saw Super Ally running in from the right side of the box and planting a diving header into the net from close range. However, the second was even better. Albertz ran half the length of the park, drifting past one Celt and then another before blasting a trademark left-footer high into the net. We went ballistic. It was more of the same the following week at Ibrox in a must-win game, with the snow – in April – drifting down. Rangers played very well and won more comfortably than the 2–0 score-line suggests. The two incredible goals were the icing on the cake. First, Swedish international Jonas Thern volleyed a 20-odd yarder high into the net in a way reminiscent of Ray Wilkins' one in that 5–1 demolition of Celtic 10 years before. Then, in the second half, Albertz scored a goal that was similar in the lead-up and the finish to the one he'd scored at Parkhead the previous week. The guy was the fans' favourite even before those two games, but afterwards he was like a god.

How typical it was that Albertz would miss the Scottish Cup Final against Hearts after having been sent off the week before in 'Gers' last League game at Tannadice, which Rangers won 2–1. Albertz had taken a fresh-air swipe at an opponent who'd fouled him, and the ref recorded that as 'violent conduct', and so Albertz was suspended for the next match even though it was in a different competition. How we could have used his talent in that dreadful game, which resulted in a sickening 2–1 defeat that left us with no trophies that season.

The Final was played at Parkhead, and for once I managed to get a ticket. It was a lovely sunny day, and I was confident that at least we would end the season on a high by winning the Cup. My ticket was for the Main Stand and I stood around in the sun, savouring the atmosphere. At one point I walked past Robert Duval, the Hollywood film star, and then I spotted the roving Sky cameraman and interviewer who get the opinions of fans outside a stadium. I told them where to find Duval, if they wanted something special to show, and off they rushed. Duval was apparently a great buddy of Celtic legend Jimmy Johnstone, but I think he was at the Cup Final that season to check it out as preparation for his film, which would be released the following year, called *A Shot at Glory* – starring himself and one Ally McCoist, no less!

If you have never had the misfortune to see this turkey of a film then watch it just to see how bad it is. To his eternal shame, Super Ally plays the part of a former Celtic legend, so when they show extracts of his goal-scoring, the film-makers had to use CGI to remove his 'Gers top and replace it with the hoops. It's an eerie and unsettling sight to see McCoist seemingly banging in great goals for Celtic. To be fair, Ally's performance is probably the best thing in this film. Meanwhile, Duval plays his manager, a Protestant bigot who just happens to be the father of the player's estranged wife. He guides his wee team, Kilnockie, to the Cup Final, where they play the big, bad Rangers team managed by the big, bad, dour, unscrupulous 'Gers manager. If you watch this film you'll probably come away with the notion that the script was written by a Celtic fan.

I had to laugh when I read about the stushie Duval had created outside the stadium in the following day's papers. The poor, naive soul had presumably been friendly towards the fans, the Rangers fans especially, and had been given various 'Gers scarves to hold above his head so that photos could be taken. The ones that appeared in the Sunday papers showed the innocent abroad holding up scarves with such slogans as 'No Surrender', '1690' and 'UVF' printed on them. There was outrage from non-Rangers fans.

I needed something to cheer me up the next day because the Final had been absolutely dreadful, from the first minute until the last. We didn't play well, but we should at least have forced extra-time. In the first minute ref Willie Young gave Hearts a penalty from which they scored, but TV pictures later proved that the foul had taken place outside the penalty area. Who says Rangers get all the decisions? Early in the second half Hearts scored again, and it looked as if the Cup was on its way to Tynecastle. However, in the final 20 minutes Rangers staged a spirited comeback and McCoist scored to give us hope. We actually had Hearts on the ropes when, in the last minute, young Italian Gattuso put McCoist through on goal. The striker was fouled, as cameras showed later, right on the 18-yard line. The ref blew his whistle. We all jumped up, knowing that we would score with this last-minute penalty. Then the ref placed the ball one inch outside the 18-yard line to give us a free-kick instead. The ref must have been 30 yards behind the play when he saw the foul – and yet he could be so precise as to place the ball where he did.

That game and Walter Smith's reign ended in defeat. Most of the players were leaving the club at the same time as the manager, so that was an awful farewell for the likes of McCoist, Laudrup, Goram and Gough. Seldom have I felt so down at the end of a season.

Walter Smith will always be appreciated for managing the club when it succeeded in winning those nine titles in a row. He guided Rangers to great domestic success, winning the treble and two doubles. He was there when Rangers most needed him, ensuring that, when Graeme Souness suddenly departed, there would be a seamless transition from that regime to Smith's own. He brought some wonderful stars to play for the club and throughout those years gave Rangers fans so much to smile about. True success in Europe never came, but most fans will never forget that tremendous European run of 1993–94 when the Holy Grail of the European Cup was almost within the club's grasp. Little did we realise that, years later, Walter's finest hour as Rangers manager was perhaps still to come.

CHAPTER SEVEN

RANGERS GO DUTCH

When Graeme Souness became Rangers' manager, my father was dying of cancer, so it was a horrible coincidence that when Dick Advocaat joined the club my mum, this time, was dying of the same disease. She had been diagnosed earlier that year and left her house in Erskine to go and live with my brother and his family in Shawlands, as they had the space. Eventually, she would die in the Princess of Wales Hospice, Glasgow, situated beside the River Clyde where she had spent virtually her entire life.

For once, when a Rangers manager had left, we didn't have to wonder who would replace him. That had been announced early in the year when David Murray presented Dutchman Dick Advocaat as Smith's successor. I had never heard of him, so I can't say that I was excited at the prospect of Advocaat taking up the reins at Ibrox, and I wondered if a foreigner would be up to the job. Following the previous trophy-less season, few fans could have envisaged Rangers winning yet another treble in season 1998–99, especially under the management of a new boss and 'Gers' first foreign manager. The former Holland coach and PSV Eindhoven manager had had months to examine his new club's players before arriving on the scene. Most of the old guard had been allowed to leave and a virtually new side had to be assembled by the Dutchman. Luckily for him, David Murray provided the necessary funds to achieve this, although 10 years later the fans might have cause to rue such spending. By the end of his first season, Advocaat would have spent £30 million on his team, which would win everything domestically and show improved performances in the UEFA Cup. Just as important, his teams would always try to play skilful, exciting, attacking football that, at times, was a joy to behold.

'The Little General', as Advocaat became known, was a strict disciplinarian, and he made sure that the players knew who was boss from the start. A system of fines was put into effect so that even turning up a minute late for lunch was penalised. Advocaat may have been a modern European coach with new methods of training and tactical ploys, but in one sense he was very much in the Rangers tradition. He insisted on his players being well-dressed and projecting a smart image on and off the field. However, despite his strict attention to time-keeping, appearance and discipline, Advocaat did have a sense of humour that he probably used more on members of the press than his players. I loved it when he made fun of the hacks. It took many of his players quite a while to work out how far they could go with him in terms of banter, but eventually they realised the boundaries.

Advocaat assembled a veritable United Nations of players for his new club. The big question was would they be united on the park? As might have been expected over the coming seasons, Advocaat seemed to rely on his Dutch contingent, which eventually swelled from originals like Numan and Van Bronckhorst to Mols, de Boer, Ricksen and Konterman. 'Gers fans sometimes wondered if the Dutch had formed a clique within the dressing room, but while trophies were being won, it didn't seem to matter if that were the case.

In Advocaat's first season the only real mishap came in November when the side lost 5–1 to Celtic at Celtic Park. By now, nobody could have doubted that Advocaat was an attacking manager and the downside of this could be seen in this match. I had managed to get a ticket for the top tier at the 'Rangers' End 'of Parkhead, unfortunately, near the empty rows of seats that separated the 'Gers fans from the Celtic fans. Even with policemen and stewards between the two sets of fans I still felt I was too close to the 'enemy' for comfort. Even worse, due to the humiliating nature of the defeat, we had to endure the taunts and songs from the home fans for practically the entire match. A ridiculous decision by the ref saw young Scott Wilson being sent off and 'Gers thus playing with only 10 men from early in the first half. Subsequently, Rangers had gone 3–0 down but had kept attacking. By halftime a goal had been pulled back but the side was still in danger of being thrashed. Most previous managers would have recognised the reality of the situation and perhaps reorganised the team in a more cautious way in order to minimise the eventual deficit. Not Advocaat though. It was as if he still thought that Rangers could salvage something from the match.

The final score humiliated Rangers fans and some of the die-hard players, like Ian Ferguson, who were still at Ibrox. Many fans wondered if the foreigners really understood what such a result meant to the 'Gers fans. That game was the start of a strange and horrible week for me both personally and as a Rangers fan. By then, my mum was spending her final couple of weeks in the hospice. That Saturday night my wife and I visited her there and she was in good spirits, kidding me on about my team 'getting cuffed'. She even told me to go across the ward to talk to an old man, who was a patient and a 'Gers fan, and tell him about the game which I duly did. I've lost count of the number of times when, driving home from a bad defeat at Ibrox, I've consoled myself with the words, 'It's only a game', but that was one of the few times in my life when I said it and really meant it. You shouldn't need to be surrounded by dying people to realise that.

The following Monday we visited my mum again and, as usual, she was smiling and asking about other people and how they were getting on. It was typical of her to be thinking of others and to keep a smile on her face. On leaving, when I said goodnight to her, I didn't realise it was to be goodbye. She died in the wee small hours of the next morning. We got a phone call from the hospice and my wife woke me up to tell me that I was to drive there as quickly as possible. I fairly raced to Glasgow on the motorway at three in the morning. I had never been on the M8 when it had been as empty as that. All I could think of was getting there before mum died.

When I arrived, I parked the car and entered the reception area of the hospice. I was directed along a short corridor and, as I walked towards the open door I saw my brother, Ian, sitting on a chair with a nurse standing beside him. He was smoking and there was something about the way he was sitting that told me that mum had already died. I remember kissing him on the top of his head while the nurse confirmed that mum had passed away. She led us along various corridors and upstairs to the bed where mum lay, looking as if she were asleep, with a flower placed above her on her pillow. She looked at peace and, in a way, so were we. We hardly spoke but spent a few minutes with her before saying our final goodbye. As we left the building we arranged to meet up later that morning to start making the funeral arrangements.

We spent most of the Tuesday doing that before having a pint together in Shawlands, and then I was going to the big game that evening. Rangers were playing Parma in the third round of the UEFA Cup, for which I had obviously already bought my ticket. I had pondered on whether or not to still go to the match, but I thought it might do me more good than brooding at home about Mum's death. Releasing my emotions by shouting and bawling at a foreign ref and players could only help in my opinion. I thought, as I was walking up to the stadium, that God owed me one. It turned out that God isn't a football fan as the match ended in a 1–1 draw, which was a creditable result for Rangers but not one likely to see us progress to the quarter-finals. We lost 3–1 in Italy, after taking the lead ,too, through a great Albertz goal before things unravelled. It was some consolation that Parma actually won the tournament that season – and that we would knock them out of the qualifying round for the Champions League in the next.

Mum's funeral at Lynn Park crematorium was the following Saturday, and I was amazed at the number of people who turned up, people that I didn't know but who obviously thought highly enough of her to come to the funeral. My mum was just an ordinary, hard-working, decent wee woman, but the sight of so many people at her funeral made me realise how she must have touched the lives of so many people. I hope that even half that number of folk turn up when it's my funeral. The reception afterwards was at the Queen's Park Hotel. I heard some Irish Celtic fans, who were obviously staying there and going to the Celtic game at Parkhead later on. It reminded me that I would be there as well the very next day at the League Cup Final between Rangers and St Johnstone.

That Sunday I was sitting in the top tier of the stand opposite the Main Stand at Parkhead, and I had a great view. The game was pretty average and, if the truth be told, my heart wasn't really in it following my mum's funeral. 'Gers won 2–1, thanks to goals from Guivarc'h and Albertz, and that completed the first leg of that season's treble.

Since the beginning of the season, the manager had added to his squad, signing stars such as Stefan Klos from Borussia Dortmund, French striker Stephane Guivarc'h from Newcastle, American Claudio Reyna from Wolfsburg and Neil McCann from Hearts. He had built a really formidable side and one that entertained as well as won. I was enjoying going to Rangers games at that time. In a thrilling climax to the season, Advocaat's side got sweet revenge over Celtic by clinching the Championship when beating Celtic 3–0 at Celtic Park.

This triumph was a memorable match for various reasons. It was the first time that a Rangers side would clinch the League Championship at the home of their greatest rivals. The side played brilliantly, humiliating Celtic on its own pitch and, as a bonus, the misbehaviour of the Celtic fans off the park made it one of the most disastrous days in that club's history. The only negative for me was that I couldn't get a ticket for this one and had to watch the live broadcast instead.

Rangers started confidently and before long were looking threatening. The first goal really gave them the impetus to go on and dominate proceedings. Deep in his own half, Tony Vidmar pushed a pass to Albertz in the centre circle. The big German slotted the ball out to the left wing for Gio Van Bronckhorst to run onto. He raced forward before releasing a precision pass into the box that was perfectly weighted for Rod Wallace to accept. Without breaking stride, he fired the ball across the face of the Celtic goal, and there was Neil McCann, on the six-yard line, stretching out a leg to steer the ball into the goal.

Later in the half, things started to look really grim for the home team when their French defender, Mahe, was sent off by referee, Hugh Dallas. This seemed to increase the incredibly hostile atmosphere inside the stadium as aggrieved Celtic fans realised that this could be a nightmare of a game unfolding. Worse was to come when Rangers were awarded a corner at the Celtic End of the stadium. As Van Bronckhorst prepared to take the corner he was pelted with coins from some fans nearby. Referee Dallas went across to protect the player and, for his pains, he was hit by a coin on the forehead, causing blood to flow. The game was held up while 'Gers players surrounded the ref and he received treatment for his injury.

From the delayed corner, Riseth, at the back post, appeared to pull Tony Vidmar over and Hugh Dallas bravely awarded a penalty. Albertz duly took the kick calmly among the bedlam and slotted the ball low into the corner of the net before running off in celebration followed by his delirious teammates, who suspected that the title had been won. Nevertheless, before half-time, a couple of Celtic fans had invaded the field, seemingly trying to get to ref Dallas. Thankfully, they were escorted away by the police before they could reach their intended victim. Even at the interval the mayhem continued when a Celtic fan, in the upper tier of the North Stand fell over onto the fans below in the lower deck. Luckily, only his pride was badly injured!

The second half was a calmer affair as both teams seemed to have accepted their respective fate, although Wallace and then Riseth were sent off in separate incidents. Then, near the end, a pass out of defence from Colin Hendry found Jonatan Johannson inside the Celtic half. The Finn slipped the ball infield and forwards first time to Neil McCann, who only had the last Celtic defender right behind him. As Marshall stretched out a foot to try and intercept the pass, he missed it and, quick as a flash, McCann was on his way, scurrying towards the goal with only the 'keeper to beat. His 20-yard, unchallenged run, took him into the box, past the diving 'keeper, enabling him to sweep the ball into the empty net right in front of the ecstatic Rangers fans.

Near the end Rod Wallace was sent off for retaliating after a dreadful tackle on him, and later Celtic's Riseth was correctly, if belatedly, sent off for totally losing the plot and attacking a 'Gers player in a corner of the pitch. A mock huddle by the Rangers players on the final whistle and Celtic's humiliation was complete as the title went to Dick Advocaat's new Rangers side for the first time. The aftermath, with the press writing about an 'Old Firm Shame Game', really annoyed me. Rangers fans had done nothing out of order. All the 'shame' had stemmed from the behaviour of Celtic's fans and players. As usual, the hacks were too cowardly to just state the truth.

Not content with that, a one-goal win over Celtic in a largely uneventful match saw the Scottish Cup won and the treble achieved in Advocaat's first season. The Cup win was 'Gers' 100th major trophy. This time, our old foes couldn't deny us that elusive treble. I was in the new BT Stand at Hampden for that Final, thanks to my mum. With some of the money she had left me in her will, I had bought a Hampden debenture ticket, which meant I was guaranteed my seat in the upper Main Stand for all games at the revamped stadium. It was one of the best things I've ever done. Since then, I've not had to worry about getting a ticket for all the big games at the National Stadium. I've seen Old Firm Cup Finals, other Cup Finals, crunch World Cup qualifiers, the Scotland versus England play-off match, the Champions League Final between Real Madrid and Bayer Leverkusen – I've even had tickets for the Robbie Williams concert!

The new revolution, the Advocaat Revolution, looked as if it had started a new era at Ibrox. Things continued in much the same vein in Advocaat's second season, and, were it not for an undeserved League Cup defeat of an under-strength 'Gers side at Pittodrie, the treble might have been repeated. Instead, Advocaat had to make do with the double, gaining revenge over the Dons by thrashing them 4–0 in the Scottish Cup Final in May. Progress in Europe, after reaching the UEFA Cup third round the previous season, continued in the Champions League. Wins home and away against his former club, PSV Eindhoven, and a draw against Bayern Munich at Ibrox had set Rangers up to qualify for the next group stage – if they could hold Bayern to a draw in Munich in the final match. In one of Rangers' best, but unluckiest, performances in Europe, a penalty goal saw Bayern go through despite Rangers having been the better side and hitting the woodwork more than once. An even bigger blow was the terrible knee injury to star striker Michael Mols, who would be out for the rest of the season and, in effect, would never be quite the same player again. It was a real shame because I thought that he could have become one of the all-time greats at Ibrox, so brilliant was he.

When Rangers won the title by 21 points from Celtic, it was the club's 49th success and they did it with six games to spare, equalling its own record from season 1962–63. Rangers only lost one home and one away game in the League that season.

The 7–0 win in the Scottish Cup semi-final against Ayr United was the club's biggest-ever win in that competition.

If this period was a new era for Rangers under Advocaat, it was also one for me personally. Since my bypass operation I had been back at work for over three years but was feeling more and more tired. I saw my cardiac consultant on a biannual basis, and at one of those examinations, which had included the annual heart scan, he revealed to me that the tissue scarring of the damaged heart muscle was stretching. When I asked him what this meant, he said that if it continued I would have to be placed on the waiting list for a heart transplant. My reaction was to ask him to find me a heart like midfield dynamo Stuart McCall's, or that of a Tory politician since that one wouldn't have been used much!

I was given more pills to take that could slow down the deterioration of the muscle and perhaps even halt it. I also figured that being a teacher in a modern comprehensive school, with all the stress that it involved, was not conducive to health. I decided to ask for early retirement on the grounds of ill health and it was granted. I officially retired in 2000. My next three books could only be written because I no longer had the school work to take up too much of my life. I still have to take 10 pills a day, but the measures seem to have worked as the damage has not increased in the decade since then.

Season 1999–2000 was Advocaat's high water mark. The Dutchman would never quite be the same manager again. Few realised it at the time, but Rangers had by now seen the best of Dick Advocaat. In his third season he faced the challenge of a new Celtic manager in Martin O'Neill, and the first Old Firm game of the season should have set alarm bells ringing when Celtic, playing at home, won the match 6–2. Although it was live on television, I didn't see this game, thankfully. It was the last Sunday in August, and I was in Edinburgh with some school colleagues to see some Fringe shows. At lunch-time we were in an Irish pub between shows, and as we were waiting for the food to arrive one of the bar staff pulled down a big screen to show the game that, by my reckoning, had just started. By the time the picture came up we could see that the score was 3–0 to Celtic. I couldn't believe my eyes. By half-time it was 3–1 and 'Gers had had a perfectly legitimate goal chalked off.

Once we had eaten, we had to leave to go to the next show, and I was grateful to get away from what turned out to be 'Gers' biggest Old Firm mauling in recent years. I didn't even know that the final score had been 6–2 until I was being driven home at midnight and was listening to the car radio. The previous red face 'Gers had received at the hands of Celtic had been the 5–1 game that I had been at just before my mum had died. At least this time I had had an enjoyable day out – as long as I kept all thoughts of Parkhead out of my head.

Despite the fact that Rangers won the next Old Firm game at Ibrox by 5–1, it was obvious that the side was struggling to keep pace with this new Celtic team. Even the purchase of Ronald de Boer from Barcelona and players such as Ricksen, Konterman, Miller, Lovenkrands, Johnston and Ritchie hadn't improved the side as devastating, long-term injuries took their toll. Halfway through the season even the acquisition of gangling Norwegian striker Tore Andre Flo from Chelsea for a record £12 million couldn't turn the team around before the end of the season in which Celtic swept the boards. I couldn't understand how we had gone from treble winners to losers, achieving nothing in a season. I should have remembered that it had happened before, in season 1976–77.

In Europe it was disappointment again after it had looked more promising than ever. After having thrashed Austrians Strum Graz 5–0 at Ibrox and beaten Monaco away, a defeat and draw against Galatasaray followed by defeat in Austria meant that Rangers had to beat Monaco at Ibrox in the final game to progress. Leading 2–1, in control, with only 12 minutes left, a silly goal was conceded and a third goal just wouldn't come Rangers' way, although Albertz had come close with a typical thunderbolt, thus propelling the team into the UEFA Cup as a consolation. It was after this disappointment that Advocaat rather brutally stripped Lorenzo Amoruso of the captaincy and awarded it to young Barry Ferguson who, despite the doubters, would make a success of it.

As Advocaat entered his fourth season in charge, he must have known that it was imperative that the initiative be seized back from Celtic. Unfortunately, despite further additions to his playing staff, the team still trailed Celtic in the League and by a long way before the season had reached its halfway point. Everybody at Ibrox realised by then that the title could not be regained that season. In football circles, the talk was that the manager had 'lost the dressing room' and that he might not survive another disastrous season. However, before such speculation could gain serious momentum, Dick Advocaat surprised everybody once again by voluntarily changing his position in the club. At the start of December 2001 he became the club's first Director of Football and was instrumental in Alex McLeish, the Hibs manager, being appointed to the Ibrox hot seat. However, within a year, Advocaat would have left the club altogether to become the coach, once again, of the Dutch national team. His revolution had been short-lived but very interesting. I have to admit, though, that by the end, I was glad to see the back of him.

Previous to Advocaat's departure, Sir David Murray decided that the club should remember and honour the achievements and contribution made to Rangers by its finest players throughout its history. Accordingly, in 2000, he set up the Rangers' Hall of Fame, the first of any club in Britain. A mahogany panel above the famous marble staircase was assigned to display the names of those former players inducted into the Hall of Fame, and an annual presentation ceremony was instigated where the players honoured received their award. The five criteria for consideration by the selections panel are service to the club, number of games played, honours won, international caps and exceptional ability.

The original panel, consisting of Sir David Murray, John Greig, Sandy Jardine, Ally McCoist and club historian David Mason, selected the candidates annually so that the fans could vote for the heroes they wished to see inducted into the elite Hall. The club historian especially tries to ensure that the players out-with living memory are not neglected when the choice from the various eras is offered. The first member elected was Moses McNeil, one of the founders of Rangers. There are now 78 members, dating from the 19th century to the present day. My fourth book, *Hall of Fame: Rangers' All-Time Greats* published in 2009 by Breedon Books, gives a detailed account of those Hall of Fame members.

If the Hall of Fame is a tribute to Rangers players of the past, the memorial to the fans who died in three terrible accidents at Ibrox Stadium is a tribute to them. In January 2001, on the 30th anniversary of the Ibrox Disaster, a memorial was unveiled outside the Main Stand. It consists of a plinth on which the names of the victims were listed, along with those of the previous two accidents at the stadium. Above it is a statue of 'The Greatest Ranger Ever', John Greig, who was the club captain at the time of the terrible accident. Until this, the only commemoration of the event had been the plaque situated on the exterior of the Copland Stand. Rangers is a club where the past can never be forgotten.

Later that year, a facility that looked to the future was opened. Rangers' new, state-of-the-art training centre at Auchenhowie, near Milngavie, a suburb north of Glasgow, was opened in 2001. Named Murray Park, it cost £12 million to build and was the brainchild of manager Dick Advocaat. The complex covers 38 acres, has 10 pitches, six of which are full size. The main pitch has under-soil heating that cost £150,000 to install. For situations when the Scottish winter is too harsh for outdoor training, the site also has an indoor pitch that uses the latest type of artificial grass and is a third the size of a regulation pitch. The surfaces of all the grass pitches are identical to that of Ibrox's so the players train on the same surface as they play actual games on, hopefully improving performances and limiting injuries.

A gym, which cost £150,000 alone, contains the most advanced apparatus to ensure maximum fitness. A hydrotherapy pool has been included that is meant to help players recovering from injury as well as developing their general strength and well-being. With restaurant facilities and the club's medical centre also being built into the complex, Rangers players have everything that they could wish for in one place. Now, they only visit Ibrox on the day of a game, a situation that, hopefully, will bring fresh enthusiasm and excitement to an appearance at the stadium.

Since Murray Park has been open, it has supplied young players for the Rangers first team including Alan Hutton, Allan McGregor, Chris Burke, Charlie Adam, John Fleck and Danny Wilson.

CHAPTER EIGHT

REGENERATION AND DECLINE

Alex McLeish was a surprising choice of manager, but maybe it was indicative of the downsizing of the club that was about to start and would continue until the end of the decade. By the time McLeish took up the management reins, there was no chance of 'Gers winning the League title. Celtic would win it again, by 18 points. However, the new manager did seem to get more out of Advocaat's players, and we actually won the two Cups in the second half of the season. Indeed, in McLeish's first four Old Firm games, he won two and drew two, leading some hacks to claim that he had the beating of Martin O'Neill.

It's fair to say that when Alex McLeish became the new Rangers manager, the fans' welcome was muted rather than disappointed. It was much the same reaction as had taken place when Walter Smith had taken over from Souness. Back then, the fans had been looking for another 'big name' but had got Smith instead. As the unassuming Smith had gone on to become one of the most successful of Rangers managers, many probably hoped that 'Big Eck' could do the same. After relatively successful spells as manager of Motherwell and then Hibs, McLeish was considered to have served an appropriate apprenticeship in management, but many wondered if he was ready to be boss of a big club like Rangers. Rangers fans were hoping that he'd picked up a lot of his managerial knowledge from his old boss at Aberdeen and current mentor, Sir Alex Ferguson. Still, with the team at a low ebb for a second consecutive season, many fans thought that the only way was up and that McLeish was as good a choice as any to give it a go.

McLeish and assistant manager Andy Watson, whom he'd brought with him from Hibs, reinvigorated the players and results began to improve. It was amazing to see the same group of underachieving players transform themselves under McLeish's guidance. By necessity, the new manager had only those same players who'd been in the shadow of Celtic for the previous 18 months to call on, but somehow he instilled the confidence in them that they'd seemingly lacked.

As far as I was concerned, one of the bonuses of having a new manager was that, like the fans, he obviously didn't rate Advocaat's signing, Bert Konterman, who, in my opinion, was one of the worst central-defenders ever to play for the club. He sometimes played the guy in midfield but, as the season wore on, he was played less and less. 'Bombscare Berti' was the nickname the 'Gers fans had accorded the gangling Dutchman. Apparently, he had been taught to play football by his mum – and she clearly wasn't the best of players! He did have one memorable moment, though, when he became a fans' hero by scoring the winning goal against Celtic in the League Cup semi-final. I was in my usual seat at Hampden that cold February night, and I couldn't believe it when Konterman, who had been jeered constantly by the Celtic fans, sent a 30-yard screamer into the top corner of the net to win the tie for us. I bet his mother hadn't taught him that! Maybe it was that goal that earned him a place in the team for the Final against Ayr United, which we won 4–0.

The Scottish Cup win that May was even more memorable. Nothing beats winning a Cup Final. Well, nothing beats it unless your opponents are Celtic. The only thing that can top that is if it's done by a last-minute goal, and that's why this game will be fondly remembered by so many Rangers fans. In a great match, the fortunes of each team see-sawed in a thrilling encounter. It was a typically robust, quick and exciting Old Firm encounter, with the play flowing from one end to the other. The first chance came to Rangers when Amoruso should have scored, having out-jumped Balde, but his header flew over the bar.

Then, at the other end, a Thompson corner was headed back across the penalty box by Balde for John Hartson, a yard from the goalline, to nod into the net. This only served to increase the Rangers' pressure on Celtic and, before half-time, the equaliser had arrived. A long pass upfield by Barry Ferguson, who was having a great game, was chased by Peter Lovenkrands. Just inside the Celtic penalty area, Mjallby and Sutton both jumped with the Dane to head the ball, but Mjallby mis-timed it and his weak header landed behind Lovenkrands. Like a flash, Lovenkrands pounced on the ball, took one touch and lashed it low, just inside the right-hand post with the despairing dive of Douglas being in vain.

Although the game ebbed and flowed, Rangers were the more dominant side and, just when they were looking superior, Celtic scored again in the second half. A Lennon free-kick on the left swirled into the box where giant Balde out-muscled Amoruso to leave himself a free header from point-blank range. Rangers would have to reinvigorate themselves and come from behind again. They were trailing by 2–1 but were playing well and so, for once, the 'Gers fans weren't in a disconsolate or defeatist mood. Inspired by skipper Barry Ferguson, who was leading by example, the team tried to hit back. A rasping Ferguson shot from over 20 yards out looked net-bound, only to swerve away and crash off Douglas's right-hand post. At this point, 'Gers fans could have been forgiven for thinking that it just wasn't going to be their day. The Rangers players, however, didn't think that for a moment as they continued to get the upper hand over their rivals. They seemed to know that it was only a matter of time.

When Balde clumsily fouled Amoruso just outside the penalty area, the situation looked tailor-made for a Ferguson free-kick, at which he had become rather adept throughout the season. The skipper fired his shot over the Celtic wall into the top right-hand corner, giving Douglas no chance whatsoever. At that point it looked like the tide had turned and that there could only be one winner of this Final – Rangers.

Rangers dominated after that, but the game looked to be heading for extra-time until the match had the perfect ending – a last-minute winner. Despite almost constant pressure, Rangers couldn't find that decisive goal, no matter how many times they surged towards the Celtic goal. Then, with one minute left on the clock and extra-time looming, Amoruso set McCann free down the left wing. The little winger made some progress before sending over a perfect cross into that dangerous area between the 'keeper and his defenders. Lovenkrands managed to get in front of his marker, Chris Sutton, to nod the ball downwards into the far side of the goal. Everybody knew at that moment that he had won the Cup for Rangers. There was simply no time for the tired-looking and dispirited Celts to make a comeback. As we jumped around in joy we knew the game and the Cup had just been won. There was barely time for the game to be restarted. As the Cup was presented, I thought that it had been one of the great experiences in watching Rangers. That was a happy day.

Those two Cup victories gave the players and the fans a fresh confidence, and we looked forward to the next season eagerly. We weren't to be disappointed as it turned out to be one of the most momentous campaigns in Rangers' history. It also helped me to produce my second book *Rangers' 50 Flags*. Two seasons previously, Martin O'Neill's first Celtic side had won the treble and I was amazed to see, a mere couple of months later, a book about this achievement in the shops already. I took a chance that season 2002–03 would be a good one for the club, knowing that if the Championship could be regained it would be Rangers' 50th – a world record. I decided to write about each game, home and away, as it happened, and I reasoned that if it didn't eventually get published at least I would have a record of that season for myself and I would have enjoyed the actual process of writing. Come what may, at least a book would be ready by the end of that season.

As it turned out, my contact at Rangers' Commercial Department, Paul Geddes, supported the idea that this should be an official Rangers publication but, at the end of the season, when I thought I had done all the hard work, he asked if I could add material that examined some of the other 49 League Championships. This I duly did, working under time constraints but enjoying researching some of the great title wins since the club's foundation. My title for this book, eventually published by Grange, was *50 Flags and a Few Trebles*, but the publisher changed this to *Rangers' 50 Flags*. The finished book comprises a first section that looks at some of the most memorable title victories from 1890 onwards, as well as all the years in which the treble was won, and the remainder of the book records all the matches of season 2002–03. And what a season that was!

Season 2002–03 produced the club's seventh treble, with Rangers beating the Celtic team that reached the Final of the UEFA Cup in the League Cup Final and by a solitary goal in the League Championship on the last day of the season. Ironically, that season had started disastrously when Rangers had been knocked out of the UEFA Cup, on away goals, in the first round by Czech minnows, Viktoria Zizkov. That might just have been a blessing in disguise because it allowed the team to concentrate on domestic matters without the distraction of Europe.

We had some really good players in the team that season, and all of them contributed to a magnificent treble. German 'keeper Stefan Klos was imperious in goal, while the defence ahead of him had Ricksen, Numan, Amoruso and Moore all at their peak. In midfield we had Barry Ferguson, Ronald de Boer, Mikel Arteta and brilliant attackers in Lovenkrands, Mols, Arveladze, Caniggia and McCann. It was a United Nations side with only two Scots regularly featuring as first-choice players. Four players scored 13 League goals or more in the 101 League goals scored.

The first Old Firm match, at Parkhead in October, perhaps set the scene for the rest of that season when a thrilling 3–3 draw was played out, suggesting that there wasn't much between the teams and that a titanic struggle would ensue that season. The next one at Ibrox in December confirmed this when Rangers won 3–2 in another exciting match. By March 'Gers had also beaten Celtic 2–1 in the League Cup Final, with goals from Caniggia and Lovenkrands, although 'Gers were to lose the final two League games against Celtic and yet still win the title. When Celtic won the last one at Ibrox in April, returning victorious from a UEFA Cup semi-final, it looked as if the pendulum had swung in Celtic's favour. However, they dropped points soon after, and it was neck-and-neck again.

When the final League games of the season were to be played on 25 May, Rangers and Celtic both had a massive 94 points and were equal on goal difference. Rangers, though, had the advantage of having scored more goals and thus were slightly ahead of their rival should goal difference be the same and it came down to counting goals scored. Celtic were away at Kilmarnock, but Rangers had the advantage of a home game against Dunfermline, whom they had already beaten 6–0, 3–0 and 3–1 earlier in the season. Both sides went into their final matches knowing that they had to win – and by as many goals as possible. Celtic would be bidding to end their season with a trophy, while Rangers were hoping to secure the club's world-record 50th League Championship, and maintain hope of the treble. Being away to Kilmarnock, logically, Celtic shouldn't have been expected to score as many goals as Rangers playing the Pars at Ibrox. Still, having just suffered a defeat in the UEFA Cup Final in Seville that week, the Parkhead side would be giving it everything to compensate for their disappointment. Nothing would be taken for granted.

As expected, Ibrox was packed on this hot, sunny day. Not only did 'Gers have to win but they had to score as many goals as possible to ensure that Celtic didn't pip them at the post. As with so many big games at Ibrox, the excitement before the game was palpable. You can always tell when the Rangers fans are really up for it, and you hope that this will transmit itself to the team. It certainly did that day. The noise, from the emergence of the teams until after the final whistle, was unbelievable. Rangers started like a whirlwind and scored in the opening two minutes, thus cranking up the already considerable volume of noise inside Ibrox. Ronald de Boer set Caniggia off on a run and the Argentinian's delicate pass,, threaded into the box, found Michael Mols. He controlled the ball and sent his shot in the opposite direction from the one all the defenders had been expecting. When the ball hit the post before entering the net the whole of Ibrox went bonkers.

We looked as if we were simply going to blow the Pars away, but before celebration mode could get into full swing, Pars' Dair sent a 22-yard shot screaming behind Stefan Klos for the equaliser. Now it seemed that Rangers were back to square one, and we were concerned about how this would affect the players' spirits.

Fortunately it didn't. Just five minutes later, the lead was regained when the determination of Ricksen saw him go into a sliding tackle, which led to the ball rebounding to Caniggia, only eight yards from goal. He calmly passed the ball into the net. Meanwhile Celtic had taken the lead at Rugby Park.

In the 29th minute Rangers' third goal only happened because of the determination and skill of Lorenzo Amoruso. He chased a lost cause out on the far side of the goalline and kept the ball in play. Not only that but he then sent over a great cross to the six-yard line, where Shota Arveladze sent his diving header into the goal. Rangers were in the driving seat again. However, by half-time, Celtic had gone 2–0 up so the sides were all square once again.

In the second half Rangers surged forward, looking for as many goals as they could to ensure that Celtic wouldn't snatch the title from them. Then, in a breakaway, the unsung hero, 'keeper Klos, saved the 'Gers' title hopes. A Brewster 22-yard shot was blasted with accuracy towards the 'Gers' goal. It had goal written all over it – until the German 'keeper threw himself to his right and miraculously palmed the ball away to safety.

As so often happens, within a minute of this escape, Rangers had scored their fourth goal. A pacy, curling McCann free-kick was met by de Boer, whose header fairly rocketed into the net. By now Celtic were 3–0 up on Killie. Then, minutes later, the pendulum had really swung in Rangers' favour when a Neil McCann dribble saw him cut the ball back a few yards from the goalline for Steven Thompson to bundle the ball into the net. Cue delirium in the stands. Rangers were now ahead on goal difference having scored this, their 100th League goal of the season.

Like thousands of other Rangers fans, I had one earphone from my radio in my ear throughout the second half so that I could keep track of what was happening at the Celtic game. The nerves were building up as it became obvious that Rangers couldn't relax and hold the lead that they had. They had to keep scoring goals, just in case. Thompson had scored 'Gers' fifth, but Celtic were now 4–0 up, having scored with a penalty and then missing a second one. If the scores stayed like that Rangers would win the title courtesy of having scored more goals. One more for Celtic, however, would give them the Championship. Those final few minutes were among the most nail-biting of my 'Gers-watching life.

However, one minute from the final whistle, a great run by McCann was halted when he was fouled inside the box, and a penalty was awarded. If this was converted we all knew that Celtic would have to score twice in the final couple of minutes to win the title. Who would take the vital kick that would surely tie up the title? The young Spaniard, Mikel Arteta, in his debut season, stepped up to do the necessary. He seemed the calmest man in the stadium as he ran forward and slotted the ball confidently away. Everyone knew then that the 50th Championship had been won. The whole stadium seemed to be bouncing. Once we had calmed down, the final whistle went and we listened nervously on our radios until the whistle was blown before one of the greatest celebrations in Rangers' history could commence. However, out on the pitch, there was a strange feeling of being in limbo as the players were reluctant to celebrate yet, just in case. When the word came through that Celtic's match had ended at 4–0 then not only the fans but the 'Gers players and management went crazy. Not only had the side won the game and the title, they had won it by playing wonderful, exciting football that had contributed to a day that no Rangers fans would ever forget. It was one of those days when, being a Rangers fan seems the greatest thing in the world.

Even Celtic's Chris Sutton's bitter comments after his game about Dunfermline 'lying down' to Rangers couldn't sour the occasion. We knew that the Pars had given everything but that we had just been irresistible. The helicopter carrying the Championship trophy had been hovering halfway between Glasgow and Kilmarnock, and now all the 'Gers fans wanted was for the trophy to arrive and be presented to Barry Ferguson. When this had been done, the celebrations really did start.

Funnily enough, winning the Scottish Cup a week later by beating Dundee 1–0 seemed a bit of an anti-climax, especially considering it completed the treble. An Amoruso header won the trophy, and despite a dull match, it was entirely fitting as he had captained 'Gers to our previous treble and would be leaving the club for Blackburn Rovers a couple of weeks later. It was maybe that Amoruso goal, clinching the treble, that ensured my book would be published later that year. Apart from that, the most memorable thing for me about that game was that I went to Hampden having had the bald part of my head painted red, white and blue. At my age!

In his first 18 months in the job, McLeish had won five out of the six available domestic trophies – and the one that was missing wasn't a feasible target by the time he had arrived at Ibrox anyway. Just as remarkable was the fact that it had been done with the same players, apart from the addition of £6 million Mikel Arteta from Barcelona and a Bosman player, Australian Kevin Muscat from Wolves.

I should have known never to be surprised by anything in football, but the following season was a poor one. Rangers were out of both Cups without reaching the Final and gave a very disappointing performance in the League, second behind Celtic by 17 points. Even in Europe, although we reached the Champions League group stage, it was an embarrassing failure, not helped by the fact that our captain and best player, Barry Ferguson, jumped ship and was transferred to Blackburn immediately after we had qualified for the group stage. In the six group matches, we won the first at home against Stuttgart, drew the next away to Panathinaikos but lost the final four to the above teams and twice to Manchester United. It's probably best to draw a veil over those games.

Perhaps an even bigger surprise for me the following season was how well we played and the fact that we won the Championship again, in dramatic circumstances, as well as the League Cup. The downside was that we failed to reach the Champions League group stage, having been knocked out by CSKA Moscow. The consolation prize was that we went into the UEFA Cup qualifiers, where we beat Maritimo of Portugal on penalties, thus qualifying for the first-ever UEFA Cup group stages, which had the strange format of groups of five clubs playing two matches at home and two away. McLeish had signed Jean-Alain Boumsong, a French central-defender who nobody had ever heard of, on a Bosman, and he proved to be an absolute star, a real hero of the Rangers fans. By Christmas he was gone. Despite appearing happy during his half-season of brilliant displays, he became unsettled just before our final match in the UEFA Cup at home against Auxerre, which we lost 2–0, putting us out of the competition. Within a week he was off to Newcastle, and cash-strapped Rangers were £8 million better off.

At least that profit was put to good use. In January McLeish brought back Ferguson, who wanted to come home to Ibrox, Greek central-defender Kyrgiakos, who admirably replaced Boumsong, Belgian attacking-midfielder Thomas Buffel and, due to a serious injury to 'keeper Klos, former Dutch international 'keeper Ronald Waterreus. This new spine of the team was, in effect, what won 'Gers the title that season, helped by a strike force of Nacho Novo and Croatian Dado Prso, who would achieve cult status at Ibrox. Those two strikers scored 37 League goals between them on the way to the title.

Things had started to look brighter when, in February, in the semi-final of the League Cup, Rangers had thrashed Dundee United 7–1. This was Ferguson's first game on his return when he was played as a substitute. The following month the Cup was won when Motherwell were beaten 5–1 in a match dubbed 'The Davie Cooper Final'. However, it was the League Championship that the Rangers fans craved. When 'Gers once again lost the final Old Firm game of the season at Ibrox, it looked a forlorn hope with only four matches left. However, the way things panned out, the destination of the title came down to the final game of the season for the second time in three years. The day, which became known as 'Helicopter Sunday', will live in the memories of Rangers fans everywhere.

For this final showdown, both Old Firm sides were away from home and Celtic had the advantage of a two-point lead at the top of the table. Rangers were at Easter Road to play a Hibs team that would finish third as long as it didn't lose by too many goals. Meanwhile, Celtic were at middle-of-the-table Motherwell. As Celtic had only lost one away game that season, I couldn't see them failing to get the win that they needed. To regain the Championship, 'Gers had to win and hope that Celtic wouldn't. As before, the SPL had arranged for a helicopter carrying the Championship trophy to be in the air, hovering between Edinburgh and its more likely destination, Motherwell.

Since I was in pessimistic mood, my wife and I had decided to spend that weekend at my aunt's house in Campbeltown, near McCartney's Mull of Kintyre. We used make the 120-mile drive down there every so often for a short break and to visit my aunt Crichton. I was happy to get away from a depressing final game of the season although both Old Firm matches were live on television on that Sunday, 22 May. I had set up my video to record the 'Gers game so that I could watch it when I got home. We had our usual great time and then left on the Sunday afternoon to come home. I had put all thoughts of football out of my mind, was enjoying the scenery on a lovely sunny day and a couple of hours later we were on the last leg of our journey as we drove alongside Loch Lomond. My wife had taken over the driving, so I was able to answer my mobile phone when it rang. It was my stepdaughter, Denise. The conversation went something like this:

Denise: 'Do you know that Rangers won?'

Me: 'Oh, right. Big deal.'

Denise: 'No, I mean they won the League!'

Me: 'You're kidding!'

Denise: 'No, really. Switch on your radio and you'll see.'

I switched on the car radio, now that we were in a part of the country where the mountains didn't interfere with reception, and heard the pundits discussing what a remarkable end to the season it had been, congratulating Rangers on winning the Championship. Once I had listened to that and interviews with the players, with the noise of the 'Gers fans in the background, I was so high I could have run the 20 miles from Loch Lomond to home. Maybe I should have paid more attention to Rangers star Marvin Andrews' motto 'Keep believing!' After that day, this became a favourite saying of Rangers fans everywhere.

A second-half goal from Novo had won Rangers the game at Easter Road, but it seemed to be to no avail as Celtic, by then, were winning 1–0. Then, in the final few minutes of their game at Fir Park, Scott McDonald equalised for Motherwell. That would have been enough to give 'Gers the title goal difference, but it got even better when the same player scored the winner within 60 seconds of his first, and the distraught Celtic players knew that they had thrown away the title, losing the League by one point. It was one of the biggest shocks of all time. Credit to 'Gers for doing their job in that final match. Celtic just didn't do theirs. When the second Motherwell goal was scored Radio Clyde commentator Peter Martin uttered the immortal words, 'The helicopter's changing direction!'

By the time we got home my other stepdaughter, Suzanne, had set up a party in her garden that was attended by the whole family. On a balmy spring evening, the 'Gers fans were in absolute heaven. I thought of my younger brother, Ian, who lived in Shawlands, and how delighted he would have been at the outcome that day. It was one of the best days of my 'Gers-supporting life, thanks to the surprise nature of the event. However, a couple of weeks later I was hit with the worst day, which came as a terrible shock. Early in June, on a lovely, sunny Saturday morning, I got a phone call from Ian's brother-in-law, Johnnie. I knew something was amiss immediately because of his hesitancy and the tone of his voice. He told me that my brother had died during the night. His daughter, Kirsty, who was not quite 10, had found him in the morning. They were awaiting the doctor, but they suspected it had been a heart attack. I couldn't believe it. He was only 50 and had always enjoyed the best of health. I told Johnnie that my wife was working and that she had my car, so I would contact her and come out to Ian's house as quickly as possible.

When I phoned my wife to tell her the terrible news, for once in my life I just couldn't speak after I had managed the initial 'Hello, it's me…' She thought that I was having a heart attack again, I think, but then, somehow, I managed to blurt it out. She told me she would be home as soon as possible. In the meantime, Denise, who lives a short walk away, came round to my house to be with me, and it was indeed a comfort to be hugged and have someone there to talk to. Once my wife had come home we drove to Shawlands right away to be with Ian's wife Janet, daughter Kirsty and other family members. The police were there because it was a sudden death, but we had to wait for the doctor and then later the undertakers. The worst part for me was when Janet wanted to see Ian's body before the undertaker came, and I offered to accompany her. I still don't know how I managed to keep myself together when we gazed upon his body, lying there as if merely sleeping. I was amazed at all the memories of Ian that suddenly flooded back, as if a dam had burst. I don't know how long I stood there looking at his body, but by the end of it I knew that I was just looking at a shell. What had made him Ian was somewhere else now. It seemed an awful long time before the official formalities had been taken care of. What can you say to the grieving family when you are feeling utterly distraught yourself? That was the longest, most painful and depressing day of my whole life.

A month prior to this, as part of the Rangers buy-a-brick scheme, I had ordered a commemorative brick with my name and the title of my first book inscribed on it. It would eventually appear on the Stefan Klos Panel at Ibrox Stadium, on the wall between my stand, the Govan Stand, and the Broomloan Stand. After Ian's death, I decided to buy a brick for him. Unfortunately, it was too late to have his brick side-by-side with mine but it was sited just round the corner with his name and the inscription 'Blues Brother'. Since Ian was cremated, there is no grave so every year, on the anniversary of his death, I take his daughter Kirsty to that part of the stadium and we lay flowers against the wall where his brick is, as hundreds of other fans seem to do for their loved ones at different times of the year. I scattered his ashes on a grassy, landscaped area in front of the modern flats at Burndyke Street, where we spent the early years of our lives. Maybe that's when Ian became a true Govanite.

Alex McLeish should have moved on in May 2005, but obviously he couldn't resist the lure of another tilt at the Champions League. That was our most successful run to date as we qualified for the knockout stages of the competition for the first time, the first Scottish club to do so. However, the League campaign was an unmitigated disaster, with the team performing poorly in a programme that ended with 'Gers finishing third in the table, our worst position since 1988.

Unfortunately, throughout the season, the spectre of the sack hung over McLeish once again as that disastrous start had seen the League title disappear well before Christmas. Even worse, 'Gers were struggling to become second in the table due to the resurgence of Hearts under new manager George Burley. I was listening to my car radio when everyone was expecting David Murray to announce the sacking of McLeish, but instead we were told that he was keeping faith with his manager. A promising Champions League campaign probably saved the manager's job – until March at least, when David Murray announced that McLeish would be leaving at the end of the season and his place taken by Paul Le Guen, former manager of Lyon, whom he guided to three consecutive French titles until he left to work for TV channel Canal+.

McLeish's finest achievement that season was in taking 'Gers to the knockout stages of the Champions League. I was at the group matches at Ibrox against Porto, Artmedia Bratislava and Inter Milan. We beat Porto 3–2 in a thrilling game, missed numerous chances and had a goalless draw against Artmedia and had a 1–1 draw in the final group game against Inter Milan. That was the third time I had seen Inter play us in European competition, and our record was two wins and a draw. Not bad against one of the European giants. After reaching the knock-out stage, McLeish's team unluckily went out 3–3 on the away-goals rule to Villarreal of Spain. It was a case of so near, yet so far. Still, it had been a campaign that had left us with some pride again.

By this time some of my friends and I had started a European game ritual by meeting up early and enjoying a pre-match curry at The Punjabi, which is located on Paisley Road West, just yards from the junction of Copland Road. It has to be booked well in advance on big match nights and is always packed to the rafters. You get the best selection of curries available anywhere in Glasgow, the Curry Capital of Britain. I can never resist their Chef's Platter for starters and a chicken jaipuri, the best I've ever tasted. Too often, though, our curry had been the most enjoyable part of our big European match experience.

It was that blank domestic season, in which Rangers could only finish third in the League, that was to cost McLeish his job at Ibrox. I was happy to see him go, though. My attitude was that anybody, no matter who, must be better than McLeish had been in his latter days in the job. How wrong can you be?

CHAPTER NINE

DEATH BY PLG, RESURRECTION BY WALTER

The first part of this chapter will be the shortest part of my book as the memory of what Le Guen did to my club is still painful. The appointment of Frenchman Paul Le Guen was announced months before the end of Alex McLeish's final season at Ibrox. The news prompted great excitement among most 'Gers fans, and the media, no less, since Le Guen was seen as one of the best young coaches in Europe, having won the French title for three consecutive seasons with Lyon before taking a sabbatical that consisted of being a pundit for French sports channel Canal+. It seemed that he was ready to get back to football management, and the challenge of reversing Rangers' fortunes was too good to turn down. I had never heard of the guy, but the same could have been said when Advocaat had been appointed. I hoped that the outcome might be the same but for a longer period of time. I was wrong on both counts.

To show the progress made by the club and its supporters in terms of combating bigotry, the fact that Le Guen would be Rangers' first Catholic manager was never an issue. Also, since the only other foreign manager of the club had been Dutchman Dick Advocaat, Le Guen was not your typical 'Gers boss. Many wondered how the new manager would cope with the club not having the millions to spend that were available in Advocaat's time, but most thought that he would bring a breath of fresh air to the club and use his Continental knowledge to attract foreign players who wouldn't cost as much as British ones might.

Le Guen brought his assistant Yves Colleau with him to Ibrox, as well as a physio and fitness coach. Later, as the season unravelled, most fans wondered just how effective these backroom guys were as the players didn't look as fit as those of Falkirk or Caley. The manager set his mark on the playing staff early when he sent Fernando Ricksen home from a pre-season tour of South Africa after a contretemps on a plane with a stewardess. Despite attending a clinic for anger management and showing a genuine contrition, Ricksen was sent away on loan, initially to former manager Dick Advocaat's new side, Zenit St Petersburg, before being sold. The fans split on this decision: one faction applauded the tough stance of the new manager; the other wondered about the sense in getting rid of our best right-back. Most, though, were willing to give the newcomer the chance to prove himself since they were already impressed by his credentials.

As Le Guen started signing new players to help turn around the fortunes of the club, some of the doubts returned. The signings were far from spectacular as most of the players were unheard of in Scotland. But, once again, the fans trusted the manager's judgement. A Chelsea youth player, Furman, was one of the first signings. He was followed by two youngsters who had been at Lyon with Le Guen. None of these cost money. Jeremy Clement, a midfielder, also came from Lyon, and he became about the only Le Guen success in the short time he played for the club. Karl Svensson, the young captain of Gothenburg, was signed for under a million, but the fans wondered if he was the finished article. Then Le Guen brought in 'keeper Lionel Letizi, who was past the flush of youth and eventually proved to be a disaster, moving back to French football in January. Eventually the new manager would plunder three players from the same club, Austria Vienna: Sionko, Papac and Sebo. Of these, only Papac would stay in the side once Le Guen had departed. In fact, striker Sebo became such a laughing stock for his inability to score that he went on to become a cult figure for some 'Gers fans. I hated this attitude shown by my fellow fans as it demeaned the club. A dud is a dud – there's no need to glorify the player.

The season got off to a winning start at Motherwell with a hard-fought 2–1 victory after 'Gers had missed a barrow-load of chances. The display, however, had the fans looking forward to the season ahead. It didn't take long for this mood to change though. Within a couple of months, points lost in terms of defeats and draws against lowly opposition, both home and away, had the fans worried. No part of the side seemed to be functioning properly, especially the central-defence, which looked weak in the air and vulnerable to even average Scottish attackers. In September I was at the club's AGM, and when it came to question time, one of the shareholders asked a question of the manager that had been obvious to the entire country before then. 'In January will you be looking for a central-defender who can actually header the ball?' Chief Executive Martin Bain whispered something in the manager's ear before he replied with the cliché, 'I'm always looking for good defenders.' I knew then that we were doomed under this man.

The only bright spot was progress in the UEFA Cup and a good sequence of results in the group stages against Livorno, Auxerre, Partizan Belgrade and Maccabi Haifa. As the autumn progressed it began to look like Rangers would be struggling to end up even third in the League as a resurgent Hearts was the only side challenging Champions Celtic. In the CIS Cup, 'Gers were even knocked out at Ibrox by First Division opposition in the shape of St Johnstone, and the 2–0 win didn't flatter the Perth side. For me, this was as bad a result as the Berwick defeat nearly 40 years before. That's how low I believed we had sunk under the Frenchman.

By now there were rumours of 'unrest' in the dressing room and of a split between the native players and the new foreigners. Whatever the truth of this, the team was going from bad to worse and the manager seemed helpless to deal with the decline. I started to get really annoyed at the constant sight of Le Guen in the dug-out looking forlorn and chewing his nails. He seemed to have no energy and worse, no answer to the ills that we could see out on the pitch. Long before Christmas he looked like a beaten man, and his side too often looked as if they had no confidence in him or his methods. Rangers were so far behind in the title race that the League was over in the eyes of just about everybody. I was fed up listening to the fans of other teams gloating at Rangers' ineptitude, and the thought that they were laughing at us made it humiliating. I will never forgive Le Guen for that. I wished him ill for the rest of his career after he went back to France and later became an international manager for Cameroon.

With the transfer window approaching, the fans hoped that Le Guen had new players in mind to bring in and stop the rot. Most were desperate for a central-defender who could cope in the air and at least head away dangerous crosses. The fans didn't get the chance to see if Le Guen would have admitted his mistakes and try to rectify them because after the first game of the new year – Motherwell again at Fir Park – the manager had gone.

Just before kick-off, everyone was stunned to hear the news that Le Guen had dropped Barry Ferguson, demoted him from being club skipper and vowed that Ferguson would never play again for Rangers as long as he was the manager. Practically every 'Gers fan would have acknowledged that Ferguson had been one of the few players to play well that season and show the necessary grit and determination to succeed at Ibrox, so the manager's decision was a hammer-blow. As with the Ricksen scenario earlier, some fans supported the manager while most didn't. Le Guen had chosen a very dangerous course of action, claiming that he had to do it as the captain had been undermining him in the dressing room. The situation, however, wasn't given time to fester. Within a day or so, after talks with Sir David Murray, Le Guen had left the club 'by mutual consent'. He landed on his feet, though, by getting the job as manager of PSG in France. Few Rangers fans, enduring the worst season in 20 years, were sorry to see the back of the Frenchman.

It was ironic that, while watching one of the worst sides in the club's history, my third book, about the brilliant 'Gers teams of the 70s, should be published during Le Guen's reign. Breedon Books published *Rangers' Treble Kings*, and that cheered me up immensely. On the other hand, remembering players like Greig, Jardine, Forsyth, Cooper and Johnstone only depressed me when I compared those guys to the ones making a mockery of the light-blue jersey at that time.

Why had the 'French Revolution' gone wrong? Most accepted that Le Guen had been the wrong man at the wrong time for the club. Until the end, though, he had enjoyed the support of the press and, in the main, the Rangers fans. Unlike at the end of the McLeish era, there had been no fan demonstrations of protest against him. Rangers had hoped that he would have been able to improve the playing staff without a tremendous outlay of money, but that proved not to be the case. In fact, Le Guen wasted £1.8 million – almost half his budget – buying Sebo, who turned out to be a disaster. If the fans had to pick one reason for Le Guen's failure, they would probably have plumped for his ineptitude in the transfer market. Only Clement had been anything remotely like a success story, while the other signings had made the fans question the manager's judgement. Another mooted factor was that many believed Le Guen had underestimated the strength of the Scottish Premier League. He must have thought that the players he had recruited had the ability and mentality to prosper in the Scottish game but was proved to be completely mistaken. Perhaps while he was the manager-in-waiting, he should have come over to Scotland to watch as many games as possible to see the standard of the game here and the type of opposition his side would be up against. It was due to his failure to do this that some fans suspected an arrogance in the man that ultimately led to his downfall.

In my 50 years of watching Rangers, Le Guen was easily the worst manager of the club. He is right up there as a 'Gers disaster with Sebo, Konterman, Prodan, Adamczuk, Capucho and Ostenstad.

As I've said before, when Rangers are faced with a managerial crisis, they turn to a tried and tested Rangers man. Walter Smith was the current Scotland manager, and he had been a success in turning around a dire international side under Berti Vogts to one performing respectably in the World Cup qualifiers. Smith immediately agreed to return to Ibrox and brought assistant Ally McCoist with him. He later added Kenny McDowell, a reserve coach at Celtic. In the meantime, while the formalities were being ironed out, Ian Durrant was caretaker manager for two matches. Unfortunately, by the time Smith took over, Rangers were out of the Scottish Cup having lost away 3–2 to Dunfermline in the third round. I watched that game on television and, at one point in the second half, Rangers were 3–0 down. In all my years of watching the 'Gers, I couldn't remember such a side beating us so easily. It was embarrassing and I was angry. That's what Le Guen had done to us. Kris Boyd pulled two goals back and we should have equalised, but we missed various chances. I was convinced that if we had managed a replay we would have beaten them at Ibrox, and with Walter Smith then in charge who knows what might have happened?

When Smith started, he had no trophies to play for. His immediate target was to make it to second place in the League and get a Champions League qualifying place – which he eventually did. He restored the captaincy to Barry Ferguson and started at Ibrox with a brilliant 5–1 win over Dundee United. The home fans showed their appreciation of his return by unfurling a banner that read, 'Walter and Ally: when duty called, you came.' That said it all. The fans believed they had two real Rangers men in charge again who actually cared about their club. Even if Le Guen couldn't see it, Walter could – so he instantly brought in two experienced central defenders who could head the ball, David Weir and Ugo Ehiogu. What a transformation. Over the remaining months of that season, 'Gers had the best defensive record in the League. We started being hard to beat, and the taunts from the fans of other clubs could be heard no longer. I will always be grateful to Smith for that.

Season 2007–08 was Smith's first full season and was one of the most enjoyable, momentous, but ultimately disappointing, in the history of Rangers. The squad was strengthened by the likes of Kevin Thomson, Lee McCulloch, Carlos Cuellar, Steven Whittaker, Daniel Cousin, Jean-Claude Darcheville, Steven Naismith, Kirk Broadfoot, Neil Alexander and, on loan, Steven Davis. These players would almost help Rangers to a quadruple while also contesting the UEFA Cup Final in Manchester in May 2008.

Walter's first task was to gain entry to the Champions League, and he did this by steering the side past Zeta from Montenegro and then Red Star Belgrade in the final qualifying round. Rangers' reward was a group that consisted of Stuttgart, Lyon and

Barcelona. 'Gers got off to a great start with a 2–1 home win against Stuttgart. For once, the brilliant Punjabi curries weren't the highlight of the evening for my pals and me. I was really proud of the team, coming from behind in the second half to win that match. It was a foretaste of the spirit in the club that would see the side go far that season. The next game was away to Lyon, and I could barely believe my eyes, watching it on live television, when Rangers thrashed the French champions 3–0 on their own patch. We started to believe then that we might get to the knock-out stage again.

As luck would have it, by the time 'Gers played Barca in the next game at Ibrox, having beaten Celtic 3–0 just days before at Ibrox, I was in Cyprus. I had booked a special surprise holiday for my wife's 60th birthday months before, so you can imagine how sick I was when the fixtures were arranged and I discovered that I would be abroad when we played Celtic and then the Spaniards the following Tuesday. Our first ever game against Barcelona and I was going to miss it. My son-in-law, Robert, to whom I had given my season ticket, phoned me to tell me that 'Gers were winning 3–0, so that added to my feeling of well-being as I walked up from the beach. For the Barca game, we found a bar that was showing the big European games. Unfortunately, the place was divided into three groups, as the 'Gers game was on one screen while Arsenal's and Manchester's were on other screens. Due to this, no sound was coming from any of the screens but the normal pub music was blaring out through all the speakers – not the best way to watch a big game.

My wife and I sat at the bar and watched one of the most negative 'Gers' displays I had ever seen. By now Walter was regularly using his cautious 4–5–1 formation and never more so than against the Catalan giants. Even my wife, who has no interest in football, asked me 'Why do Rangers players keep punting the ball up to that guy up front by himself? Why are 'Gers players nowhere near a Barcelona one when they get a pass?' Rangers were lucky to get to half-time with the score at 0–0, and so boring and embarrassing was the game that I couldn't take it any longer. We left to go to a different bar with no screens, and I didn't find out the final score until the next day. The draw was a pleasant surprise. It wouldn't have amazed me if Barca had won three or 4–0.

Despite my feelings about Rangers' display, that match turned out to be the high point of our campaign as we had a total of seven points out of a possible nine. However, we lost the final three matches and went out of the Champions League and into the UEFA Cup knockout stages. The Lyon match at Ibrox was a huge disappointment to me as 'Gers only needed a draw to progress to the last 16 of the tournament, and they lost 3–0. The French side started the match better than Rangers and could have scored before they did, but when they eventually opened the scoring it was the result of poor goalkeeping by Allan McGregor. Going in at half-time 1–0 down we still realised that one goal would be enough to put us through.

In the second half, a brilliant 'Gers move ended with the ball being passed into the six-yard box, where Darcheville arrived and had only to tap it into the net from a couple of yards out. Somehow the Frenchman managed to put it over the bar. At that point I felt it wasn't going to be our day. Later on, the brilliant young striker, Benzema, finished us off with two late goals. We hadn't deserved to lose by that margin, so it was a sore one to take, but at least we were still in Europe.

The rest of that season domestically was a real roller-coaster of a journey. In the League, the lead switched between 'Gers and Celtic, but in January Rangers were seven points ahead and looking good for the title. A fixture pile-up, mainly due to our success, eventually cost us the treble.

The first trophy was won in March when 'Gers beat Dundee United in the League Cup Final. What a game that was. Twice Rangers went behind and, thanks to substitute, Kris Boyd, twice came back to equalise. With things looking bleak and only five minutes left of regulation time, Boyd equalised to give us a lifeline. In extra-time, United struck first and it took another Boyd goal seven minutes from the end to send the game into a penalty shoot-out. As befits the Boyd story, it was he who scored the winning penalty to win the Cup. That would not be the end of Kris Boyd deciding the destination of Cups that season.

Meanwhile, in the chase for the League title, Rangers kept their lead, although at various times in the second half of that season Celtic had games in hand and both the final Old Firm matches were to be played at Parkhead. This was due to the fact that the Old Firm match in January was postponed at Celtic's request, following the death of Motherwell player Phil O'Donnell, who had played for Celtic 10 years previously. I was disappointed by that postponement because, had the game gone ahead, Celtic would have been minus their two most creative and dangerous players while Rangers would have been at full strength. At that point 'Gers were playing really well while Celtic were suffering from poor form. All in all, I expected have to beaten them if that January game had gone ahead.

For me, there were two crucial games that ultimately cost Rangers the Championship. One was in the first of the two Old Firm games to be played at Parkhead. Rangers were playing well, but in the second half the wheels came off when Carlos Cuellar, who would be voted Player of the Year weeks later by the sportswriters, was sent off and then 'keeper Allan McGregor had to be subbed when he was injured with less than 15 minutes to go. Stand-in 'keeper Neil Alexander had the daunting task of coming on in that frenzied game as 'Gers tried to hold out for a draw that would probably have won the title at the end of the season. It looked like they would succeed when, in the second of three minutes of injury time, Celtic scored. A punt from deep by Caldwell towards the back post saw Scott McDonald give Whittaker a little nudge in the back as the ball was in flight. This meant that McDonald was able to head the ball into the six-yard box where his strike partner, Jan Vennigoor of Hesselink, had an easy header past Alexander on his line. Watching this live on television left me gutted because I knew that it had given Celtic a lifeline. Celtic also won the second of those games, rather unjustly in my opinion, and suddenly it was neck-and-neck, with Rangers up against it due to the fixture pile-up thanks to their UEFA Cup run to the Final and making it to the Scottish Cup Final.

The club tried to have the season extended, but the authorities merely made a token gesture, which they could hardly avoid as it would have meant playing three games in four days if they hadn't. Meanwhile a desperate Celtic saw their Chief Executive, Peter Lawwell, bleat about 'sporting integrity' as they strove to give Rangers no leeway whatsoever. The lack of cooperation by the football authorities meant that Rangers couldn't even get the weekend before the UEFA Cup Final off, unlike their Russian opponents. That Saturday saw us have a titanic and controversial struggle with Dundee United, which we eventually won 3–1 in an Ibrox atmosphere that I have rarely felt as tense.

Before that game I went into the Rangers/JJB shop at Ibrox to see what souvenir items and leisure wear it was selling with the UEFA Cup Final the following week. A cheap-looking t-shirt (that wasn't cheap) and scarf was all that was on offer. Meanwhile the street traders across from the Main Stand were doing a roaring trade in innovative tops, scarves, hats, badges, the lot. As I said at the following AGM to Sir David Murray, maybe 'Gers should have teamed up with the street traders rather than JJB Sports.

We played Zenit St Petersburg in the Final the following Wednesday, and when we came back we had to play Motherwell at Fir Park on the Saturday. That was the other crucial game that lost us the Championship. I was happy enough watching this live broadcast with Rangers 1–0 up, and in the second half Daniel Cousin was right through on goal. All he had to do was put it in the net and we would have had the three points. Instead, he missed and after that Motherwell equalised. Those two spilled points turned the advantage over to Celtic. Now we had to play St Mirren away on the Tuesday evening followed by Aberdeen away on the Thursday evening with the Scottish Cup Final on the Saturday against Queen of the South. That meant in the final 10 days of a 69-match season, Rangers players were being asked to play five games – three away and two at neutral venues.

It was never going to happen. We beat St Mirren 4–0, resulting in a final evening when the Championship would be decided. Celtic had to win at Tannadice to make sure of the title, but 'Gers had to win at Pittodrie to have a glimmer of a chance. Rangers and Celtic were both drawing 0–0 at half-time, so it seemed that there was hope of success. Two second-half goals by Aberdeen sank 'Gers' hopes but it wouldn't have mattered anyway as Celtic won 1–0. I remember feeling cheated out of that Championship. Smith and his team had deserved to win it, but fate was against them – not to mention everybody else in Scottish football.

Two days later the team had to pick itself up for the Scottish Cup Final. I can't remember any team having had to play a crunch game less than 48 hours before the showcase match at the end of the season. The one saving grace was that it was 'only' a First Division side. I watched from my usual debenture seat at Hampden and was very relaxed at half-time since Rangers had gone in 2–0 up, thanks to goals from Boyd and Beasley, who had been out injured since November. Then, early in the second half, like the team I was reeling when Queens pulled the two goals back. Now we really were in a game. I could see the season ending even more disastrously at that point with a humiliating defeat by a team from a lower division. Then, with 18 minutes left, a Kris Boyd header proved to be the match-winner. He had won us a Cup again. At least we could celebrate another Cup victory when the final whistle went, but it didn't really make up for losing the Championship and the UEFA Cup in the previous 10 days.

CHAPTER TEN

THE ROAD TO MANCHESTER

Our march to the 2008 UEFA Cup Final in Manchester was Rangers' greatest European achievement since appearing in the Final of the Cup-Winners' Cup in 1972 in Barcelona. As had happened 36 years before, I was at every game at Ibrox, but this time I actually managed to get to see the Final in person.

Walter Smith, all the way through this tournament, stuck to his tried-and-tested 4–5–1 system, which was designed not to lose a match rather than win it. Perhaps it was no surprise that of the four matches at Ibrox, three were 0–0 draws, with our best display coming in a 2–0 win against Werder Bremen. Also, in every round, we had the disadvantage of playing the first leg at home. Our first game was in the round of 32 against Panathinaikos at Ibrox. As usual, my friends and I had a great pre-match curry at The Punjabi, but the fare on offer later at Ibrox wasn't as tasty. We should have beaten the Greeks comfortably, but Nacho Novo, in particular, missed three or four really good chances to take a lead to Greece. I thought we would be out of the tournament.

When the return in Greece was being shown live on TV, I was driving and listening to it on the radio. Typically, Rangers lost an early goal and I was convinced that that was it. An hour later, when I got into my car to return home, I switched on the radio and was quite happy that at least 'Gers were still only losing by that solitary goal. Then, as I was driving across the Erskine Bridge, Nacho Novo scored the goal that would put 'Gers through on the away-goals rule. I nearly crashed the car into the River Clyde, so shocked was I. We hung on and made it to the round of 16, and since we were up against the German cracks,

Werder Bremen, I assumed that this would be the end of our European adventure for that season.

When we played Werder Bremen at Ibrox in the first leg at the start of March, for once the match outdid the curry. Amazingly, Rangers beat Bremen by 2–0, mainly thanks to the dire display of their 'keeper. Having said that, Rangers did play well and could have won by another couple of goals. The bonus was that we hadn't lost a goal at home. I watched the second leg on television, and what a nail-biter that was. Rangers defended well but still needed 'keeper McGregor to bail them out quite a few times as the Germans pounded us. A goal late in the second half put the team under extreme pressure until the final whistle, but 'Gers held out to qualify for the quarter-finals where we were to meet the Portuguese side Sporting Lisbon with the first leg, again, at home.

This time it was back to watching a 0–0 draw, but the team didn't create the chances that we had against the Greeks in the earlier round. It was a far cry from the previous game I had attended against Lisbon in 1971, when 'Gers had won 3–2 in a thrilling game that eventually saw us win the Cup-Winners' Cup in Barcelona. Again, I was convinced that we were out, but again, I was wrong.

I watched the second leg of the Lisbon tie on television and experienced the most pleasurable performance of our campaign to date. Against dangerous opponents, Rangers played well, none more so than 'keeper Allan McGregor. Then, in the second half we got the first goal, a vital away goal, and that made me start to believe we might just eliminate the Portuguese team. A quick break out of defence found Steve Davis running towards the Sporting goal before sliding his pass across into the box for Darcheville to net. Near the end, 'Gers sealed their win with a brilliant solo effort from Steven Whittaker, dribbling past various opponents for half the length of the park, belying the fact that he is actually a right-back.

Next up it was Fiorentina at Ibrox. The Italian club had denied 'Gers its first European trophy all those years before when I had watched the first leg live at my gran's, a few hundred yards away from Ibrox Stadium. Now, here I was 47 years later, watching another first leg against Fiorentina, this time from inside the stadium. To be truthful, this game provided none of the fireworks of that match in the early 60s, and it ended in another 0–0 draw. This time, however, I wasn't writing Rangers off. I had at least learned something from that European campaign.

A week later I sat down to watch the second leg from Florence and was as nervous as I have ever been while watching a Rangers game. Talk about role reversal! This time it was the Italian side doing all the attacking while Rangers defended in depth with true-blue, backs-to-the-wall determination. Rangers barely had an attack while the home side pummelled us relentlessly. Despite brilliant performances from Weir and Cuellar in central defence, and from stand-in 'keeper Neil Alexander, it seemed to be only a matter of time before Fiorentina scored, necessitating an away goal from us to progress to the Final. It never came.

The match went into extra-time, and by then I knew that Rangers' best hope lay in forcing the conclusion to a penalty shoot-out. Our task was made harder in extra-time when Daniel Cousin got himself sent off for a second yellow-card offence, thus missing the Final. However, at that stage it didn't look like 'Gers were going to make it to the Final. With my nerves virtually in shreds, Rangers got to the end of extra-time with our goal intact. Now all I had to worry about were those penalty-kicks. When Barry Ferguson missed our first, not for the first time that season, I thought that we had had it. However, Alexander saved an Italian shot and Vieri ballooned their last attempt over the bar. Now it all came down to Novo taking his kick. If he scored, we would be on our way to the Final. When the wee Spaniard sent his shot into the net, he and the rest of the 'Gers players went crazy. So did I, jumping around the room like a madman. It was one of the greatest feelings.

In 1967, losing in Nuremberg against Bayern had been harder to take because Celtic had won in Lisbon the week before. 'Gers fans have never heard the end of that triumph in Lisbon. Equally, since Celtic's losing appearance in the 2003 UEFA Cup Final in Seville, the Hoops supporters haven't shut up about it. Now, having equalled that feat by reaching the UEFA Cup Final in Manchester, we had a riposte for Celtic fans trying to gloat. I was so proud of the players for achieving that.

Unlike Barcelona 36 years earlier, I was hopeful of getting to see this European Final in Manchester. For years, as well as being a season-ticket holder, I had been a member of the Rangers Continuous Credit Card scheme that meant that the club could charge my account when a non-season ticket match was involved and I would get a ticket for the said match. I would also have priority for a ticket for games not played at Ibrox. Despite this, getting a ticket for the UEFA Final was not a certainty as there were thousands of Rangers fans in this scheme and obviously only a limited number of tickets. A ballot was to be held, and every day for over a week I waited anxiously for the post to see if my ticket would arrive. It didn't.

We decided the week before the match to hold a UEFA Cup Final party at our house, inviting all of the family round to share food, drink and the excitement of the Final. Thankfully, before we could buy any of the necessary booze and food, I had a phone call on the Monday evening, two days before the game. A woman informed me that she was from Rangers' ticket office, that they had had some extra tickets given to them and that I was next in line to get one. Did I want this ticket? The answer was obvious. When I heard that the price was £90 I realised that it must be a great seat in the stadium, too. However, I was told that, due to time constraints, the tickets would be in Manchester and that I would have to pick mine up at the Midland Hotel after 10 o'clock on the day of the match. No problem.

Then my initial joy turned to suspicion. I started to wonder if this call had been a hoax. It seemed strange that the ticket was to be picked up in Manchester. Just in case, I called my credit card company to check that Rangers had actually taken the money from my account, and when I was told that they had, I accepted that it was genuine. I was going to be at Rangers' biggest game in 36 years! The question was how was I going to get there?

My son-in-law, John, told me that someone he knew in Erskine was a member of the Rangers Supporters' Club and that it was running a bus to Manchester. He gave me the guy's address, which was near my house. When I spoke to him, though, he told me that the bus was already full. He suggested the Bishopton Supporters' bus, but I discovered that this was full too. I had no alternative but to drive down to Manchester. In the meantime, my other son-in-law, Robert, who lives near me, told me that he fancied going down for the match just to soak up the atmosphere and be in the city even though he didn't have a ticket. He decided to come with me, and we shared the driving down to England.

Days before the game the newspapers were full of stories about how all the accommodation anywhere near Manchester was full to capacity with 'Gers fans coming from all over the world. Even Blackpool was bursting with fans. I thought that I was being really clever when I went onto the Internet and succeeded in booking one night, bed and breakfast for us at a hotel in Lytham St Annes. The plan was to arrive there on the morning of the game, get a bus into Blackpool and the train from there to Piccadilly station, Manchester. It was simple in theory and perfect for going to the match, but it was a different story afterwards.

The night before the Final I went to bed about 9 o'clock to get a few hours sleep before getting up at three in the morning to pick up my son-in-law and drive to Lytham. I drove the first half of the trip before Robert took over for the remainder. Once we had crossed the border and were on the motorway, what amazed me was the unbelievable number of cars transporting Rangers fans to the match. How did I know the cars were full of 'Gers fans? Every one of them seemed to be flying a Union Jack and/or a Saltire from its windows. That convoy of cars was like a friendly invading army. We stopped at Southwaite services and there were hundreds of 'Gers fans there, even at that unearthly hour of the morning. What amazed me most was the evidence of the thousands of Rangers fans who must have stopped there before us. The car park was littered with debris that was going to be an unwelcome sight for the poor soul whose job it was to keep the place clean and tidy.

We arrived at our hotel around 7.30am and knocked on the door. The lovely landlady looked as if she had just got out of bed but was very welcoming, told us where our room was, gave us keys to get in after the match and said just to let ourselves in whenever we got back from Manchester. We parked the car in her tiny car park and set off for the bus to Blackpool. We reached the station in time for the 8.45 train, and the place was already awash with Rangers fans waiting to go to Manchester. Trains were leaving every half hour, and I didn't think we'd get on that first one but we did and we even got a seat. A husband and wife draped in Rangers' gear sat beside us and, once chatting to them, we discovered that they came from Bishopton – three miles away from our home.

After a couple of stops, the train could take no more 'Gers fans, and I must admit that I felt sorry for the would-be passengers, who were probably daily commuters, as they stood on each platform, unable to board the train. On a beautiful sunny morning, the trip was as enjoyable as any train journey I have ever been on. When we arrived at Manchester, my first task was to pick up my ticket at the Midland Hotel. When I got there, dozens of Rangers fans seemed to be there for the same reason. I certainly felt a whole lot better once I had my ticket for the match inside my pocket.

When we emerged from the hotel, we noticed that, just across the road, there was one of the 'fan zones', specially created for 'Gers supporters without tickets to see the game on huge screens. We decided to check it out. This was the one in Albert Square, just in front of the Town Hall. Before that, right on the corner, there was a nice little café doing a roaring trade, and, since we were starving, we went inside first to get a great breakfast served up to us.

The square had been cordoned off by the police, with narrow entrances guarded by officers who were checking the bags or boxes that were being carried in by the fans. Beer was allowed if it was in cans but not bottles. By the time we returned in the afternoon, this policy had obviously been abandoned by the police and fans were walking about with bottles of beer. We walked through the Square while some fans kicked a ball about and others drank. Even that early a few looked the worse for wear. I shuddered to think what they would be like eight hours later.

Since Robert was going to be watching the game from one of these fan zones, we decided to check out the other one nearby, in Piccadilly. As soon as we walked into this area, Robert told me he had a bad feeling about it. It seemed more restricted than the one we'd just been in, had a greater number of fans in it and more seemed to be under the influence already. As we left, Robert had already decided that he would watch the match from the zone in Albert Square, which turned out to be lucky because it was at Piccadilly that the trouble erupted when its screens broke down just as the game was about to begin.

After that we looked for a pub to get a drink, but every place we tried was full-to-bursting with thirsty Rangers fans. We abandoned this idea and decided to walk to the City of Manchester Stadium to check out the journey that I would be making later that day. It was sunny and hot, and with every step we took towards the venue, the more desperate we became for a drink. Unfortunately, our route, using a map, took us nowhere near any pubs until we actually reached the stadium. Once at the stadium we discovered that it had been cordoned off by the police and we couldn't get really close to it, but at least I knew where I was going now.

We had a welcome pint in a wee pub right beside the stadium and then had to walk back to the train station as Robert had arranged to meet his brother, Tam, who was coming from Chester. Once we met up, it was into a pub nearby to get a drink. That was easier said than done by that time. Every pub seemed to be full to capacity with Rangers fans singing a medley of 'Gers songs. One drink was enough before we got out into the sunshine, looking for a place to buy beer before going back to the fan zone. As we walked along, I couldn't believe the number of places that had signs up saying that they were out of beer. It was then that it dawned on me that the city and its traders had no idea of what was going to be needed to satisfy what was later estimated to be 200,000 Rangers fans spending a day in their city. It was the same with the train authorities and police.

Once inside Albert Square we got a pint from the beer tent, and then Robert's brother decided that he would leave and go searching for a place to buy some cans of beer. About an hour later the poor soul returned with the beer and some sandwiches. He had had to walk about a mile to get a place that was still selling alcohol. When he returned he was like an intrepid explorer come back with goodies from another world. By now the square was really filling up, and all the fans seemed to be in a great mood, chatting, laughing and singing. I saw one guy in a wheelchair, although I had no idea how he was going to be able to see the screens.

Just after 6 o'clock I told Robert that I was going to head off to the stadium. We arranged to meet at the train station as soon as I could get there after the game. Trying to get out of that square, though, was easier said than done, so dense was the throng of people. I had to squeeze my way past fans to get to the edge of the fan zone and then out on to the street. At one point I had the terrible thought that there was I with a £90-ticket in my pocket but I would have to watch the match on the screens because it seemed impossible to make my way through the crowd. Thankfully, I gradually made progress and eventually emerged on to the street, able, at last, to head for the stadium.

It was still warm and sunny as I started the 20-minute walk to the stadium. It was a great feeling, joining the thousands of other 'Gers fans in their blue tops, scarves and flags, heading for our biggest game in 36 years. After nearly 50 years of going to Rangers matches I was going to see the team play in the Final of a European competition. When I reached the stadium the Manchester police had made life difficult by not allowing fans to enter through the perimeter fence at the entrances nearest the main road. We were all funnelled to entrances further along, where huge numbers of fans were congested as the police checked their tickets before allowing them through. I was cursing inwardly at such incompetence.

Once in, I had to double-back as I was well away from the stand entrance that I had to go to in order to get into the Main Stand. I was getting really excited by now and could hardly wait to get inside the City of Manchester stadium but I made sure I took plenty of photos first of all. By the time I was inside, and up in the top tier of the stand, I was so hungry that I just had to join the long queues waiting to buy burgers and drinks. I ate underneath the stand before going up the steps to emerge into the stadium and take my seat. And what a seat it was! I found myself right on the halfway line, halfway towards the rear of the top tier and in the row of seats right behind the foreign press with their television monitors beside them. My first thought was that this could be handy to review replays during the game, but I never did because I was usually so excited or distraught that I forgot to look down at the monitors at the time.

I surveyed the scene before me and it was an amazing sight. Three quarters, if not more, of the stadium was filled with Rangers fans, a sea of blue and Union Jacks. To my right, from behind the goal to just past the corner flag opposite me was the small section of Russian fans who added to the colour. It was great to see 'Gers' banners showing that fans had come from all over the world to be there. It had been an unforgettable day…and then the match started.

For one of the few times in my 'Gers-watching life I went into a match not really believing that we could win it. I had decided that the Russians were better players than us and had a better team. I thought that, for us to succeed, they would have to have an off-day, we would have to be at our best and we would have to have any luck that was going. None of it happened. I suspected as much when I heard the Rangers team announced over the tannoy. I had been hoping that our cautious manager might actually have a go now that we were in the Final, but it was not to be. He played *two* right-backs in the side, with one of them, Whittaker, in left midfield. He played defensive midfielder Hemdani, who had hardly played all season, and one man up front, Darcheville, who wasn't even our top goalscorer. Due to this line-up, I felt deflated even before the match had begun.

The game itself was instantly forgotten so little happened in it, especially from a 'Gers attacking viewpoint. I have the DVD of it, but two years later, I still can't bring myself to watch it again. We rarely threatened in that first half, but when we got to half-time at 0–0 I consoled myself with the fact that maybe, with a bit of luck, we could snatch a goal and hang on. We did have a good 10-minute spell in the second half when we had a couple of chances and a penalty claim, but we fizzled out after that. By then, I was looking for a penalty shoot-out as our only way of succeeding, something we had done three times already that season.

Then, with only 18 minutes left, the Russians cut us open and scored. As soon as that happened I knew we had blown it. The manager put Novo on and minutes later McCulloch, and we were all crying out for Boyd to be brought on. Our top goalscorer eventually appeared with only four minutes left. Just after that, Novo missed a good chance to equalise before the Russians raced up the park and killed us off with a second goal. With a minute to go I left to make sure I got to the train station before thousands of others did. It was a dejected walk once I had left the stadium.

I didn't know what to expect as I neared the station. I phoned Robert on my mobile and he told me he was inside the station already and where to meet him. I imagined a long queue of fans outside but as I arrived there just seemed to be hundreds of them walking towards the station entrance, where policemen were on duty. Then, when I was a few yards away, the shutters were pulled down at the glass doors and I could hear policemen tell fans that the station had been shut temporarily because there were too many people inside. Instead of getting the fans outside to form an orderly queue, the policemen on duty just let this crowd grow larger and larger in what was a pretty confined space. I could feel the pressure of the crowd building up behind me and decided it would be safer to move across to be at the side of this area rather than right in front of the doors. I just couldn't believe that the police were allowing this to happen. Even more unbelievably, after about 10 minutes of this, when the shutters went up and the doors opened, the policemen just stood aside and left the fans rush towards the narrow entrances. I could hear women at the front screaming in terror as a crush developed. Thankfully, it was alleviated, no thanks to the Manchester police, and eventually I got into the station and met up with Robert.

Getting into the station turned out to be the least of our problems. After another congested area was negotiated, we found ourselves in a queue, four abreast, that stretched hundreds of yards into the distance, up two escalators that had been stopped so that fans could stand on them as part of the queue. Coming to Manchester from Blackpool, there had been a train every half hour. We had discussed this throughout the day and come to the conclusion that the train company, knowing how many return tickets had been sold that day, would put on extra trains. Not a bit of it. After hours of standing in this queue it was obvious that only the scheduled trains were running – one every hour. In effect what happened was that a train filled up, took the fans to Blackpool, turned around to come back to Manchester and fill up again. We stood in that queue from around 10.30 until 5.30 the next morning. It was while we were standing in this queue that we heard other fans say that there had been trouble in the streets after the game. Neither of us had seen or heard anything, so that was quite a shock.

Maybe it was lucky for the railway authorities that 'Gers had lost because the fans inside the station were too tired and too dispirited to cause any trouble while waiting for all those hours. Nevertheless, at around one in the morning, about a dozen policemen in riot gear suddenly arrived and positioned themselves across the queue, dividing it in half for some reason. I suspect that they had been called in just in case the by-now really frustrated fans decided to take it out on the station. Eventually we got our train to Blackpool and thought that we would just get a taxi at the station to take us to Lytham. When we arrived, there was just one taxi waiting to pick up fans. Do the taxi drivers of Blackpool not need the work? Are they too rich? Or too lazy? We must have walked the Golden Mile before we were able to stop a taxi.

We got to our bed around 7.30 and set the alarm for 11 o'clock as we wanted to get our breakfast before having to vacate the premises at midday. Falling asleep immediately was easy – we were so tired and the adrenalin of a European Final had long since deserted us.

Manchester was a great adventure. The whole day leading up to the game had been so enjoyable, helped by the fact that it had been warm and sunny. It was gratifying to see thousands upon thousands of Rangers fans walking the streets decked out in 'Gers colours, looking as happy as I've ever seen the supporters. I felt that we were all in this together. What a pity that our memories of the occasion have been scarred by the aftermath, when a few hundred out of the estimated 200,000 'Gers fans fought with police in the streets. At least now you don't hear Celtic fans banging on about Seville as much as you had prior to Rangers' own UEFA Cup Final.

CHAPTER ELEVEN

53 AND COUNTING

After the disappointments of season 2007–08, it was barely conceivable that the following one could start in such a traumatic manner. Firstly, in a Champions League qualifier, Rangers were eliminated by Lithuanian side Kaunas. After a 0–0 draw at Ibrox, in which 'Gers missed three or four great chances, 'Gers went ahead in the away game, getting the vital away goal. Near half-time, the home side equalised with a 30-yard thunderbolt – a shot in a million. Nevertheless, Rangers would still go through if the score stayed the same. 10 minutes from time, Rangers missed a great chance to seal the tie and, as you might expect, minutes from the end, Kaunas scored a second and we were not just out of the Champions League but out of Europe completely. Even worse, within a week our star defender, Carlos Cuellar, had been transferred to Aston Villa for £8 million.

Along with practically every other Rangers fan, I was horrified and disgusted. The fans started lobbying for something to be done and for players to be bought. A protest movement quickly sprang up. Whether it had any effect, who knows? However, the manager was allowed to strengthen his squad, but many reasoned that it was too late. He bought Steve Davis, Pedro Mendes, Kyle Lafferty, Madjid Bougherra and Maurice Edu. He had previously brought Kenny Miller back to Ibrox to the annoyance of many 'Gers fans because he had played for Celtic for a season.

These signings, on the whole, paid off as Rangers went on to win the League and Cup double by the end of that season. In a great display at Parkhead in the first Old Firm game of the season, 'Gers won 4–2, and until the final minute had been 4–1 up on their bitter rivals. I didn't know what had pleased me more: the tremendous long-range goal by Mendes or the two goals scored by former Celt, Kenny Miller. When Celtic won the next one at Ibrox in December, thanks to a Scott McDonald goal, it put them seven points ahead of Rangers and things were looking bleak. A 0–0 draw at Parkhead later suited us as, by that time, the sides were neck-and-neck and we had the final Old Firm game to look forward to at Ibrox.

Thanks to a Steve Davis goal, Rangers won that match, and now we were in the driving seat with a two-point lead and only three games left. On the Wednesday I watched the live broadcast of our game against Hibs at Easter Road. We played well but went behind to a goal by ex-Celt Derek Riordan. However, we fought back and created chance after chance, but good defending, goalkeeping, bad luck and officiating prevented us from equalising. At one point near the end I was convinced we had equalised, but the ref and linesman decided that the ball hadn't crossed the goalline, although the television pictures suggested it was more of a goal than not. Eventually we did equalise but had dropped two vital points. If Celtic won at Easter Road in their next game, they would be in poll position to win the title. It was like the previous season all over again.

On the Saturday Rangers beat Aberdeen at Ibrox in a nervy game. The next day, I was driving my car while Celtic were playing Hibs. I hate listening to games on the radio so, near the end, I switched it on to find out what the score was. I was relieved to hear that Celtic were only drawing, but I just had to listen to the final few nail-biting minutes as I drove, hoping that they wouldn't score. They didn't, and that meant that Rangers went into the final game at Tannadice knowing that if they won, they would be the League Champions. I could have finished the rest of that journey without my car – I was flying.

When it came down to the final Sunday of the season, I was as tense as I have ever been when I sat down to watch the game on live television. At least we knew that the destiny of the title was in our own hands. I wish I'd known prior to this that Rangers were about to produce their best display at Tannadice, our bogey ground, in years. Within five minutes Lafferty had given us the lead, and that settled the nerves both on the park and in my stomach. Before half-time Pedro Mendes scored a beauty from 20 yards out and I really started to believe that we would win the title. A third from Boyd in the second half sealed our win and, with Celtic only drawing against Hearts at Parkhead, we knew the Championship was coming home. Watching that win was one of the best days since I had started going to Rangers' games.

A week later I was in my usual seat at Hampden to watch the Scottish Cup Final against Falkirk, who had been toiling at the foot of the League all season. I should have known it would have been an anticlimax after that Tannadice experience. It seemed as if the 'Gers players just couldn't lift themselves for the occasion. Rangers played badly and Falkirk out-played us in the first half. Then Novo came on as a substitute at half-time and, within a minute his brilliant long-range shot won the Cup and secured the double for the club. Seeing the players parade around Hampden with the Cup made it the perfect end to a difficult season.

I thought back to January, when the news of Rangers' financial troubles was the sensation of the back pages of the newspapers. The club needed money badly and the debt to the bank had soared. Rangers even accepted an offer of over £3 million from Birmingham for our top striker, Kris Boyd, but he refused to go. While this was still in doubt, banners appeared with the message 'No Boyd = No goals = No title'. How accurate that would have been if the player had accepted Birmingham's offer of a contract.

Winning the title allowed Rangers direct entry to the following season's Champions League group stages, with the millions that this would bring the club in extra revenue, but the financial situation was still perilous. The manager was unable to buy players to freshen up his squad, and eight or nine players were allowed to leave the club or were transferred if money could be received for them. The running costs of Rangers were being reduced while the majority shareholder, Sir David Murray, sought a buyer for his shares. Most Rangers fans, like me, shuddered at the thought of where the club would have been without that extra £10–15 million from the Champions League.

The biggest disappointment of season 2009–10 was our dreadful performance in the Champions League. Having drawn Seville, Stuttgart and unknown Romanians Unirea Urziceni, most of us fancied our chances of progressing to the knock-out stage. It was not to be. We drew two of the away games and lost by a goal in Seville, but we lost all our home matches – two of these by the same scoreline, 4–1. I think it was our most humiliating campaign ever – and, in my opinion, the club's crippling debt wasn't the major factor in it either. It was a horrible experience that all 'Gers fans would rather just forget about.

That September I was back in Cyprus again to attend the wedding of my daughter, Heather, and fiancé, Donald. This time, though, I didn't miss any big Rangers games. It was an international week and we were only there, in Pafos, for four days anyway. As it turned out, I flew into Glasgow on the Saturday morning in time to drive to Hampden to watch Scotland beat Lithuania 2–0 in a World Cup qualifying game, with the Holland match being played the following Wednesday. As the entire country had probably expected, we lost 1–0 in that game and were out of the World Cup.

At least, for Rangers, things went better domestically. We beat Celtic twice at Ibrox and drew at Parkhead in January, all of which helped us build up a 13 point lead in the League by the middle of March. The first trophy of the season was also won in that month when we lifted the League Cup for the 26th time. Playing against St Mirren, Rangers went into that Final as hot favourites, despite being without their top 'keeper, McGregor, and top defender, Bougherra. They also lost top midfielder Davis at half-time to the illness that had almost prevented him from starting the game.

If I had thought that these absences were a disadvantage, the second half produced a couple more when referee Thomson sent off Kevin Thomson early on and young Danny Wilson 20 minutes from the end. With only nine men it looked bleak for Rangers, but seven minutes from time a great breakaway by Naismith ended with a headed goal by Kenny Miller to win the Cup. I had never seen the renowned 'Rangers spirit' better illustrated. When Miller scored we all went crazy in the Main Stand at Hampden. There might have been no cloud of dust kicked up by the celebrations as there had been in the 1966 Scottish Cup Final when Johansen scored, but the feeling was just as ecstatic. Exactly 46 years previously I had attended my first Rangers' League Cup Final when we beat Morton 5–0, but I have seldom been as proud of a Rangers side as I was of our nine men in beating St Mirren.

Towards the end of the season there were two great moments for the Rangers fans. Firstly in April, following a humiliating 4–0 defeat by St Mirren in Paisley, Celtic sacked their manager, Tony Mowbray, more or less admitting defeat in the race for the title. Neil Lennon was made caretaker manager, and a month later he was in charge when Celtic sensationally got knocked out of the semi-final of the Scottish Cup by lower division side Ross County. In my opinion this was the biggest upset in the history of the Scottish Cup – far worse than 'Gers' defeat at Berwick. That Saturday it would have taken sucking a lemon, to get the smile off my face.

The Championship was finally clinched before the end of April with three games to spare, including the final Old Firm match of the season – quite a difference from the previous final-day deciders. Rangers beat Hibs 1–0 at Easter Road, and the 53rd League title was confirmed. It was the first time that Rangers had won consecutive Championships since the Advocaat era 10 years previously. It was a real luxury for players and fans to go into the final Old Firm match of the season already knowing that the title had been won. Unfortunately 'Gers lost 2–1 in a hard-fought game and, in truth, should have come away with at least a draw. Still, for once I, and most of the Rangers fans, didn't care…at least not much! Between 2000 and 2010, a decade that Celtic fans consider to have been a great one for their club, in which they 'dominated' Scottish football, the haul of League Championships reads Celtic 6, Rangers 5. That's not bad considering the fact that, throughout that spell, Rangers was supposed to be on its uppers financially.

When I started going to Ibrox in season 1960–61, Rangers won the League Cup and League Championship. As I write this, 'Gers have won the same two trophies again, with many more in between. Over the 50 years of watching Rangers, I have seen the good times and bad times. Being the world's most successful club, the good times have far outweighed the bad. Whatever happens though, you will still find me watching the Teddy Bears from the best seat in the stadium: Govan Rear, Row N, Seat 160.

CHAPTER TWELVE

MY GREATEST...

In 50 years of watching Rangers I have seen so many great players, fantastic matches and special occasions, and I have felt a whole range of emotions, so, ending with this chapter is a difficult thing and is bound to be controversial. Feel free to disagree with me, but what follows is my genuine opinion.

MY GREATEST RANGERS TEAM

Throughout Rangers'history there have been hundreds of fantastic players. I could compose dozens of brilliant 'Gers sides, but here, just for fun, would be my best-ever team. The list of possible candidates could be longer, but I have only included players from the 1960s onwards and who held the position for a suitable length of time.

GOALKEEPERS:

George Niven, Billy Ritchie, Eric Sorensen, Norrie Martin, Peter McCloy, Stewart Kennedy, Nicky Walker, Jim Stewart, Chris Woods, Andy Goram, Theo Snelders, Ally Maxwell, Anttii Niemi, Lionel Charbonnier, Stefan Klos, Ronald Waterreus and Allan McGregor.
MY CHOICE: ANDY GORAM.

RIGHT-BACK:

Bobby Shearer, Kai Johansen, Sandy Jardine, Alex Miller, Gary Stevens, Jimmy Nicholl, Fraser Wishart, Alex Cleland, Sergio Porrini, Fernando Ricksen,

Mo Ross, Alan Hutton, Kirk Broadfoot and Steven Whittaker.
MY CHOICE: SANDY JARDINE.

LEFT-BACK:

Eric Caldow, Davie Provan, Willie Mathieson, Alex Miller, John Greig, Ally Dawson, Stuart Munro, John Brown, David Robertson, Arthur Numan, Tony Vidmar, Michael Ball, Paolo Vanoli, Gregory Vignal and Sasa Papac.
MY CHOICE: JOHN GREIG.

CENTRAL-DEFENDERS:

Bill Patterson, Ronnie McKinnon, Dave Smith, Colin Jackson, Tom Forsyth, Derek Johnstone, Gregor Stevens, Craig Paterson, John McClelland, Terry Butcher, Richard Gough, Graham Roberts, David McPherson, John Brown, Oleg Kuznetsov, Alan McLaren, Gordan Petric, Basile Boli, Joachim Björklund, Craig Moore, Lorenzo Amoruso, Colin Hendry, Bert Konterman, Marvin Andrews, Henning Berg, Jean-Alain Boumsong, Soti Kyrgiakos, Frank de Boer, Carlos Cuellar and Madjid Bougherra.
MY CHOICES: TOM FORSYTH and TERRY BUTCHER.

CENTRAL-MIDFIELDERS:

Ian McMillan, Harry Davis, Billy Stevenson, Jim Baxter, John Greig, Andy Penman, Alex McDonald, Bobby Russell, Ian Redford, Robert Pritz, Cammy Fraser, Derek Ferguson, Ian Durrant, Graeme Souness, Ray Wilkins, Ian Ferguson, Nigel Spackman, Trevor Steven, Stuart McCall, Paul Gascoigne, Alexei Mikhailichenko, John Brown, Rino Gattuso, Jonas Thern, Barry Ferguson, Jorg Albertz, Gio van Bronckhorst, Claudio Reyna, Tugay Kerirroglu, Ronald de Boer, Mikel Arteta, Stephen Hughes, Alex Rae, Kevin Thomson, Steven Davis, Lee McCulloch, Mo Edu and Pedro Mendes.
MY CHOICES: PAUL GASCOIGNE and JIM BAXTER.

WINGERS:

Alex Scott, Willie Henderson, Davie Wilson, Willie Johnston, Orjan Persson, Tommy McLean, Bobby McKean, Quinton Young, Davie Cooper, Ted McMinn, Mark Walters, Pieter Huistra, Brian Laudrup, Andrei Kanchelskis, Neil McCann, Peter Lovenkrands, Chris Burke and DaMarcus Beasley.
MY CHOICES: WILLIE HENDERSON and WILLIE JOHNSTON.

STRIKERS:

Jimmy Millar, Ralph Brand, Jim Forrest, George McLean, Alex Ferguson, Colin Stein, Alfie Conn, Derek Johnstone, Derek Parlane, John McDonald, Colin McAdam, Iain Ferguson, Gordon Smith, Ally McCoist, Sandy Clark, Bobby Williamson, Colin West, Robert Fleck, Trevor Francis, Mark Falco, Kevin Drinkell, Mo Johnston, Mark Hateley, Duncan Ferguson, Gordon Durie, Marco Negri, Oleg Salenko, Seb Rozental, Gabriel Amato, Rod Wallace, Stefan Guivarc'h, Michael Mols, Shota Arveladze, Claudio Caniggia, Billy Dodds, Tore André Flo, Thomas Buffel, Nacho Novo, Dado Prso, Kris Boyd and Kenny Miller.
MY CHOICES: ALLY McCOIST and DEREK JOHNSTONE.

In formation my greatest side from all the players I have seen in the past 50 years would be:

	GORAM		
JARDINE	FORSYTH	BUTCHER	GREIG
HENDERSON	GASCOIGNE	BAXTER	WILLIE JOHNSTON
	McCOIST	DEREK JOHNSTONE	

THE PLAYERS:
ANDY GORAM

Lancashire lad Goram started out playing between the sticks for Oldham and, thanks to a Scottish grandparent, even gained his first Scottish cap while playing for them. He would make another 42 appearances for Scotland. A move from Oldham to Hibs saw him spend the next four seasons there until Walter Smith signed him to replace Chris Woods, a victim of UEFA's three-foreigner-only rule. It certainly was a case of being in the right place at the right time, and Goram would continue being in the right place at the right time while guarding the 'Gers' goal. His saves and personality made him a Rangers legend. He was voted Rangers' greatest 'keeper by the fans and was elected to the Hall of Fame.

At only 5ft 11in, Goram was relatively small for a goalkeeper, but his sturdy build meant that he could take care of himself in a crowded penalty box. Due to his size, he stayed on his line more than most 'keepers when crosses were put in and, when he did come for a cross, his favoured method of dealing with them was to punch the ball away to safety. If this was a handicap, it never seemed like that to the fans, who could only admire him for all his other qualities.

Goram was fast on his feet, with the quick reflexes that any top 'keeper must have. His confidence spread itself to the rest of his defence, and the defenders must

173

have felt safe in the knowledge that he was behind them should a forward break through. This was perhaps where Goram was seen at his best. In a one-on-one situation, he would stay on his feet, making himself look as big as possible to the onrushing forward and make them decide how they was going to get the ball past him. Invariably the striker didn't. A dive at the forward's feet, an outstretched palm, a leg in the way – the ball stayed out one way or another. By the time he'd established his reputation, he must have held a psychological edge over any striker bearing down on his goal.

SANDY JARDINE

Jardine was signed by Scot Symon as a wing-half (that's a midfielder to you younger readers) but was played in various positions by various managers before Willie Waddell finally found his ideal spot at right-back. Jardine had great skill, speed, stamina, determination and intelligence, and he eventually became a world-class full-back. So good was he that Celtic's classy Danny McGrain was required to play at left-back for the Scotland side of the mid-to-late 70s. In his 38 Scotland appearances, Jardine seldom put a foot wrong.

Sandy Jardine, even today, would be considered a class act. His qualities would see him thrive in the modern game as they did in the 70s and 80s. He was intelligent, fast, exciting, reliable, consistent and elegant. A bonus was that he was more two-footed than most players, capable of shooting with either foot. He had mobility and pace as well as stamina, allowing him to run up and down the flank all day. He was a wing-back before such a position had been created. As a defender, he could use his speed but also his brain to tackle at the opportune moment, to intercept, to nip danger in the bud. He also had the vision to cover for teammates in-field when necessary.

As a modern, attacking full-back, this foresight and pace were also invaluable as Jardine was capable of creating goals as well as scoring them. For a player who was invariably joining in the Rangers' attacks, he was seldom caught out by a swift counter-attack as he always managed to get him back into position to do the necessary defending. By the end of his Ibrox career, Jardine would have amassed 77 goals – a great tally for a player who was essentially a defender.

TOM FORSYTH

Fans of all clubs have always had a special place in their hearts for the sort of player who used to be known as the 'iron man' of the team. This usually meant that he was the type of player who'd be hard and ferocious, the kind who'd tackle a rhino and win, thanks to his strength, determination and fearlessness. He was also usually the guy who wore his heart on his sleeve and genuinely seemed to play for the jersey rather than merely kiss it. Tom Forsyth was such a player.

The Rangers fans who adored Forsyth's style and christened him 'Jaws' – a nickname he detested – a homage to the 1970s blockbuster film and the fact that his tackles could bite your legs. However, this nickname didn't reflect the ability of the man. He was always a fair, honest player with more skill than he was given credit for, especially in his passing. After all, he'd started out a midfield player at Motherwell before being converted to a central-defender at Ibrox by Jock Wallace.

Wallace obviously believed that Forsyth was the player who could best complement Colin Jackson in central defence, and how it worked. His strength in the tackle, his mobility and his reading of the game made him the ideal foil for Jackson.

Forsyth was part of the team that brought the League title back to Ibrox in 1975, after an 11 year gap, before going on to win two trebles in three seasons in 1975–76 and 1977–78. Forsyth's contribution in the winning of those trebles can't be underestimated. His defensive expertise, allied to a determination, strength and will-to-win, combined to make him a formidable barrier to opposing forwards. It is significant that the barren season in between those trebles saw Forsyth miss almost a third of the League games played due to various injuries.

TERRY BUTCHER

At 6ft 4in, Terry Butcher really was a rock. A big, brave, powerful, 'traditional' centre-half, he had the physical presence to hold a defence together and inspire his teammates. Naturally, he was supreme in the air when defending but was also a great threat to the opposition at corners and free kicks. Butcher's timing and aggression in the tackle made it difficult for forwards to get away from him, and he showed a fleetness of foot that belied his size. Perhaps, surprisingly for the Scots, who hadn't paid much attention to him while he had been in England, he had a tremendous left foot that could send long, raking, but very accurate passes up to his forwards. With all those qualities that Souness already admired, Butcher was the obvious choice to be his captain on the field.

The Rangers fans took to the quintessential Englishman from the start, recognising that he was a very good defender but also a player who would give his all for the club. It soon became obvious that Butcher was also a great ambassador for Rangers in the way he conducted himself off the field and dealt comfortably with the media. These communications skills were put to good use when it came to talking his colleagues through certain games.

JOHN GREIG

John Greig is officially Mr Rangers. A few years ago the club organised a poll to find the Greatest Ranger, and Greig was accorded that honour by the fans. He was the ultimate one-club man who played for Rangers, became its manager and worked as its public relations officer after that. A quick survey of his achievements will also support his credentials. He captained club and country, earning 44 caps. He played in a record three treble-winning sides, captaining two of those. He made 857 appearances for Rangers, scoring an incredible 120 goals for a defender and in that time was twice voted Player of the Year by Scottish sportswriters. He won every domestic honour at least four times and captained Rangers to the European Cup-Winners' Cup trophy in 1972. On retiring as a player he was awarded the MBE for his services to football.

Throughout his long career, Greig showed a versatility that would have been an asset to any team. He played in either full-back position, central defence or in midfield. During the darkest days of Celtic's nine-in-a-row years, it was Greig who was the 'Gers' inspiring skipper, frequently scoring the goal from long-range that won his side the points. In most games it seemed that Greig covered every blade of grass in his determination to ensure that he and his teammates didn't let their fans down. For many years, fans and pundits alike agreed that Greig carried Rangers on his back – and never let them down.

Greig was a great competitor with a talent for leadership that meant no cause was lost while he was still on the field. In the brilliant team of the early 60s, he was the perfect foil for Jim Baxter, allowing him time and space to destroy the opposition because Greig would take care of any danger. Having said that, Greig's own passing ability was better than most people gave him credit for. His never-say-die spirit was in keeping with those great 'Gers' captains of the past. At his peak, he could have left Ibrox for any number of top English clubs, but his loyalty to Rangers was never in question. That loyalty was richly rewarded in the 70s when he captained the club to two trebles and European success.

WILLIE HENDERSON

Wee Willie, as he was affectionately termed, used pace coupled with trickery. His flexibility and his talent for twisting and turning, tying his opponents seemingly in knots, was the precursor for Celtic's 'Jinky' Johnstone a few years later. Henderson was the traditional Scottish 'tanner ba' player supreme, bamboozling defenders with his excellent ball control and complemented by his weaving runs that mesmerised opponents, teammates and fans alike.

Even in the early 60s, Henderson seemed a throwback from the good old days when such players had been the norm rather than the exception. So good was his tight control that, at times, it must have seemed as if he had the ball tied to his bootlaces. Perhaps this was just as well because he was so short-sighted that he had to wear contact lenses to be able to see anything at all.

As with all great wingers, Wee Willie was a brave player, always ready to take stick from frustrated defenders and come back for more. Sometimes he seemed like the ball itself in his ability to be bounced about before getting up after persistent fouls and taking on the same defenders. Those opponents who didn't know him probably thought that, at only 5ft 4in tall, he'd be 'easy meat'. How wrong they were. In order to even foul him, they first had to catch him! His pace, trickery, bravery and supreme confidence made most defenders' task a nightmare. Also, although small in stature, he was quite a muscular player and could use this to good effect too.

Henderson didn't score as many goals as other 'Gers' wingers, such as Scott and Wilson but he made so many more. He was a far more profitable player in terms of creating chances for his colleagues. His forté was in racing to the byline, having left umpteen opponents in his wake, before cutting the ball back low across the face of the goal for his strikers to run on to and crash the ball into the net. With brilliant forwards like Millar and Brand in the centre, not to mention fellow winger Davie Wilson coming in from the back post, it was no wonder that Henderson's runs resulted in so many goals.

Despite his talent for bobbing and weaving and dribbling round defenders, making them look foolish, Henderson, in the eyes of many, was a superior winger to the later Jimmy Johnstone due to the fact that Wee Willie was more direct and effective. Henderson's trickery and speed were used simply to get into a position to deliver a telling cross or cut-back. Seldom would you see him beat the same defender two or three times, á la Johnstone, with no progress having been made.

PAUL GASCOIGNE

When Rangers signed Gazza in the summer of 1995 from Lazio for a fee of £4.3 million, it was probably the biggest coup ever seen in Scottish football. Here was the English hero of Italia '90 and the midfielder acknowledged by English fans as the most talented player of his generation coming to Scotland – and he wasn't even at the veteran stage yet.

A modern midfield player, Gazza combined strength with skill. His surging runs would create many goals, and sometimes he would score off the back of his own run.

177

He showed great vision and had a variety of passing skills that meant he could open up defences at will. Excellent ball control and an instant first touch gave him the time and space to set off on a penetrating run that sometimes became almost a mazy dribble through the opposition. He used his upper body strength to ward off any challenges and sometimes his elbows too, – a tactic that caused some controversy at times. A genuine creative, goalscoring midfield player who got himself ahead of forwards into good positions, Gascoigne was very difficult to mark. No wonder he would amass 57 caps for England.

Gascoigne's greatest weakness was his discipline. A tendency to retaliate against opponents who spent the whole match trying to stop him illegally and a penchant for dissent made referees show him the yellow card too easily.

Throughout his first season, Gascoigne's brand of football magic and fun lit up Ibrox and the other stadia of Scotland. He controlled matches, set up goals and scored some memorable ones himself. In the crunch match at Ibrox against Aberdeen, when a 'Gers' win would seal the title, Rangers were a goal down before Gazza took on the Dons' defence single-handedly to equalise before half-time. A penalty and another stunning goal gave Rangers the necessary victory and eight-in-a-row. His second goal will never be forgotten by fans who were there that day.

As often as not, Gascoigne's great technique saw him passing the ball into the goal rather than blasting it. This was seen at its best in the League Cup Final at Parkhead against Hearts, who had come from two goals behind to equalise in the second half. With Rangers looking for inspiration, it was Gazza who provided it. His two goals exemplified his movement, vision and skill perfectly as he passed the ball into the net once he had made the space to try it.

JIM BAXTER

If John Greig was rightly voted 'The Greatest Ranger', then Jim Baxter, in the eyes of most fans, could rightly be considered 'The Best Ranger Ever'. Sir Bobby Robson called Baxter 'sheer genius', icon Denis Law stated that 'a pass from Baxter was like a guided missile' and our old enemy, Liverpool's Emlyn Hughes said that he was 'a fabulous, fabulous player'. Even his friend and one-time Old Firm rival, Pat Crerand, claimed that Baxter's talent was 'a gift from God'. Baxter won the admiration of practically every player, manager and supporter who ever saw him in his heyday.

God's gift, innate ability, natural talent – call it what you will, it was not the result of coaching or a strict training regime. When Baxter was transferred to Rangers for £17,500, it was a Scottish record.

For a newcomer, Baxter stood out immediately. His self-confidence and ability meant that he became a star from his first games in a Rangers shirt. He was also lucky in that he was joining what would become, arguably, the greatest Rangers side of all time. His elegance, arrogance, vision and sublime passing skills with his left foot made him not only fit into the 'Gers side from the start but control it too. Baxter was the maestro, his left foot the baton, conducting an orchestra full of virtuoso performers who composed a symphony on so many memorable occasions in the early 60s. The silky passes of Slim Jim were tailor-made for wingers like Henderson and Wilson, not to mention the route through the middle where Millar, Brand and latterly, Jim Forrest ran on to score from a defence-splitting passes.

So great was Baxter that he was accorded the honour of playing in the Rest of the World side that faced England in its Centenary match at Wembley in 1963. The following season saw Baxter at his peak, and with Rangers going well in the European Cup, the signs were promising. However, in Vienna, in the second leg of their European Cup second-round match, disaster struck Rangers and Baxter. With the game all but over and 'Gers cruising into the quarter-final following a magnificent Baxter performance, Slim Jim was tackled by a frustrated Austrian and his leg was broken. The loss of Baxter for the quarter-final against Inter Milan was too much for Rangers, who went down 3–2 on aggregate. Every 'Gers fan wondered what might have been if only the great Baxter had been available to play in those two matches.

WILLIE JOHNSTON

Although Willie Johnston had been signed in 1964 from a Fife Junior side, 'Bud' as he became known, was actually a Glaswegian. Making his debut for 'Gers at the age of 17, so spectacular were his performances that within six months he was playing for Scotland in World Cup qualifying matches, becoming the youngest internationalist since Denis Law, with whom he formed a left-wing partnership.

As a winger, Johnston was a combination of Henderson and Wilson in that he had electric pace (faster than either of those two) and a mesmerising dribbling ability. He was more like Wilson in his goalscoring prowess, though. Indeed, at various points in his career he'd play on the wing or as a striker through the middle with equal effect even scoring great goals. Unfortunately, his temperament was his Achilles heel. A short fuse when fouled once too often by frustrated defenders would normally lead Bud to retaliating and end up getting himself sent off

As well as being brave, skilful and exciting to watch, Johnston was also a character – the type of which we see too few of nowadays in Scottish football. He was the sort who could gleefully pat a defender on the head if he'd just scored an own-goal or, like Baxter, sit on the ball and tease his opponents. He was a player who gave everything and liked to play with a smile on his face, remembering that the game was there to be enjoyed.

Not only did Johnston score goals throughout 'Gers' journey to eventual success in Barcelona in the European Cup-Winners' Cup in 1972, he even scored two of the three goals in the Final. He forged a great partnership with Colin Stein, who scored the other goal in that game.

ALLY McCOIST

Put quite simply, Ally McCoist MBE is the most prolific goalscorer in the history of Rangers. Fifteen years as a Rangers star gave him the platform to achieve his huge goal tally, but who knows what the number might have been but for a broken leg and the fact that he had turned down Rangers twice before he arrived at Ibrox?

By the time the fans had become worshippers of the man, another manager in the form of Graeme Souness had to be convinced of the striker's worth. McCoist had picked up the nickname 'Super Ally' and had been capped for Scotland by the time of Souness' appointment. He was scoring goals by the barrow-load and, as if that wasn't enough to make him the fans' hero, he had an engaging personality that perhaps was a factor in his ability to score goals. McCoist was a bubbly, chirpy, extroverted character who always looked happy to be playing.

At only 5ft 10in tall and weighing 12 stones, Ally was not a physical forward, although he could handle himself in the penalty box, as all great strikers must be able to do. He was brave, alert, quick off the mark and brilliant at getting into the right place at the right time to finish off moves with a goal. When he scored with his head, it was not the type of soaring header that players like Mark Hateley would later become renowned for. McCoist's headers normally came about because his anticipation and quick reflexes enabled him to get across or in front of his marker allowing him the deadly header. As McCoist matured he seemed to score with more headers – and better ones at that!

It was in season 1989–90 that McCoist broke the Premier Division scoring record and, by scoring two goals in the final Old Firm match of that season, he overtook Derek Johnstone's post-war Rangers' record of 132 League goals. In 1991–92 he scored 41 goals, which brought him to a career total of 200 for the

Scottish League. His spectacular season resulted in him being awarded both the Scottish sportswriters' and players' Player of the Year awards, as well as winning the European Golden Boot for being top League scorer throughout Europe. Had he peaked? Not a bit of it! The following season Rangers' treble, and Ally's goals made a huge contribution to that achievement.

Once again, Ally won the Golden Boot award with 34 goals in 34 League games, and his total in all competitions was 49. This record was even more remarkable considering the fact that he broke his leg that spring while playing for Scotland in a World Cup match in Portugal. Who knows how many goals could have been added to his tally if he'd played until the end of the season?

By season 1995–96, McCoist had created a new Rangers' scoring record when he surpassed the legendary Bob McPhail's League total of 233 and, although injury restricted his appearances in his veteran seasons, he could still do the business, as witnessed when he scored the opening goal against Celtic at Parkhead in a 2–1 Scottish Cup semi-final victory in 1998. His final goal against Celtic saw him equal Jimmy McGrory's Old Firm match total, only surpassed by the feat of R.C. Hamilton's haul 100 years previously.

DEREK JOHNSTONE

For such a versatile player, it's really amazing that Johnstone still ended up as one of Rangers' highest ever goalscorers – despite the fact that for quite a chunk of his career he played at centre-half, not to mention the occasional spell in midfield. It's become a cliché in football to talk about certain players having a storybook career, being a real life Roy of the Rovers, and the aforementioned Super Ally was one of those. However, Derek Johnstone had already acted out a similar script in the 70s.

The most memorable feature of Derek Johnstone's game was his heading ability. It was this that won many a match for Rangers, especially important games. It was this skill that brought him to the attention of the general football public at the tender age of 16. The start of his Ibrox career was truly fairy-tale stuff. Although he had made his Rangers debut at Ibrox against Cowdenbeath in a 5–0 win, where he scored twice, his real fame started a month later when Willie Waddell and Jock Wallace decided to throw this skinny kid in at the deep end in the League Cup Final of 1970 against Celtic at Hampden. Heading the winning goal was written in the stars.

It's a truism that there is no better way for a newcomer to get the Rangers fans on his side than to score a winning goal against Celtic. From the moment Johnstone's golden head nodded in the winner, DJ became an instant hero. Although still a boy, he was 6ft tall, with power and determination, not to mention that great ability to leap. He could also shoot with both feet. For a big lad he was mobile without being fast, and he was good at linking with his fellow forwards and midfield men. When playing at the back, he was obviously great in the air, but he could also read a game and anticipate danger. His tackling was efficient, and as a ball-playing centre-half he was useful at starting counter-attacks. He was simply a great all-rounder.

In that debut season Johnstone scored six goals from 13 starts, but that was just the beginning of an avalanche of Rangers goals. Even this early in his career, he was showing his versatility. For instance, in the European Cup-Winners' Cup run to Barcelona, Johnstone played as a striker in the quarter and semi-finals but in the Final itself played at centre-half in place of the injured Colin Jackson. It was this ability that led sportswriters to call him 'the new John Charles' – a reference to the giant Welshman from the 50s who played for Juventus and Wales in both positions with distinction.

If Johnstone had spent his entire career up front, who knows how many goals he would have scored by the end of it? As it was, he ended up with an impressive 210. This is especially intriguing when we remember that he had strike partners who ranged from Colin Stein and Derek Parlane to Gordon Smith and that he could have benefited from crosses by Tommy McLean and Davie Cooper.

BEST TEAM OF 'FOREIGN' RANGERS:

WOODS

GARY STEVENS	GRAHAM ROBERTS	TERRY BUTCHER	ARTHUR NUMAN
MARK WALTERS	PAUL GASCOIGNE	JORGE ALBERTZ	BRIAN LAUDRUP
	MARK HATELEY	MICHAEL MOLS	

SIX OF THE BEST, 1960s–PRESENT
TOP SIX GOALSCORERS:

1. Ally McCoist (355 goals)
2. Derek Johnstone (210 goals)
3. Ralph Brand (206 goals)
4. Jimmy Millar (162 goals)
5. Davie Wilson (157 goals)
6. Jim Forrest (145 goals)

TOP SIX RANGERS GOALS:

1. Paul Gascoigne (second goal versus Aberdeen at Ibrox, League, May 1996)
2. Davie Cooper (versus Celtic in Drybrough Cup Final 1979)
3. Ally McCoist (second goal versus Leeds away, European Cup 1992)
4. Paul Gascoigne (second goal versus Celtic at Parkhead, League, September 1995)
5. Ally McCoist (first goal versus Aberdeen at Ibrox, League, December 1990)
6. Bobby Russell (third goal versus PSV Eindhoven away, European Cup, November 1978)

TOP SIX CAPTAINS:

1. John Greig
2. Terry Butcher
3. Richard Gough
4. Eric Caldow
5. Bobby Shearer
6. John McClelland

TOP SIX 'KEEPERS:

1. Andy Goram
2. Chris Woods
3. Billy Ritchie
4. Stefan Klos
5. Peter McCloy
6. Stewart Kennedy

TOP SIX DEFENDERS:

1. John Greig
2. Tom Forsyth
3. Terry Butcher
4. Richard Gough
5. Sandy Jardine
6. Ronnie McKinnon

TOP SIX MIDFIELDERS:

1. Jim Baxter
2. Paul Gascoigne

3. Barry Ferguson
4. Stuart McCall
5. Jorge Albertz
6. Gio van Bronckhorst

TOP SIX WINGERS:

1. Willie Henderson
2. Willie Johnston
3. Brian Laudrup
4. Davie Cooper
5. Davie Wilson
6. Mark Walters

MOST ENJOYABLE VICTORIES:

1. 3–2 versus Celtic (Scottish Cup Final, May 1973)
2. 6–1 versus Dunfermline (Ibrox, League, May 2003)
3. 3–2 versus Celtic (Scottish Cup Final, May 2002)
4. 5–1 versus Celtic (Ibrox, League, August 1988)
5. 2–0 versus Bayern Munich (Cup-Winners' Cup semi-final, April 1972)
6. 2–0 versus Juventus (Ibrox, European Cup, September 1978)

MOST SICKENING DEFEATS:

1. 4–2 versus Celtic (Parkhead, League, May 1979)
2. 1–0 versus Berwick (away, Scottish Cup, 1967)
3. 1–0 versus Bayern Munich (Nuremberg, Cup-Winners' Cup Final, 1967)
4. 1–0 versus Hamilton (Ibrox, Scottish Cup, January 1987)
5. 4–0 versus Celtic (Scottish Cup Final, May 1969)
6. 3–0 versus Lyons (Ibrox, Champions League, December 2007)

GREATEST ACHIEVEMENT:

Completing nine-in-a-row (1988–97)

I had considered winning the 1972 European Cup-Winners' Cup in Barcelona for this accolade due to the calibre of opposition and the fact that it is the club's only European trophy. However, winning nine successive titles must overtake that feat. In my opinion, 'Gers nine-in-a-row was a greater achievement than Celtic's under Jock Stein for these reasons:

Rangers lost their manager after the first three titles but completed the job under Walter Smith, whereas Celtic had the same manager throughout their run;

the League was harder to win when 'Gers won their nine titles due to the fact that all the clubs in the smaller League were full-time professionals and each had to be played against four times. In Stein's era, there were 18 clubs, many only part-time, and each was played against twice;

nowadays changes in the pace and style of football mean there are more injuries and suspensions that can affect a team;

the pressure was greater on the Rangers team because when Celtic won their nine, there was no pressure on them past seven, which was the previous record. Rangers had to achieve nine titles to equal the record.

APPENDIX

50 YEARS OF RANGERS' HONOURS

The honours won by the club since I have been following it are as follows:

EUROPEAN CUP-WINNERS' CUP
winners – 1972
runners up – 1961, 1967

UEFA CUP
runners up – 2008

LEAGUE CHAMPIONSHIP (22)
1961, 1963, 1964, 1975, 1976, 1978, 1987, 1989, 1990, 1991, 1992, 1993, 1994, 1995, 1996, 1997, 1999, 2000, 2003, 2005, 2009, 2010

SCOTTISH CUP WINNERS (19)
1960, 1962, 1963, 1964, 1966, 1973, 1976, 1978, 1979, 1981, 1992, 1993, 1996, 1999, 2000, 2002, 2003, 2008, 2009

SCOTTISH LEAGUE CUP WINNERS (24)
1961, 1962, 1964, 1965, 1971, 1976, 1978, 1979, 1982, 1984, 1985, 1987, 1988, 1989, 1991, 1993, 1994, 1997, 1999, 2002, 2003, 2005, 2008, 2010

LEAGUE SEASONS

SEASON	POSITION	P	W	D	L	GF	GA	PTS
1960–61	1	34	23	5	6	88	46	51
1961–62	2	34	22	7	5	84	31	51

SEASON	POSITION	P	W	D	L	GF	GA	PTS
1962–63	1	34	25	7	2	94	28	57
1963–64	1	34	25	5	4	85	31	55
1964–65	5	34	18	8	8	78	35	44
1965–66	2	34	25	5	4	91	29	55
1966–67	2	34	24	7	3	92	31	55
1967–68	2	34	28	5	1	93	34	61
1968–69	2	34	21	7	6	81	32	49
1969–70	2	34	19	7	8	67	40	45
1970–71	4	34	16	9	9	58	34	41
1971–72	3	34	21	2	11	71	38	44
1972–73	2	34	26	4	4	74	30	56
1973–74	3	34	21	6	7	67	34	48
1974–75	1	34	25	6	3	86	33	56
1975–76	1	36	23	8	5	60	24	54
1976–77	2	36	18	10	8	62	37	46
1977–78	1	36	24	7	5	76	39	55
1978–79	2	36	18	9	9	52	35	45
1979–80	5	36	15	7	14	50	46	37
1980–81	3	36	16	12	8	60	32	44
1981–82	3	36	16	11	9	57	45	43
1982–83	4	36	13	12	11	52	41	38
1983–84	4	36	15	12	9	53	41	42
1984–85	4	36	13	12	11	47	38	38
1985–86	5	36	13	9	14	53	45	3
1986–87	1	44	31	7	6	85	23	69
1987–88	3	44	26	8	10	85	34	60
1988–89	1	36	26	4	6	62	26	56
1989–90	1	36	20	11	5	48	19	51
1990–91	1	36	24	7	5	62	23	55
1991–92	1	44	33	6	5	101	31	72
1992–93	1	44	33	7	4	97	35	73
1993–94	1	44	22	14	8	74	41	58
1994–95	1	36	20	9	7	60	35	69
1995–96	1	36	27	6	3	85	25	87
1996–97	1	36	25	5	6	85	33	80
1997–98	2	36	21	9	6	76	38	72
1998–99	1	36	23	8	5	78	31	77
1999–00	1	36	28	6	2	96	26	90
2000–01	2	38	26	4	8	76	36	82
2001–02	2	38	25	10	3	82	27	85
2002–03	1	38	31	4	3	101	28	97
2003–04	2	38	25	6	7	76	33	81

SEASON	POSITION	P	W	D	L	GF	GA	PTS
2004–05	1	38	29	6	3	78	22	93
2005–06	3	38	21	10	7	67	37	73
2006–07	2	38	21	9	8	61	32	72
2007–08	2	38	27	5	6	84	33	86
2008–09	1	38	26	8	4	77	28	86
2009–10	1	38	26	9	3	82	28	87

SCOTTISH CUP FINALS

Wins are in bold.

1960　**Rangers**　**2–0**　**Kilmarnock**
1962　**Rangers**　**2–0**　**St Mirren**
1963　**Rangers**　**3–0**　**Celtic** (after 1–1 draw)
1964　**Rangers**　**3–1**　**Dundee United**
1966　**Rangers**　**1–0**　**Celtic** (after 0–0 draw)
1969　Rangers　0–4　Celtic
1971　Rangers　1–2　Celtic (after 1–1 draw)
1973　**Rangers**　**3–2**　**Celtic**
1976　**Rangers**　**3–1**　**Hearts**
1977　Rangers　0–1　Celtic
1978　**Rangers**　**2–1**　**Aberdeen**
1979　**Rangers**　**3–2**　**Hibernian** (after two 0–0 draws and extra-time)
1980　Rangers　0–1　Celtic (after extra-time)
1981　**Rangers**　**4–1**　**Dundee United** (after 0–0 draw)
1982　Rangers　1–4　Aberdeen (after extra-time)
1983　Rangers　0–1　Aberdeen (after extra-time)
1989　Rangers　0–1　Celtic
1992　**Rangers**　**2–1**　**Airdrie**
1993　**Rangers**　**2–1**　**Aberdeen**
1994　Rangers　0–1　Dundee United
1996　**Rangers**　**5–1**　**Hearts**
1998　Rangers　1–2　Hearts
1999　**Rangers**　**1–0**　**Celtic**
2000　**Rangers**　**4–0**　**Aberdeen**
2002　**Rangers**　**3–2**　**Celtic**
2003　**Rangers**　**1–0**　**Dundee United**
2008　**Rangers**　**3–2**　**Queen of the South**
2009　**Rangers**　**1–0**　**Falkirk**

SCOTTISH LEAGUE CUP FINALS

Wins are in bold.
1961　**Rangers**　**2–0**　**Kilmarnock**

1962	**Rangers**	**3–1**	**Hearts** (after 1–1 draw)
1964	**Rangers**	**5–0**	**Morton**
1965	**Rangers**	**2–1**	**Celtic**
1966	Rangers	1–2	Celtic
1967	Rangers	0–1	Celtic
1971	**Rangers**	**1–0**	**Celtic**
1976	**Rangers**	**1–0**	**Celtic**
1978	**Rangers**	**2–1**	**Celtic** (after extra-time)
1979	**Rangers**	**2–1**	**Aberdeen**
1982	**Rangers**	**2–1**	**Dundee United**
1983	Rangers	1–2	Celtic
1984	**Rangers**	**3–2**	**Celtic** (after extra-time)
1985	**Rangers**	**1–0**	**Dundee United**
1987	**Rangers**	**2–1**	**Celtic**
1988	**Rangers**	**3–3**	**Aberdeen** (after extra-time, 5–3 on penalties)
1989	**Rangers**	**3–2**	**Aberdeen**
1990	Rangers	1–2	Aberdeen (after extra-time)
1991	**Rangers**	**2–1**	**Celtic** (after extra-time)
1993	**Rangers**	**2–1**	**Aberdeen** (after extra-time)
1994	**Rangers**	**2–1**	**Hibernian**
1997	**Rangers**	**4–3**	**Hearts**
1999	**Rangers**	**2–1**	**St Johnstone**
2002	**Rangers**	**4–0**	**Ayr United**
2003	**Rangers**	**2–1**	**Celtic**
2005	**Rangers**	**5–1**	**Motherwell**
2008	**Rangers**	**2–2**	**Dundee United** (after extra-time, 3–2 on penalties)
2009	Rangers	0–2	Celtic (after extra-time)
2010	**Rangers**	**1–0**	**St Mirren**

RANGERS MANAGERS

1	Scot Symon (1954–67)
2	David White (1967–69)
3	Willie Waddell (1969–72)
4	Jock Wallace (1972–78)
5	John Greig (1978–83)
6	Jock Wallace (1983–86)
7	Graeme Souness (1986–91)
8	Walter Smith (1991–98)
9	Dick Advocaat (1998–2001)
10	Alex Mcleish (2001–06)
11	Paul Le Guen (2006–07)
12	Walter Smith (2007–)